PREHISTORIC KIVAS

OF ANTELOPE MESA

NORTHEASTERN ARIZONA

PAPERS OF THE PEABODY MUSEUM OF ARCHAEOLOGY AND ETHNOLOGY
HARVARD UNIVERSITY, CAMBRIDGE, MASSACHUSETTS, U.S.A.
VOLUME 39, NO. 1

a

b

Frontispiece. *a*. View of the Western Mound at Awatovi from the northeast. Rooms 218, 229, and 240 are on the left slope just below the summit. Test 14 is in the low area in the middle ground at the left.

b. The Spanish convento at Awatovi from the north, with Test 31 in the foreground.

PREHISTORIC KIVAS
OF ANTELOPE MESA

NORTHEASTERN ARIZONA

Watson Smith

Reports of the Awatovi Expedition

No. 9

PEABODY MUSEUM OF ARCHAEOLOGY AND ETHNOLOGY

HARVARD UNIVERSITY, CAMBRIDGE, MASSACHUSETTS

1972

ISBN 0–87365–115–4
LIBRARY OF CONGRESS CATALOG CARD NUMBER 72–92005
PRINTED AT HARVARD UNIVERSITY PRINTING OFFICE
CAMBRIDGE, MASSACHUSETTS, U.S.A.

Contents

Figures

Foreword

The Peabody Museum of Harvard University conducted five seasons of excavations, 1935–1939, on Antelope Mesa in the Hopi Indian Reservation, northeastern Arizona. Although our major efforts were made at two large sites, at Awatovi, which was occupied for some five centuries — well into the historic period — and at Kawaika-a, a similar large town, twenty-one sites were examined in all. They ranged in time from the seventh century A.D. to 1700. At eight of them, structures were excavated which can be classified as belonging to the tradition of Pueblo Indian ceremonial architecture known as the *kiva*. These buildings are the subject of this ninth report on the work of the Awatovi Expedition.

The author, Watson Smith, is well qualified as an historian of prehistoric kiva development. Before joining the Awatovi Expedition he had dug in kivas at the Lowry Ruin in Montezuma County, southwestern Colorado, and at Marsh Pass on the Navajo Reservation in northeastern Arizona.

At Awatovi he was in charge of kiva excavations and is the author of a definitive monograph, *Kiva Mural Decorations at Awatovi and Kawaika-a.** The present monograph, *Kivas of Antelope Mesa, in the Hopi Country, Northeastern Arizona*, may be considered as a sequel to his study of the kiva paintings. In addition to the late prehistoric and early historic kivas, of which the murals were described in the earlier work, this paper deals with the ground plans, structural details, and special features of all kivas discovered by the Expedition, including the predecessors of those in which wall paintings were found.

Unlike the better known circular kivas of the Mesa Verde and Chaco divisions of the San Juan Anasazi and those of the Rio Grande Valley, the Hopi and other western Anasazi kivas early developed a rectangular form through a transitional period of subterranean D-shaped structures. That development is traced in this report.

The director of an archaeological expedition has to be blessed by fortune if he is to achieve any reasonable measure of success. He must be lucky in the sites he picks out to dig, and in the spon-

sors he selects or who select him. He must, above all else, be lucky in his staff.

I was especially fortunate at Awatovi. Members of the Expedition staff have been listed in previous reports (Peabody Museum Papers, vols. 33 to 38). Without their superb skills, devoted loyalty, and just plain hard work we would have got nowhere: Al Lancaster, the best field man the Southwest has produced; our cook, Lin Thompson, whose imaginative creations were matched only by his good humor and his skill in joinery; Hattie Cosgrove, who herded upwards of half-a-million sherds a season over the classification tables in the pottery tent; Johnny Hack, who not only mastered the crumbling topography of our Dakota sandstone but also the Hopi's incredible agricultural techniques and their coal-mining prowess; Ross Montgomery, the resurrector of our Franciscan Mission; Dick Woodbury, who breathed life into the stone implements; Ned Hall, who made our tree-ring calendar; the long list of students, seasonal helpers, and technical volunteers; our twenty-nine extraordinarily able and enthusiastic Hopi excavators; and then there was Watson Smith.

After graduating from Brown University and taking a degree at the Harvard Law School, Watson Smith practised law in Providence and Cincinnati. One springtime, about 1933 I think it was, he observed to a friend that, since the sedentary nature of the legal profession produced not only boredom but increasing weight, he would like to spend the summer at hard labor that might also prove interesting. The friend was acquainted with Paul Martin at Chicago's Field Museum and, by June, Watson was digging at Lowry Ruin in Colorado. At the end of the summer, before resuming practice of the law, he decided to visit a classmate in California. Driving through Flagstaff he saw a sign: *Museum of Northern Arizona*. By now intrigued by archaeology, he turned right, off U.S. Highway 66, and encountered Harold Colton and Lin Hargrave. This led to eight months in one of the Monte Vista Hotel's far from palatial bedrooms and to lending editorial assistance to Colton and Hargrave's *Handbook of Northern Arizona Pottery Wares*.

The virus had by now a firm grip. Having heard

* Papers of the Peabody Museum of American Archaeology and Ethnology, Harvard University, vol. 37, Cambridge, Massachusetts 1952.

of the Gila Pueblo Museum, Watson moved to the Old Dominion Hotel at Globe, Arizona, and repeated the exposure. At that time there was no more enthusiastic proponent of archaeology in the nation than the proprietor of Gila Pueblo. Harold Gladwin completed the infection and when Watson finally reached California he ran into Ansel Hall and signed up for work in the field at Marsh Pass, where he met Ralph Beals and George Brainerd. By now it was 1935, and we had begun to dig at Awatovi. The season on the Navajo Reservation ended early and Wat moved south across Black Mesa to see what we were up to. This monograph bears testimony that he never did escape from that one. He became the anchor man of the Awatovi staff, our chief writer and editor, and a close personal friend. And Awatovi, as his bibliography attests, has been only one of his projects during the ensuing thirty years. Now, as Honorary Curator of Archaeology in the American Southwest in the Peabody Museum, he can look back on, and still continues a career of effective research and publication in which any archaeologist would take pride. This is one way in which an archaeologist is made.

The work of the Peabody Museum Awatovi Expedition was made possible, during the fieldwork and subsequently, through liberal contributions by Mr. and Mrs. William H. Claflin, Mr. Donald Scott, Mr. and Mrs. Raymond Emerson, Mr. Henry S. Morgan, Mr. and Mrs. Philip R. Allen, and the Wenner-Gren Foundation for Anthropology.

J. O. Brew
Director, Awatovi Expedition

Peabody Museum
Cambridge, Massachusetts
August 1, 1972

Acknowledgments

This report has been compiled and written at the Peabody Museum West of the Pecos in Tucson, Arizona, from field notes, photographs, and maps of the Expedition's files, which have been made available through the helpful collaboration of Dr. Stephen Williams, Director of the Peabody Museum, and Dr. J. O. Brew, Field Director of the Awatovi Expedition. Especial gratitude is due to Dr. Brew for his constant and helpful assistance and advice throughout the gestation of this report and for his painstaking reading of the manuscript.

The dating of wood and charcoal specimens was done by Dr. Edward T. Hall, a member of the field staff, and by the Laboratory of Tree-Ring Research of the University of Arizona (Hall 1951; Smiley 1951; Bannister et al. 1966, 1967).

Mr. Barton Wright, Curator of the Museum of Northern Arizona, Flagstaff, Arizona, executed the drawing of a kiva interior, which appears on the cover of this volume.

Beyond the acknowledgment that is due to all members of the Expedition and Museum staffs, as expounded in earlier reports, several others have assisted directly and significantly in the actual preparation of this volume. The manuscript was typed by Miss Chloe Haynes, and the excellent line drawings were executed by Mrs. Karen Sue Young. The onerous task of editing and production was carried out by Mrs. Martha Smith and Mr. Burton Jones of the Publications Staff of the Museum. To all these friends and supporters I wish to express my sincere personal gratitude. My errors of omission and commission are not to be ascribed to them.

Watson Smith

Peabody Museum West of the Pecos
Tucson, Arizona
May, 1971

PREHISTORIC KIVAS

OF ANTELOPE MESA

NORTHEASTERN ARIZONA

I

Introduction

The universe is queerer than we suppose, and queerer than we can suppose.

J. B. S. Haldane

During the years 1935–1939 the Peabody Museum Awatovi Expedition under the direction of Dr. J. O. Brew carried out extensive and intensive archaeological investigations in the Jeddito Valley–Antelope Mesa region of northeastern Arizona, in several large and small sites that had once been the homes of ancestors of the modern Hopi Indians (fig. 1). The major focus of the work was upon the great village of Awatovi, a large pueblo that had flourished from at least middle Pueblo III times until the end of the 17th century. Its first European visitor was Don Pedro de Tovar of Coronado's expedition in 1540, and it later became the site of the first Spanish mission church in the Hopi Country, San Bernardo de Aguátubi, established by Franciscan friars in 1630.

The history of Awatovi is reasonably well known, and both it and the story of the Peabody Museum Expedition have been comprehensively summarized in earlier reports of this series (Montgomery, Smith, and Brew 1949, pp. vii–ix, xix–xxiv, 3–40; Smith 1952a, pp. vii–xii; Smith 1971, pp. 1–12). Other publications reporting special phases of the expedition's work are Hack 1942a, 1942b, Lawrence 1951, Woodbury 1954, and Daifuku 1961. During the course of the fieldwork several preliminary reports were also published: Brew 1937, 1939a, 1939b, 1941.

The expedition devoted some of its time and effort also to the partial excavation of three other large and relatively late pueblos and to the investigation of about seventeen smaller and earlier sites in the vicinity. At Awatovi (fig. 2) and at Kawaika-a, a large Pueblo IV village a few miles east of Awatovi (fig. 3), more than thirty kivas were excavated. Among the striking features of those kivas was an unexpected bonanza of mural

paintings, relating to the ceremonial observances of their time. These paintings have been exhaustively discussed and illustrated in a previous volume (Smith 1952a) of this series, but the architectural features of the kivas were not considered therein.

The present volume is in a sense a sequel to the earlier one, and presents a detailed account of the architecture of the same kivas from the two sites. In addition there are included descriptions of several structures from other and earlier sites in the region that were identified at the time of the excavation as kivas. Some of these were constructed during Pueblo II, and others during Pueblo III, while all those at Awatovi and Kawaika-a date from early to late Pueblo IV. We have, thus, a regional sequence of ceremonial chambers from about 1000 to 1700.

In the present report every effort has been made to record and illustrate the complete data from the field notes, and to point up relevant and productive comparisons within the context of the material under immediate consideration. It has not been the purpose, however, to expand the discussion into a comparative survey of Southwestern kivas in general, either structurally, historically, geographically, or philosophically. Such an essay, provocative and useful as it would be, is left to others better fitted for the task and with greater vision and vigor than are possessed by the author. I hope that this small contribution will add a new cairn in the underground of Anasazi prehistory even if not a beacon to cleave the darkness.

It became evident from our excavations at Awatovi and Kawaika-a that rectangular kivas were a commonplace at those villages. But, before our

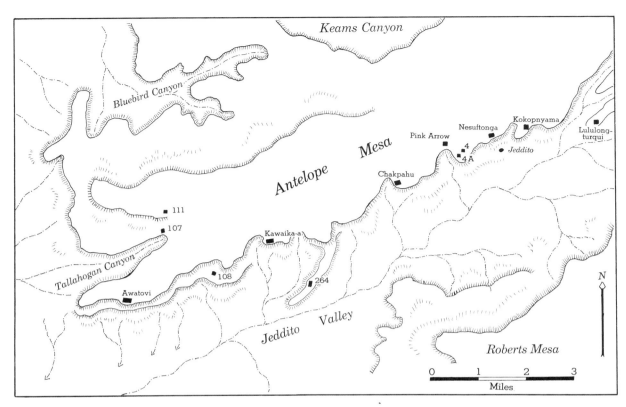

Fig. 1. Map of Antelope Mesa and its immediate vicinity, showing major sites in the area, including those at which kivas have been excavated and reported herein.

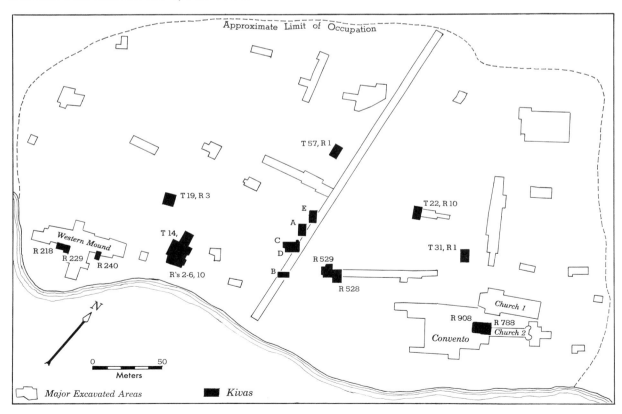

Fig. 2. General plan of Awatovi, showing major excavated areas, including kivas.

discoveries there, such a situation was anything but evident. After his visit in 1885 Victor Mindeleff (1891, p. 50) wrote:

Awatubi is said to have had excavated rectangular kivas, situated in the open court similar to those used in the modern village. . . . No trace of these kivas was visible at the time the ruins were surveyed.

Fewkes, however, believed kivas to be rare because of a conviction (Fewkes 1898b, p. 612, note 1) "that the kiva was of comparatively recent introduction into Tusayan," and in the same report he expressed the opinion (p. 611) that if kivas did exist at Awatovi,

. . . . they were probably to be looked for in the open court east of the western mounds and in the space north of the mission. In all the inhabited Tusayan pueblos the kivas are separated from the house clusters and are surrounded by courts or dance plazas. No open spaces existed in the main or western mounds of Awatobi, and there was no place there for kivas unless the pueblo was exceptional in having such structures built among the dwellings, as at Zuni. . . .

There is no reason to suppose that the kiva was a necessity in the ancient performance of the Tusayan ritual.

First impressions were misleading, however, as Hargrave's work at Kokopnyama in 1929 showed

(Hargrave 1931), and as our excavations emphasized. Perhaps we must now guard against an overemphasis toward the other extreme as a sort of pro-kiva backlash engendering the belief that the inhabitants of pre-Spanish Tusayan suffered from a kind of kiva-mania. I do not think this was so, but it is evident that the place and style of ceremonial observances in the 14th, 15th, and 16th centuries were remarkably close to what they are today. How close they were will become apparent as we consider their surviving remains, kiva by kiva, and the cumulative evidence provided by comparative data.

In the pages that follow we shall describe each excavated kiva as carefully and objectively as possible, with a minimum of speculation, and finally we shall review the entire scene more broadly to arrive at some general conclusions inferable from the detail.

The numbering of rooms in the field had no relation to their original chronology, but was in an arbitrary series representative simply of the sequence in which they were excavated. In the presentation in this volume the rooms are arranged first in three groups according to locations, (a) at Awatovi, (b) at Kawaika-a, and (c) at other sites. Within each group they are described, as nearly as possible, in terms of their probable chronology, as inferred from all relevant data.

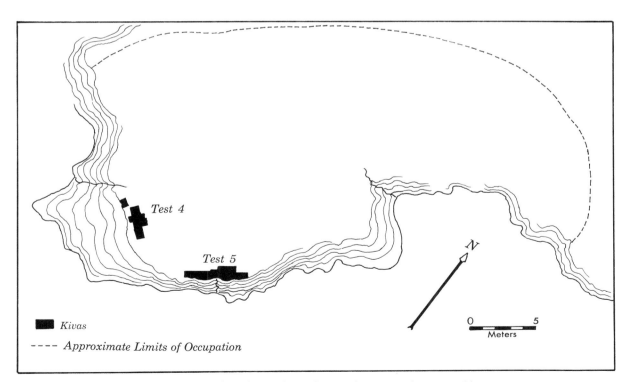

Fig. 3. General plan of Kawaika-a, showing locations of excavated kivas.

Explication of Specialized Terminology

Oh, that mine enemy had written a book!

Book of Job, 31:35

For the most part in this report the technical and esoteric terms used will be clear enough to the Southwesternist, but a few specialized expressions will require brief definitions and explications to assist the reader to a better understanding.

ARCHITECTURAL FEATURES

Considering a rectangular kiva as basically a parallelepipedal box, there commonly occur at least five kinds of extensions of its enclosed space. Various terms have been applied to these in other publications, but the following are adopted herein.

A *niche* is a small aperture in the wall of a room or kiva, usually not more than about 30 cm. in any dimension, used for the deposit of food or small ceremonial objects.

A *cist* is an aperture much larger than a niche, penetrating the face of the broad rear bench usually found in a rectangular kiva, just below its surface, and frequently but not always occupied by a large globular pottery jar, in which quantities of food and ceremonial objects are kept.

An *alcove* is a large bay extending outward from one side of a kiva, its floor either at or above the level of the main floor of the kiva, to which it bears a relation almost like that of a subsidiary apartment or annex.

A *recess* is a specialized form of alcove, not present in the rectangular kivas of the Jeddito area, but usual in earlier circular kivas, especially those with pilasters of the Mesa Verde type, where it occurs above the ventilator tunnel at the south or southeast side. This recess is morphologically and probably ceremonially analogous to the area above the rear bench in rectangular Jeddito and Hopi kivas, but since the latter are usually of the same width as the central area of the kiva, they are better considered simply as parts of the entire area.

A *bench* is a flat area raised above the level of the floor and abutted against one of the walls of the kiva. It may extend into the main area of the kiva or be set into an alcove or recess.

Pits are excavations through and below the floor, used normally as fireplaces or as sipapus.

It has seemed convenient in the following descriptions of kivas to adopt a consistent terminology with respect to their orientation and the positions of their several parts. In doing so, each kiva is described from the point of view of an observer seated upon the broad bench that normally existed at one end of the kiva, and which was penetrated by a ventilator tunnel. In modern Hopi kivas, observers of a ceremonial sit upon this bench facing the opposite end of the kiva, where ceremonial paraphernalia is arranged.

It is thus appropriate to regard the end containing the bench as the rear of the kiva, the opposite end the front, and the sides as respectively right and left relative to the front-facing position of the observers. Furthermore, inasmuch as the positions of kivas vary widely in terms of compass directions, consistency demands the use of constant terms like rear, front, right and left, instead of relative terms such as north, south, northeast, southwest, etc. The latter have therefore been usually omitted altogether; but for the purpose of indicating the actual compass position of each kiva, its orientation has been recorded in terms of the degree of declination from true north of an imaginary line through the kiva running from rear (bench) end toward front end and parallel to the right and left sides. Thus the compass direction of each wall or other feature can be calculated by the reader if desired.

MASONRY DESIGNATIONS

Although no exhaustive analysis or discussion of the masonry of kiva walls has been made in this report, certain gross chronological changes in masonry techniques have been recognized, and their resultant manifestations have been designated as early, intermediate, and late, respectively. A summary of the characteristics of these styles is presented on pages 108–112 and in figures 67 and 68, and will not be elaborated here.

CERAMIC TERMINOLOGY

References to pottery types are mostly expressed in well-established terms used elsewhere in the literature and particularly defined in a report on the ceramics of the Western Mound at Awatovi (Smith 1971). Certain qualifications should be noted, however. It is recognized that the types Awatovi Black-on-yellow and Jeddito Black-on-yellow blend into each other in such manner that many sherds cannot be definitely assigned to either type in distinction from the other. This fact was observed in the field during the excavations and was confirmed later in the laboratory, with the result that such indeterminate sherds were assigned to a twilight category called "Equivocal Black-on-yellow." In the ceramic tables this category is sometimes combined statistically with one or the other of the two bracketing types.

Sikyatki Polychrome has long been a well-known type, characteristic of middle and late Pueblo IV, and being in essence a polychrome version of the bichrome Jeddito Black-on-yellow. It became apparent in the field that each of these rather flamboyant and variable types later evolved into one or more distinct and separable types both prior to and after the coming of the Spaniards. Definitions and nomenclature for these potential types and varieties have not been formulated, however, and we have therefore used the term "post-Sikyatki" to refer generally to specimens that differ from the norm of Sikyatki Polychrome and Jeddito Black-on-yellow but are yet clearly affiliated with them.

The differentiations from the norms of Jeddito Black-on-yellow and Sikyatki Polychrome were usually in the direction of heavier construction, thicker vessel walls, less carefully smoothed surfaces, less nicely executed painting, changes in shape, less well-controlled firing with resulting variations in color from yellow to pink, all together producing a general appearance of inferior quality and degraded virtuosity.

The term "post-Sikyatki" suggests a chronological placement subsequent to that of "classic" Sikyatki Polychrome, and in general that inference is warranted. It is very likely, however, that an undetermined number of sherds called "post-Sikyatki" may in fact have been merely inferior examples of the established types, but actually contemporary with them.

This uncertainty creates an admitted fuzziness in the chronological statistics, but in general the term "post-Sikyatki" may be taken as equivalent to "late" Sikyatki as well as literally "post" Sikyatki. For the purposes of the discussion herein that is precise enough.

In the ceramic tables for kivas at Awatovi and Kawaika-a only painted sherds have been considered, whereas in the tables for kivas at the other sites, all sherds have been included. Direct comparisons of sherd counts between the two groups cannot therefore be exact, although the ultimate significance is not materially affected.

CERAMIC GROUPS

Throughout the discussion, the term "ceramic group" is used in the sense defined by Colton (1953, p. 65) as an assemblage of contemporary, usually painted, pottery types occurring together in a site or in particular components or strata of a site. The subject has been fully explicated in a study of the ceramics of the Western Mound (Smith 1971, pp. 18–22, figs. 12–14), where the several ceramic groups occurring there have been defined. It is necessary here merely to note the distinctive characteristics of those groups that occurred in the kivas herein discussed.

Group A-1. Almost completely Jeddito Black-on-yellow, Sikyatki Polychrome, and post-Sikyatki types. This group can be subdivided into early and late phases, on the basis of relatively small or large components of post-Sikyatki types in relation to Jeddito Black-on-yellow and Sikyatki Polychrome.

Group A-2. Mostly Jeddito Black-on-yellow, Sikyatki Polychrome, and post-Sikyatki types combined, with a very small component of Awatovi Black-on-yellow.

Group A-3. From one-half to three-fourths Jeddito Black-on-yellow, Sikyatki Polychrome, and post-Sikyatki types combined, with from 10 to 25 percent Awatovi Black-on-yellow and not over 10 percent Jeddito Black-on-orange.

Group B-4. Less than one-half Jeddito Black-on-yellow, Sikyatki Polychrome, and post-Sikyatki types combined, with one-half to two-thirds Awatovi Black-on-yellow, and less than 10 percent Jeddito Black-on-orange.

Group B-5. Less than 20 percent Jeddito Black-on-yellow and Sikyatki Polychrome combined, almost no post-Sikyatki examples, with more than one-half Awatovi Black-on-yellow, about one-fourth Jeddito Black-on-orange, and small quantities of Tusayan Black-on-white.

Group C-6. Negligible components of Jeddito Black-on-yellow and Sikyatki Polychrome combined, and no post-Sikyatki examples, with one-fourth to one-third Awatovi Black-on-yellow, 30 to 45 percent Jeddito Black-on-orange, and 20 to 25 percent Tusayan Black-on-white.

Ceramic groups characteristic of earlier horizons at Awatovi and Kawaika-a are irrelevant here, because no kiva excavated at either of those villages contained examples of them.

MURAL PAINTING LAYOUT GROUPS

Most kivas excavated at Awatovi and Kawaika-a were embellished with elaborate ceremonial decorations painted upon the successive layers of plaster that coated their walls. These designs have been exhaustively analyzed, described, and illustrated (Smith 1952a). In the analytical procedure, the paintings were classified into several design styles on the basis of inherent artistic features, which made possible their arrangement in a chronological seriation.

Seven layout groups were recognized and were designated respectively from latest to earliest as I, II, III (3), III (2), III (1), IV (2), and IV (1), as explained in Smith (1952a, pp. 106–162, 315–319; tables 5, 6, and 9). Occasionally with reference to the dating of kivas discussed herein, mention will be made of the layout groups of mural paintings found on their walls. For this purpose the stylistic characters of the paintings are of no concern; it is sufficient to note their chronological implications for the kivas in which they were executed. Those of Group IV were associated with the earliest kivas, for example Rooms 218 and 229 at Awatovi, whereas those of Group I, which were by far the most numerous, were associated with the very latest kivas, for example Rooms 529 and 788 at Awatovi.

Thus, the layout groups of mural decorations, taken together with the ceramic groups represented in the fill and the dendrochronological data from structural remnants, all combine to provide evidence for estimating the probable dates at which the several kivas were constructed and used.

III

Excavations of Kivas at Awatovi

Then we gather as we travel
Bits of moss and dirty gravel,
And we chip off little specimens of stone;
And we carry home as prizes
Funny bugs of handy sizes,
Just to give the day a scientific tone.

Charles E. Carryl

As has been noted above, the major work of the Awatovi Expedition centered at the village of that name, situated near the southwesterly extremity of Antelope Mesa. The initial occupation of Awatovi had occurred probably during the 12th century in the period of Pueblo III and continued until the winter of 1700–1701, when a tragic series of events culminated in the violent and final destruction of the village and the dispersal of its people (Montgomery, Smith, and Brew 1949, pp. 18–23; Wilson 1972, pp. 125–130).

During the four and a half centuries of its existence, Awatovi covered an expanse of more than 20 acres, although probably not more than one-third of that area was ever actively inhabited at any one time. The earliest settlement was established on the bare caprock of the mesa at the westerly extremity of the area ultimately occupied, and there, at the time of excavation, a mound of cultural accumulation had risen to a height of almost seven meters. Within this mound were the remains of solidly built masonry structures, an earlier one of probably two stories, and a later one superimposed upon it and occupied after some or all of the earliest rooms had been abandoned and filled.

Subsequently this later building was in turn abandoned, though perhaps gradually, and the inhabitants expanded their living space toward the north and east, where they were living when Coronado's men briefly confronted them in 1540. When the Spaniards returned in 1630, this time to stay, they established the church and convento of San Bernardo within the southeasterly part of the village, partly upon existing and occupied native structures, which were filled with debris and abandoned.

The Awatovi Expedition cleared the entire Spanish complex and also excavated several hundred native rooms at numerous other portions of the site. An extensive area was dug to bedrock in the Western Mound, other areas which had been occupied during the middle period of about the 15th century were tested or extensively excavated, and finally numerous tests were made in places that had been occupied contemporaneously with or just before the Spanish period.

Kivas were found in all parts of the site except the earliest and lowest levels of the Western Mound. Surely the Awatovians of that time had used kivas, as had their kinsmen in other parts of the Western Anasazi area, but our limited investigations simply failed to discover them.

The earliest excavated kivas, thus, were located in the upper and later levels of the Western Mound, and had been built and used apparently during early or middle Pueblo IV. Other and later kivas were found widely distributed throughout the other parts of the site, and these were associated with intermediate and late periods of occupation.

In the discussions that follow, each excavated kiva is individually described and discussed, and they are arranged in sequence corresponding as nearly as possible to their original chronology. Collectively they span approximately the period of Pueblo IV, with a few of the latest possibly having survived into the time of Spanish hegemony.

ROOM 218

The kiva designated as Room 218 was located slightly below and south of the summit of the Western Mound and had apparently been constructed within a series of contemporary or pre-existing domestic apartments. A semblance of subterraneousness and insulation had been achieved, however, by the fact that the walls of the kiva on its left, rear, and right sides were not common to those of any of the surrounding rooms, but were separated from them by narrow earth-filled areas. This situation did not obtain along the front of the kiva, however, where the wall was common to the adjoining room, No. 229, which was also a kiva (fig. 4). These two kivas had apparently been built as a unified structure, and had originally been interconnecting by means of two openings through their common partition. Except along this wall, Room 229 was also insulated from its surrounding rooms by areas of rubble and fill.

The floor of Room 218 lay from 3.50 to 3.85 m. above the caprock of the mesa, on which the earliest rooms of the pueblo had been built, and although no investigation was made beneath it, there had probably been two or more earlier occupational levels there, such as were found a little to the east, where excavation was carried down to caprock (Smith 1971, pp. 598–600).

The kiva was roughly rectangular, but its walls were unevenly laid and far from straight, and its corners were only approximately square. Total length of the floor area varied slightly from 4.46 m. along the left wall to 4.22 m. along the right, and total width from 2.90 m. across the rear to 2.43 m. across the front. Its orientation was about N. 75° E.

A bench extended across the rear of the room, 1.08 m. broad and from 47 to 55 cm. high. Another bench extended along the left wall from the face of the rear bench to the front wall, from 50 to 60 cm. broad and from 45 to 70 cm. high. The two benches were separated from each other by a masonry pier that extended into the room from the left-rear corner to the extent of their respective breadths. The rear bench had been part of the original architecture of the room, but the left bench had been added later, as will be explained below. The surfaces of both benches had been paved with stone slabs.

Slightly to the left of the center line of the rear bench a rectangular horizontal tunnel, 30 cm. wide and about 50 cm. high, extended to a point just beyond the rear wall, where a roughly circular vertical shaft rose to the surface within an irregular mass of clumsily piled rocks that could hardly be called masonry. This rock pile was within the rubble-filled area that surrounded the kiva. The bottom of the horizontal tunnel was at floor level and was formed with stone slabs, as were the sides; small cross sticks above the tunnel supported the surface paving slabs of the bench.

The floor of the kiva was completely paved with irregular but neatly fitted sandstone slabs. Since the room had been built on fill, however, the floor had settled unevenly, and the walls had slumped and bowed so that the entire structure was in a state of advanced decrepitude at the time of excavation.

A rectangular slab-lined firepit, 40 by 39 cm. in dimensions, was sunk into the floor midway between the right and left edges of the floor and about 1.00 m. from the face of the rear bench. Halfway between the firepit and the face of the bench was a vertical stone slab set into the floor as a deflector; it was 63 cm. wide but its height was not recorded.

The masonry of the walls and of the faces of the benches was very poor and insubstantial, and consisted of single-faced blocks of sandstone irregularly placed in a matrix of copious mortar. Its construction was characteristic of the slovenly manner of building used throughout the later pre-Spanish period of the pueblo, in contrast to the much more neat and substantial style of the earlier structures. The walls were in various stages of collapse, but the highest section stood at 2.25 m. above the floor at the left-front corner.

Near the right end of the front wall, about 25 cm. from the center, was a small niche, the dimensions of which were not recorded.

As originally constructed, a doorway had pierced the front wall giving access into Room 229, but it had been filled with masonry prior to the application of the first coating of plaster on that wall. This doorway was a rectangle 42 cm. wide by 90 cm. high, and was situated 1.45 m. from the right wall and 1.10 m. from the left. Its sill was 54 cm. above the floor.

There had also originally been a small window opening into Room 229 through the front wall of

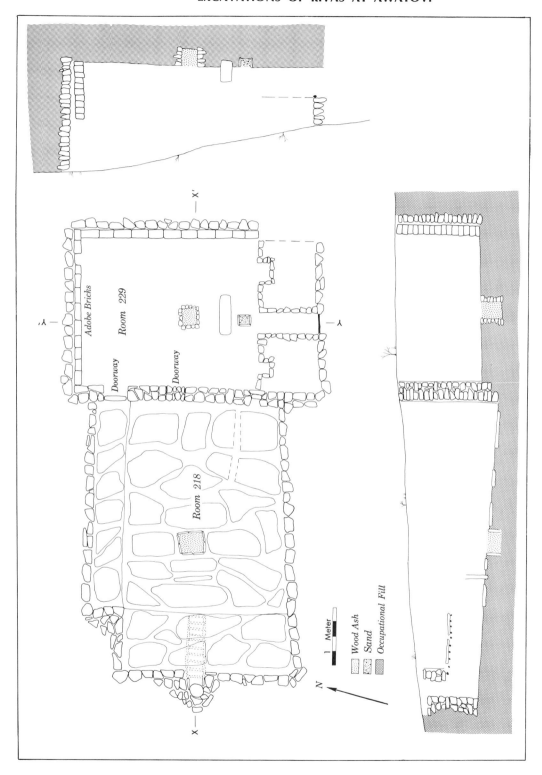

Fig. 4. Plan and profiles of Rooms 218 and 229 at Awatovi, showing their relative positions and the two sealed doorways between them. The original front and right walls of Room 229 were of stone masonry, but secondary adobe-brick walls had later been erected inside and snugly against them.

Room 218 near its left corner, in the form of a rounded square. It was 44 cm. high by 41 cm. wide, 15 cm. from the corner, and 25 cm. above the floor. It had clearly remained open for some time while both rooms were in use as kivas, because numerous layers of plaster, some of which bore painted decoration, could be traced continuously from the front wall of Room 218 around the edges of the opening and on to the left wall of Room 229. Corresponding layers of plaster had been applied to the left wall of Room 218 and extended downward to the floor, behind the subsequently constructed bench. Later the window opening was closed with a carefully shaped and fitted slab, and at the same time the bench along the left wall was constructed, obscuring the lower part of the opening and the lower areas of the early layers of plaster. After this event subsequent layers of plaster were applied continuously over the front wall, across the slab, around the corner, and along the left wall above the bench.

This kiva was the first one at Awatovi in which decipherable painted mural decorations were discovered, although their presence had already been adumbrated by the fragments in Kiva C. In terms of its own date of construction, however, Room 218 was the earliest painted kiva excavated. More

than 100 layers of plaster were defined along the front wall, of which 26 or 27 were painted. These have been discussed elsewhere in detail (Smith 1952a), and belonged to Layout Groups III and IV. They are illustrated therein in figures 37, a, 40, a–d, 41, b, d, 42, a–d, 44, a–c, 45, a–c, 46, a, 74, a, 90, e. The maximum thickness of accumulated plaster was about 11 cm. (fig. 70, in the present report). Layers of plaster existed on both left and right walls but no painting was discovered on them. The discovery of mural decoration was in itself an exciting circumstance, though at the time we did not realize that these paintings were but the harbinger of many more to come in other kivas, most of them indeed much more spectacular and significant than these.

The fill within the kiva was excavated in five strata, in all of which the ceramic contents were dominated by sherds of Jeddito Black-on-yellow and Sikyatki Polychrome, with lesser but still relatively large quantities of Awatovi Black-on-yellow. Black-on-white and black-on-orange sherds were extremely rare and post-Sikyatki types were absent. The ceramics of all strata were essentially similar and fell within Ceramic Groups A-2 to B-4. The period of filling after abandonment must have been rapid. No specimens of wood on charcoal were recovered.

ROOM 218, SHERD COUNT

Depth in cm.	B/W		B/O		Awa. B/Y		Equiv. B/Y		Jed. B/Y		Siky. Poly.		post-Siky.		Totals
	No.	%	No.	%	No.	%	No.	%	No.	%	No.	%	No.	%	
0–50	—	—	2	1	61	24	120	49	42	17	24	9	—	—	249
50–100	—	—	1	—	28	9	125	41	138	46	12	4	—	—	304
100–150	2	1	4	2	68	23	160	54	40	13	20	7	—	—	294
150–200	4	2	7	3	23	10	98	43	87	39	6	2	—	—	225
Floor	4	3	7	5	5	3	111	84	3	2	2	1	—	—	132

No absolute date for the construction or occupancy of this kiva can be ascertained, but on the basis of its position within the upper levels of the Western Mound, the large number of plaster layers on its walls, and the nature of ceramic debris in the fill, it must have been in use for a long time (perhaps 50 years) during the middle part of Pueblo IV, or a little earlier than that.

ROOM 229

Room 229 (fig. 4) was a roughly rectangular kiva, although its sides were highly irregular. The room had originally measured 3.80 m. along its right side, 4.00 m. along its left, 2.73 m. across the front, and about 2.75 m. across the rear, although this dimension was indeterminate due to erosion of the right-rear corner. Subsequent to the original construction, however, and after a period of use during which five or six coats of plaster had been

applied to the walls, secondary walls of adobe brick were erected inside and against the front and right walls, thus reducing the dimensions of the floor area by about 12 to 15 cm. The kiva was oriented about N. 15° W.

Across the rear of the kiva a bench had been erected, with a breadth of 1.07 m. at its left end and 1.00 m. at its right. It varied in height from 33 to 39 cm., and terminated about 30 cm. short of the right side of the floor area, the right wall at that point being thicker and extending into the room by the same amount so as to form a kind of pilaster. Such a device also occurred in Room 218 and in several other kivas, but its purpose is unknown. The bench was faced with masonry and had probably been originally covered with sandstone slabs, but these had disappeared before excavation. A cist was let into the left face of the bench, 34 cm. from the left wall and 7 cm. above the floor; it was 18 cm. wide by 16 cm. high. Another cist occurred in the right face of the bench, 40 cm. from the right wall; it was about 31 cm. square by 26 cm. deep, and was open on the top, probably having been originally covered by the slabs of the bench surface. Perhaps this cist had once contained a large-mouth storage jar, such as occurred in corresponding positions in several other kivas.

Through the bench extended a horizontal ventilator tunnel at floor level, 34 cm. wide and without a surviving roof, though one small cross stick helped to support the rear wall where it extended over the tunnel. It was 1.20 m. from the left wall and about 1.60 m. from the right. The sides of the tunnel were of masonry. Some evidence of a vertical shaft remained outside the rear wall, but this area had been badly damaged by erosion.

The floor of the kiva was between 3.89 and 4.00 m. above the caprock of the mesa, and thus only insignificantly higher than that of Room 218. It was bereft of stone paving slabs, which had probably been scavenged at some time after abandonment. An almost square firepit existed near the center of the room, 1.95 m. from the face of the bench, 1.10 m. from the left wall and 1.20 m. from the right. Its sides were of masonry; it measured about 26 cm. square by 37 cm. deep, and was filled with wood ashes.

About 50 cm. behind the firepit rose a deflector in the form of a single sandstone slab with rounded edges 66 cm. long by 28 cm. high, and with the unusual thickness of 23 cm. Between the deflector and the mouth of the ventilator tunnel was a small slab-lined pit measuring 18 by 11 cm., its longer dimension parallel to the longer axis of the room, and 13 cm. in depth. This pit was filled with clean white sand. Its purpose was not apparent, though it might have served as the footing for a pole ladder leading to a hatchway in the roof.

The original walls of Room 229 were of the poorly constructed late style (pp. 109–110), composed of unshaped sandstone blocks laid in abundant mortar, roughly adjusted to a fairly even face on the interior, but quite irregular on the exterior. The kiva had been placed within the main block of domestic apartments, but was separated from adjacent rooms on the front, left, and right sides by a narrow intervening zone filled with earth and debris. The west (or left) wall, however, was integral for most of its length with the front wall of Room 218, and was originally pierced by the two openings that have been described in connection with that kiva (pp. 8–10), but which were subsequently closed and plastered over. All original walls had been covered with five or six layers of plaster, the surviving portions of which showed no traces of painted decoration.

Later, perhaps at the time of the closing of the openings into Room 218, new walls were constructed against the interior faces of the front and right walls. The new walls were unusual in being made of preformed adobe bricks, sun-dried and hand-modeled, and laid in even courses with mud mortar between. In length the bricks varied from 26 to 36 cm., the norm being between 29 and 32 cm., but in the other dimensions they were nearly uniform, 12 to 13 cm. in breadth, and 9 to 9.5 cm. in thickness. They were evenly laid in horizontal courses with broken vertical joints (fig. 5).

The bricks were unquestionably pre-Spanish, and had not been formed in molds. One face was flat while the others were very slightly rounded and showed finger and hand imprints suggesting that they had been modeled by hand on a flat slab of stone. Into the adobe had been mixed grass and other vegetal matter. The use of adobe bricks by the Anasazi was unusual but not unique, and a résumé of known instances has been compiled in Smith (1952a, p. 9).

In the front brick wall three niches were inset, as shown in figure 5. Two occurred within the same course of bricks, their lower edges about 76 cm. above the floor. Both were 9 cm. high by 16 cm. wide, the left-hand one 44 cm. from the left wall, the other 24 cm. from the right wall. The third niche was only 9 cm. above floor level and 26 cm. from the left wall. It was roughly arched above a flat sill 24 cm. wide at the base and 20 cm. high. Subsequent layers of plaster, when applied to the face of the wall, had been carried around the edges and into each of the niches so that the latter became progressively smaller as new layers were added.

The total number of plaster layers applied to the walls of Room 229 was not exactly determined, but definable remains of painting survived on nine of them, all on the front wall. Plaster on the other walls had mostly fallen, but no indication of paint was discovered on the fragments. The designs have been fully discussed in Smith (1952a, figs. 41, *a*, *c*, 43, *a*, *c*, *d*, 46, *c*, 70, *a*), but we may point out here that all were within Layout Groups III and IV, except the outermost, which was classifiable with Layout Group I. This situation suggests that all except the latest were probably contemporary with those in Room 218, but that Room 229 may have remained in use a little longer than did Room 218, its occupational life overlapping somewhat with that of the kivas in Tests 14 and 19.

The fill that had collected in the kiva after abandonment contained a ceramic complex heavily dominated by black-on-yellow, with very small components of Tusayan Black-on-white and Jeddito Black-on-orange, a small amount of Sikyatki Polychrome, and a complete absence of post-Sikyatki types, being thus representative of Ceramic Groups A-2 or A-3.

ROOM 229, SHERD COUNT

Depth	B/W		B/O		Awa. B/Y		Equiv. B/Y		Jed. B/Y		Siky. Poly.		post-Siky.		Totals
	No.	%	No.	%	No.	%	No.	%	No.	%	No.	%	No.	%	
0–floor	6	1	20	2	66	6	321	30	527	50	116	11	—	—	1056

No datable specimens of wood or charcoal were recovered from the excavation, and no absolute date can be assigned for either construction or occupancy beyond the general one of middle Pueblo IV, as inferred from the ceramics in the fill.

Fig. 5. Secondary front wall of Room 229 in the Western Mound at Awatovi, made of hand-modeled adobe bricks, with earlier, plastered stone-masonry wall behind.

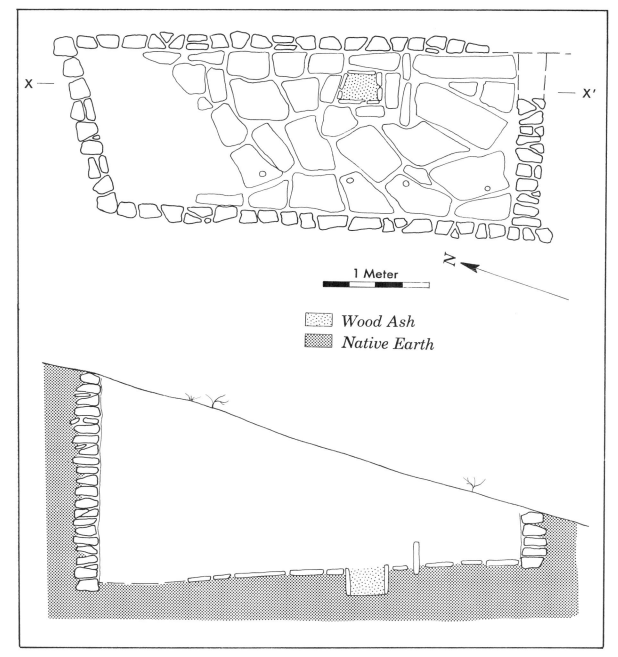

Fig. 6. Plan and profile of Room 240 at Awatovi, showing the off-center firepit and deflector. The point at which a ventilator tunnel might have existed had been entirely destroyed by erosion.

ROOM 240

Room 240 was located in the upper part of the Western Mound, about 16.50 m. east of Room 229, and within the same extensive block of domestic apartments, with the adjacent units of which it shared its left, front, and right walls; the

area beyond the rear wall had been almost entirely eroded away (fig. 6).

It was considered to have been a kiva, although it lacked some of the characteristics thereof. One of the persuasive factors in this identification was the presence on the front (north) wall of approximately 50 layers of plaster, one of which was painted with a large stylized bird figure (Smith 1952a, fig. 43, *b*).

The room was unusually long and narrow, roughly rectangular with exceedingly uneven walls of very poor "late" style masonry. The surviving walls stood about 2.00 m. high at the front, but had almost disappeared at the rear. The dimensions at floor level were 1.53 m. across the front, 1.69 m. across the rear, 3.92 m. along the left side, and 4.33 m. along the right. There was no evidence of a bench. Orientation of the room was about N. 15° W.

The floor was mostly paved with fitted sandstone slabs although some had been removed from the northerly area, which had slumped considerably. The floor level varied, but was originally about 3.60 to 3.70 m. above the caprock of the mesa, and thus very nearly on the level of Rooms 218 and 229. A slab-lined firepit occurred, considerably to the right of the midline of the floor area, 26 cm. from the right wall and 1.25 m. from the rear wall. It was irregularly trapezoidal, with sides varying from 28 to 36 cm., 27 cm. deep, and was filled with wood ash. About 25 cm. behind (south of) the firepit was a deflector, 73 cm. long, 27 cm. high, and 10 cm. thick. It was composed of two vertical sandstone slabs, set edge-to-edge, the right extremity almost in contact with the right wall. That part of the rear wall

directly behind the firepit had been destroyed, so that if there had ever been a ventilator there it had entirely disappeared.

The only other floor feature was a row of four small holes approximately circular, drilled through the floor slabs. These were placed from 33 to 40 cm. from the left (west) wall, and were unevenly spaced along a span of about 2.40 m., the end ones being 16 cm. and 1.43 m. from the rear and front walls, respectively.

Only small quantities of sherds were found in the fill, but the dominant category was black-on-yellow, with few black-on-white or black-on-orange, few Sikyatki Polychrome, and no post-Sikyatki examples, the complex being representative of Ceramic Group A-3.

This complex resembled those in Rooms 218 and 229 and in the other adjacent rooms and suggested a date of construction and abandonment during middle Pueblo IV. The single mural painting belonged to Layout Group IV which also suggested contemporaneity with Rooms 218 and 229.

No wood or charcoal specimens were recovered.

As said above, the identification of this room as a kiva is uncertain, but it was tentatively classified as such on the basis of the mural decoration, the firepit with deflector, the slab floor, the row of circular holes in the floor, and the relatively large area.

ROOM 240, SHERD COUNT

Depth	B/W		B/O		Awa. B/Y		Equiv. B/Y		Jed. B/Y		Siky. Poly.		post-Siky.		Totals
	No.	%	No.	%	No.	%	No.	%	No.	%	No.	%	No.	%	
0–floor	1	1	5	6	15	20	20	25	32	41	6	7	—	—	79

TEST 14, GENERAL

Between the summit of the Western Mound at Awatovi and the rising ground northwest of the Franciscan mission area, about 70 meters from the former and 120 meters from the latter, lay a shallow swale through which drained the run-off from the higher land to northwest and northeast.

In this unlikely place, and close to the escarpment of the mesa, not actually in the lowest part of the swale but along the gentle slope of its

westerly side, occurred a tightly integrated cluster of at least six kivas. At the time of excavation they were collectively designated Test 14, and while one of them (Room 10) lay beneath the general level of the others and was therefore of an earlier horizon, the other five must have been built nearly simultaneously, since they were nested together like the domiciliary rooms of a compact pueblo (fig. 7). They had almost certainly been occupied contemporaneously, during a period between the abandonment of the Western Mound and the subsequent development of the Eastern Village, northwest of the site of the later Christian church.

Other rooms of a domestic nature surrounded the kivas of Test 14, but although they were not fully investigated, surface spoor did not suggest the presence of extensive solid house blocks. Since the accumulation of sand and soil in this area was minimal, the floors of the kivas were close to bedrock, and much of their superstructure must have been above ground, rather than sunk into a subterranean pit or confined within other buildings.

Why such a cluster of kivas was built in this place was not apparent. But the practice of contiguity in kiva location was not uncommon, as evidenced elsewhere at Awatovi (for example Rooms 218 and 229; Rooms 788 and 908; Kivas A, C, D, and E) and at Kawaika-a (for example Tests 4 and 5). Whatever the purpose, the kivas of Test 14 were clearly intimately related to each other and will be considered together.

TEST 14, ROOM 2

Room 2 in Test 14 (fig. 8) was almost rectangular except that the rear wall was not quite at right angles to the side walls, and was also somewhat shortened at its right end by a masonry buttress that protruded coextensively with the depths of the rear and right benches. The total length of the left side of the room was 6.00 m., that of the right about 5.56 m.; the width across the front was 4.10 m., that across the rear 3.75 m. The area of the main portion of the kiva, exclusive of the rear bench, was almost square, measuring 4.10 m. across the front, 4.12 m. across the face of the rear bench, 4.16 m. along the right side, and 4.50 m. along the left side. The kiva was oriented about N. 20° W.

As stated above, a broad bench extended almost across the rear of the kiva, its left end flush with the left wall, but its right end terminating a little short of the right wall. This shortening was produced by a buttress that protruded from the right wall about 45 cm. at the face of the rear bench and about 38 cm. at its back, and extended forward about 1.40 m. The bench had probably been originally paved with slabs, but only a few remained scattered about. Its face was of masonry. It was 1.64 m. broad at its left end, 1.40 m. broad at its right end, stood from 50 to 55 cm. above the floor, and was pierced by a rectangular ventilator tunnel almost exactly at right angles to its face, but placed about 25 cm. to the left of the midline of the kiva. The tunnel was 49 cm. wide, but its original height was indeterminate because all evidence of its roof had disappeared. The exterior vertical shaft was not excavated.

The rear bench had apparently originally contained two large rectangular cists, one on each

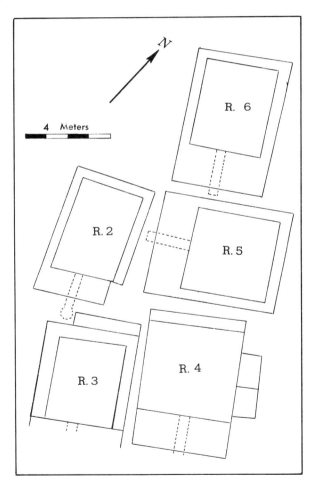

Fig. 7. Diagrammatic plan of all kivas excavated at Test 14 at Awatovi, showing their positional relations to one another. Room 10 was beneath Room 4, but its exact outlines are not indicated hereon.

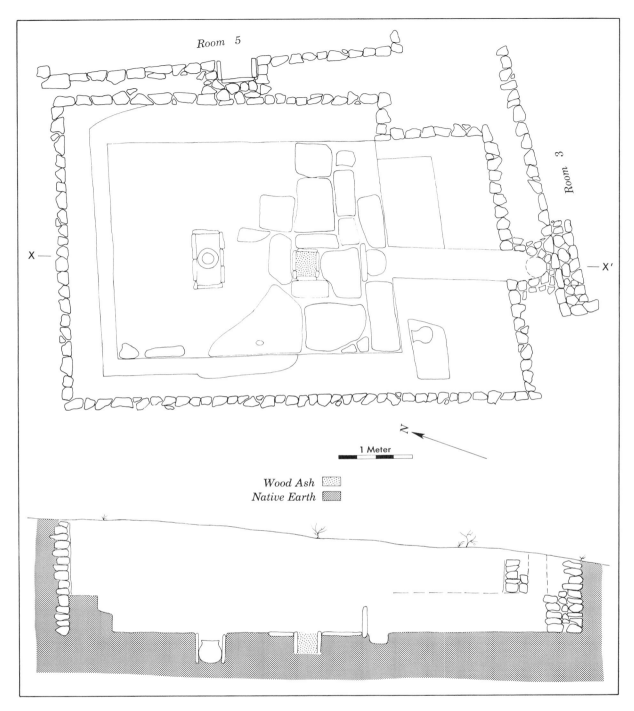

Fig. 8. Plan and profile of Test 14, Room 2, at Awatovi, showing the positions of a utility jar beneath the left-hand side of the rear bench, and another in a subfloor pit that served perhaps as a sipapu or footdrum. The two-level, unpaved front bench was unusual.

side of the ventilator tunnel. Although both were badly broken down so that their dimensions could not be determined, they could be equated with correspondingly located features in numerous other kivas. The one on the left side contained a large yellow utility jar, its orifice flush with the face of the bench and directed upward at a slight angle above the horizontal. Doubtless the other cist had once held a similar jar, although it had disappeared. Analogous jars in other kivas often contained various small objects, but nothing was found in this one.

Narrow benches surrounded all other sides of the kiva, and these had apparently been modified during the period of occupation, although the exact sequence of events was not determinable. Apparently these benches had originally extended around the kiva at the same level as that of the rear bench, and had varied in breadth between 50 and 60 cm. Later, however, they appeared to have been partially reduced in height by about half, so that in their secondary phase they stood only 25 to 30 cm. above the floor. The right-side bench was lowered over its entire area, but the front and left-side benches were lowered for only approximately the outward half their breadth, leaving a steplike contour. It is possible that this apparent lowering was an illusion, however, because all three benches were badly broken down and no facing or surfacing slabs remained to define them sharply.

The floor of the kiva, which was almost on the caprock of the mesa, was paved with fitted slabs, although only those in the rear half of the area remained *in situ*. A rectangular slab-lined firepit, measuring 28 cm. longitudinally by 33 cm. transversely, was situated about 1.00 m. in front of the mouth of the ventilator tunnel, 1.58 m. from the left wall, and 2.08 m. from the right wall. It contained wood ash. At about one-third the distance from the ventilator opening to the firepit stood a large slab functioning as a deflector. It was 53 cm. long, 30 cm. high, and 6 cm. thick. The area between this slab and the ventilator was occupied by an irregularly shaped pit that may have served as an ash collector, or as a socket to support a ladder.

Embedded below the floor, almost exactly on the longitudinal midline of the kiva, and about 1.70 m. from the front wall, was a globular yellow jar, 28 cm. in diameter by 40 cm. deep. It was con-

tained within an elongated rectangular pit that had probably been covered with a slab of stone or wood to serve as a sipapu or footdrum. The sides of this pit were slab-lined, but its exact dimensions were not recorded.

In one floor-paving slab and 26 cm. from the left-side bench were two circular holes, 6 cm. in diameter, probably once used for the insertion of loom anchors.

The upper parts of the walls of this kiva had collapsed and stood only 1.30 to 1.50 m. above the floor. They were built in the rather unevenly laid style characteristic of the masonry of the late prehistoric period. The left wall was the third that had successively formed that side of the kiva. The two earlier walls stood directly behind it without appreciable spaces between any two of them. Why they had been replaced was not clear — perhaps for reinforcement.

Fragments of plaster survived in several places on all the walls, but only near the front end of the right wall was there an intact area sufficiently large to warrant investigation. Here were found 20 layers, of which 9 were painted. Decipherable parts of 8 designs were recovered, the outer 7 classified with Layout Group I and the earliest with Layout Group II. They are illustrated in Smith (1952a, figs. 47, *d*, 64, *a*, 65, *a–d*, 85, *a*, *c*; pl. E).

The fill in this kiva gave the appearance of having been deposited from a central point, sloping downward in all directions. This fact supported the hypothesis that the roof of the kiva had contained a central hatchway for entrance, although no remnant of the roof itself had survived.

The ceramics in the fill were within Ceramic Group A-2 or A-3, heavily dominated in all three excavated strata by Jeddito Black-on-yellow and Sikyatki Polychrome, and quite without post-Sikyatki representation. This fact, together with the character of the mural paintings, pointed to a date of occupancy and abandonment during middle Pueblo IV, but not the very latest part of the prehistoric period, closely contemporary with the other kivas of this cluster in Test 14.

A hexagonal abrader was found in the upper-

TEST 14, ROOM 2, SHERD COUNT

Depth in cm.	B/W		B/O		Awa. B/Y		Equiv. B/Y		Jed. B/Y		Siky. Poly.		post-Siky.		
	No.	%	No.	%	No.	%	No.	%	No.	%	No.	%	No.	%	Totals
0–70	9	1	3	—	*	—	*191	27	338	48	163	23	—	—	704
70–100	20	1	14	1	*	—	*860	43	800	41	262	14	—	—	1957
100–150	6	—	4	—	*	—	*354	37	392	42	179	20	—	—	935

* Awatovi Black-on-yellow and Equivocal Black-on-yellow combined.

most stratum and a circular jar lid in the second stratum (Woodbury 1954, figs. 21, *m*, 39, *i*).

Eight charcoal specimens, found in the lowest excavated stratum, were dated by Dr. Edward T. Hall as follows: 1372, 1374 (2 specimens), 1383, 1384, 1403, 1423, 1429. Since these were not bark dates and since the specimens were casually scattered through the fill, they are of only incidental chronological value. They are, however, consistent with an ascription to the room of a date within middle Pueblo IV, during the late 14th century.

TEST 14, ROOM 3

Room 3 in Test 14 (fig. 9) was located immediately southeasterly of Room 2 and southwesterly of Room 4 in the cluster. While the walls of each of the three rooms had been independently constructed, the front (or northwest) wall of Room 3 was almost contiguous with part of the rear (or southeast) wall of Room 2. The right (or northeast) wall of Room 3 was almost contiguous with the left (or southwest) wall of Room 4, but a few centimeters of fill lay between the adjacent walls.

Although the three kivas were evidently not built as integral parts of an architectural unit, they were constructed at nearly the same time. Room 3 was, however, built later than Room 2, as evidenced by the fact that the front wall of Room 3 had to be adjusted by an angular offset toward its left end to prevent interference with the already existing and probably still functioning ventilator shaft of Room 2 (fig. 9).

The rear wall of Room 3 had entirely disappeared before excavation, due to natural processes of erosion, since that part of the room lay very close to the south edge of the mesa, where runoff was heavy. Overall dimensions were unobtainable, therefore, but can be postulated with a reasonable degree of accuracy.

Two courses of masonry that had once formed the face of a rear bench still remained intact defining the main area of the kiva below and in front of the bench. This area was almost perfectly rectangular as originally constructed, being 4.00 m. wide along the front wall, 3.87 m. wide along the face of the rear bench, 5.16 m. long on the right side, and 4.75 m. long on the left side. The difference in length between the left and right sides was accounted for by the existence of the offset already mentioned at the left extremity of the front wall, which extended forward into the room a distance of 25 cm. and outward from the left wall a distance of 1.20 m. as required by the ventilator shaft of Room 2 behind it.

At a subsequent time a second front wall was constructed about 60 cm. inside the central part of the original front wall and parallel to it, shortening the floor area to a length of 4.41 m. along the right wall and 4.38 m. along the left, and eliminating the offset. The kiva was oriented about N. 25° W.

As indicated above, a rear bench had formerly existed, but except for the remnant of its masonry face, it had been almost entirely eroded, so that its elevation and breadth could only be hypothesized. Assuming that it had originally been of a height equal to that of the side benches, it would have been about 45 cm. high, and on the basis of analogy to benches in similar kivas at Awatovi, it might have been from 1.50 to 1.70 m. in breadth. A ventilator tunnel about 30 cm. wide had extended beneath the rear bench, its center line about 5 cm. to the left of the midline of the kiva.

At the time of excavation, benches existed along both sides and across the front of the kiva, but these had been installed during a period of renovation after the time of original construction. As stated above, a secondary front wall was built about 60 cm. in front of the original front wall and the benches must have been put in at a still later time. The evidence for this inference lies in the fact that numerous layers of plaster on the left, right, and secondary front walls extended downward to the floor behind the benches. There were thus at least three phases in the architectural evolution of this kiva. Faces of all benches were of coursed masonry, covered with one or two coats of plaster. Whether the tops of any of the benches had been paved was not determinable, for their surfaces were either eroded or otherwise damaged and no stone slabs remained upon them. These benches were 45 cm. high and varied from 48 to 60 cm. in breadth.

The floor of the kiva had probably been fully paved, but slabs remained in position on only about one-fourth of the area, mostly in the right-rear portion around the firepit and between it and the rear bench. The level of the floor was about 40 cm. above caprock, which seemed to have been covered with a leveled layer of sand as a support for the floor slabs.

A rectangular firepit, measuring 30 and 32 cm. along its fore-and-aft sides, 28 and 31 cm. along its transverse sides, and 35 cm. deep, was situated

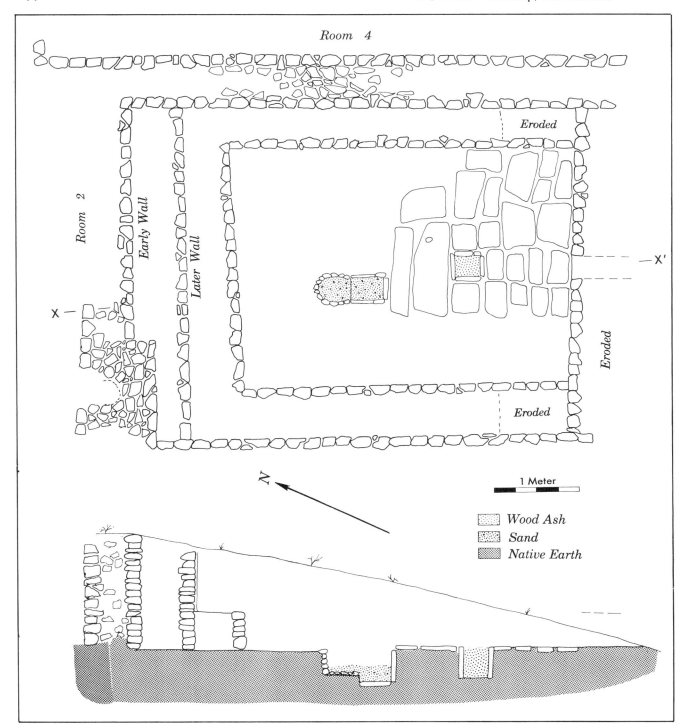

Fig. 9. Plan and profile of Test 14, Room 3, at Awatovi, showing the offset in the early front wall, made necessary by the already existing ventilator shaft of Room 2. The double pit toward the front of the room contained only sand.

96 cm. in front of the mouth of the tunnel. Its sides were formed by vertical stone slabs, their upper edges flush with the floor. No deflector was found but it could have been removed for use elsewhere when the kiva was abandoned.

Another rectangular firepit was located 2.16 m. in front of the rear bench and about 26 cm. leftward of the midline of the kiva. It measured 38 and 41 cm. along its fore-and-aft sides and 25 and 26 cm. along its transverse sides, and was 43 cm. deep. Three sides were formed of vertical sandstone slabs, but any slab that may have formed the front side of the pit had been removed. The bottom of the pit was of clean sand, burned red, as were the side slabs, but no ash remained. A mano lay on the bottom. The side slabs extended a few centimeters below the level of the sand and rested upon an adobe base, which showed no evidence of burning.

The side slabs of this pit extended upward only to the level of the underfaces of the floor slabs, and one such slab extended partly across the firepit. It appeared, therefore, that the pit had been used at an early date and subsequently abandoned and covered. Its use may have been contemporary with the period prior to the installation of the secondary front wall and the side benches, after which it was superseded by the other firepit nearer the rear bench.

Contiguous to the early firepit, and between it and the front wall was a roughly hemispherical pit 30 to 40 cm. in diameter and 35 cm. deep containing earth and debris. Its bottom and circumference were lined with small irregularly shaped stones, but there was no dividing barrier between it and the firepit. Probably there had once been a vertical slab in this position. This pit may have served as a sipapu or perhaps as an ashpit in conjunction with the contiguous firepit.

Near the right end of the front bench and leaning against the front wall rested an enormous rectangular sandstone slab. It had been pecked to shape, with fairly straight edges and rounded corners. It measured 86 cm. by 1.15 m. and was 6 cm. thick. The purpose of this slab was not evident; it was thicker and larger than normal paving slabs, and was far larger than necessary to close any known door or hatchway. It appears in the background in figure 10.

Only the successive front walls and the front portions of the side walls remained even partly intact. The rear wall had completely disappeared and both side walls had mostly fallen. They stood at their highest points not more than 1.30 m. above the floor.

The original front wall also stood about 1.30 m. above the floor. It had been coated with approximately 22 layers of plaster, of which 15 were painted. The later front wall carried approximately 13 layers of plaster, of which 5 were painted. These latter extended downward behind the bench. The right wall carried at least 34 layers of plaster, 19 of them painted, the surviving fragments almost wholly behind the bench. Evidence of painted plaster existed on the left wall, but was too fragmentary for recovery.

Of the 13 painted designs that could be recovered from the early front wall, 8 were classified as belonging to Layout Group I, 4 to Layout Group II, and 3 to Layout Group III. There were only 3 recoverable designs from the later front wall, 2 of them belonging to Layout Group I, and 1 to Layout Group III. On the right wall, of the 16 designs that were recoverable, 8 belonged to Layout Group I, 5 to Layout Group II, and 3 to Layout Group III.

The quantity and character of these paintings on all walls suggested a fairly long period of occupation during the middle and later years of Pueblo IV. They are illustrated in Smith (1952a, figs. 37, b, c, 47, e, 48, a, b, 49, a, 50, b, 51, d, 52, a, 53, a, 54, a, b, 55, b, 57, a, 58, a, 59, a–c, 64, c, d, 73, a, 74, d, 75, a, 78, c, 82, b, 83, a, b, 84, a, 87, a, 88, b, 91, b; pls. C, H).

The fill of Room 3 was of the usual sand and debris mixture and was excavated in three strata. All were closely similar in ceramic content, and were dominated by Jeddito Black-on-yellow and Sikyatki Polychrome, with very small components of post-Sikyatki types, and a few sherds of Jeddito Black-on-orange and Tusayan Black-on-white, thus representing Ceramic Groups A-3 or B-4.

TEST 14, ROOM 3, SHERD COUNT

Depth in cm.	B/W		B/O		Awa. B/Y		Equiv. B/Y		Jed. B/Y		Siky. Poly.		post-Siky.		Totals
	No.	%	No.	%	No.	%	No.	%	No.	%	No.	%	No.	%	
0–50	7	3	9	4	*	—	*97	40	95	40	22	9	10	4	240
50–100	11	2	8	1	4	1	249	43	180	32	61	10	64	11	577
100–130	9	1	12	2	8	1	230	38	180	29	107	18	69	11	615

* Awatovi Black-on-yellow and Equivocal Black-on-yellow combined.

Fig. 10. Test 14, Room 3, from the rear, showing benches on all sides, large stone slab upright on front bench, and Room 2 in background.

A grooved stone abrader and a polished stone cylinder, possibly a nose plug (?), were found in the fill (Woodbury 1954, figs. 20, *d*, 28, *t*).

No datable wood or charcoal specimens were recovered.

The mural paintings and the ceramic remains both indicate a period of occupation during the middle and later parts of Pueblo IV, but ending just as the post-Sikyatki pottery types were getting established, and well before the Spanish period. This kiva would thus appear to have been somewhat later than Room 2, a conclusion further borne out by the architectural relationship between the two, as already discussed.

TEST 14, ROOM 4

Room 4 in Test 14 (fig. 11) was located just northeasterly of Room 3 and southeasterly of Room 5 in the cluster. Each of the three kivas had been independently constructed and their walls, although almost contiguous, were separated by narrow intervals of fill about 25 to 40 cm. broad. Although Room 4 had undergone at least two changes in shape and considerable renovation during its occupational life, as will be explained below, its final form was, like that of the other kivas, an almost perfect rectangle, measuring 4.03 m. across the front, 4.00 m. across the rear, 6.43 m. along the right side, and 6.25 m. along the left side. The orientation was exactly parallel to that of Room 3, about N. 25° W.

A very wide bench extended across the rear, 1.75 m. broad at its right end, 1.71 m. broad at its left, and about 40 cm. high (figs. 11, 13). This bench had been completely paved with carefully fitted sandstone slabs, but those from the right-hand area had been robbed before excavation. The face of the bench was supported in part by coursed masonry and in part by upright slabs.

A ventilator tunnel penetrated the bench but

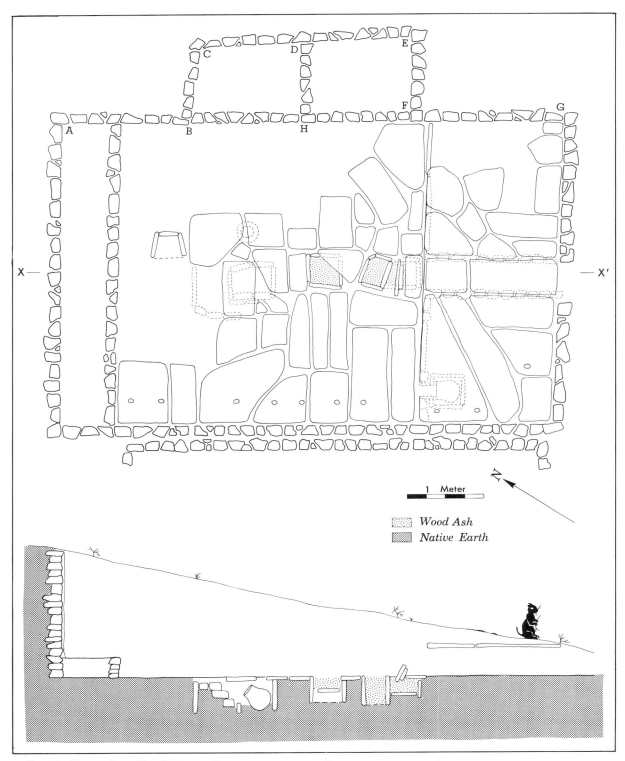

Fig. 11. Plan and profile of Test 14, Room 4, at Awatovi, showing it as a more than commonly complex kiva. The emplacement of a large utility jar is indicated beneath the left-hand side of the rear bench. There were four firepits, probably used at different periods of occupancy, and an elaborate subfloor pit containing a utility jar, which may have served as a sipapu or footdrum. See also figure 14. The superimposed letters refer to successive building periods, as discussed on page 27.

was not precisely at right angles to its face. Its frontal opening, 38 cm. wide, was almost exactly in the midline of the kiva, but at the point where it penetrated the back wall it lay 7 cm. to the left of the midline, and was expanded to a width of 50 cm. The bottom of the tunnel was even with the floor of the kiva, but was not slab-paved. Its side walls were of coursed masonry, and it was covered by large slabs that formed parts of the paving for the surface of the bench. There was no evidence of wooden poles or other internal supports for these slabs. The area of the exterior ventilator shaft had been almost completely eroded away.

A cist was constructed within and behind the face of the rear bench. Its opening was rectangular, 12 cm. long by 11 cm. high, 6 cm. above the floor, and 41 cm. inward from the left wall of the room. This aperture extended backward 15 cm. through the masonry that formed the face of the bench, and was lined on top, bottom, and sides with thin stone slabs. Immediately behind the aperture was an enlarged chamber about 32 cm. square in plan and of slightly lesser height. This chamber was lined on both sides and back with vertical slabs, but was not paved. A horizontal slab, supported by the upright slabs, formed the cover. Within the cist lay about half of a large post-Sikyatki jar, which had been split vertically and placed on its side, its concave face upward and the neck orifice just inside the inner edge of the cist. The jar contained two hammerstones and a small worked bit of obsidian.

A bench also existed across the front of the kiva, 77 cm. broad at its right end, 71 cm. at its left end, and about 25 cm. high. Its face was of coursed masonry but its surface was not paved.

The floor of Room 4 had been fully paved with slabs, but a few had been robbed from the right-front area.

Four firepits were discovered at various places in the floor although they had not all been in use simultaneously. One firepit lay directly in front of the ventilator opening and 50 cm. from it. This pit was almost rectangular in shape but its sides were not quite parallel with the main dimensions of the room. It measured 37 cm. transversely, 22 cm. fore-and-aft on one side and 27 cm. on the other, by 36 cm. in depth. Its sides were supported by vertical slabs, their upper edges flush with the floor slabs, its bottom was composed of clean sand, and it was filled with wood ash.

Between this firepit and the ventilator opening was erected a deflector. This feature was formed

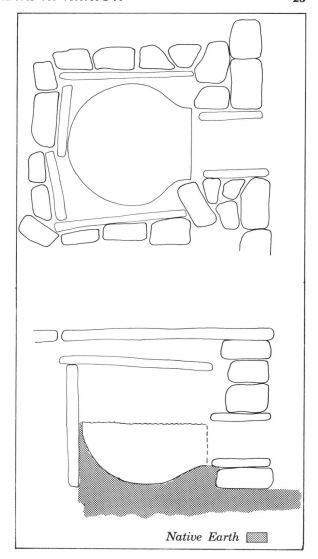

Fig. 12. Plan and profile of cist containing half of a utility jar beneath the rear bench of Test 14, Room 4, at Awatovi.

of two slabs set snugly face-to-face, the larger 47 cm. long and 16 cm. high above the floor, the other somewhat shorter and lower. Their combined thickness was about 6 cm. and they slanted backward toward the bench at an angle of about 30° from the vertical. The deflector was exactly parallel to the shorter dimension of the kiva and was therefore at a slight angle to the firepit, the interval between being 5 cm. on the right and 11 cm. on the left.

Farther forward, and about 1.05 m. from the face of the bench, was another rectangular firepit,

41 and 38 cm. on its transverse sides and 41 and 39 cm. on its fore-and-aft sides. It was almost exactly in the midline of the kiva, with sides parallel to the walls. Its sides were lined with upright slabs, their upper edges flush with the floor surface. The pit contained wood ash to a depth of 16 cm. where a horizontal stone slab 5.5 cm. thick with rounded edges was tightly fitted to form a bottom. Directly below the slab was a solidly packed mass of charcoal to an additional depth of 11 cm., and beneath that was a bed of clean sand.

A third firepit, not visible from the surface, was found beneath the floor slabs about 50 cm. from the front bench, 1.48 m. from the right wall and 2.20 m. from the left wall. The pit was a trapezoid in plan, its fore-and-aft sides measuring 37 and 27 cm., respectively, its transverse sides 30 cm. each. Three sides were lined with slabs but the fourth and longest slab was missing. There was no clearly defined bottom, but the slabs extended downward about 48 cm. thus bringing them to a level only 5 or 6 cm. above bedrock. The pit was

filled mostly with sand and small amounts of charcoal and coal ash.

A fourth firepit, also completely obscured by the flooring, was found 16 cm. in front of the ventilator opening and directly beneath the deflector. It had been more carefully made than any of the others and measured 32 cm. on its transverse sides by 30 cm. on its fore-and-aft sides. All sides were lined with slabs, one of which also formed one side of the first firepit already described. This slab and the one parallel to it were considerably longer than the dimensions of the pit. Each of the other sides was lined with two slabs face-to-face.

This pit contained sand, wood ash, and charcoal to a depth of 20 cm., where a horizontal stone measuring 18 by 22 cm. and 3 cm. thick was emplaced approximately in the center of the pit. Below it occurred 2 cm. of clean sand, below that 3 to 4 cm. of wood ash, and then several centimeters of clean sand extending to bedrock.

In a pit obscured by floor slabs 1.37 m. from the right wall and 1.90 m. from the front bench

Fig. 13. Test 14, Room 4, from the front, showing rear bench, pavement, firepits, and sipapu.

was a large yellow corrugated jar standing upright and filled with sand, bits of charcoal, and small rodent bones. It was 33 cm. tall, 36 cm. in maximum diameter, with a slightly ovoid mouth 20 to 22 cm. in diameter (fig. 14). Several large stones had been set around the vessel as if to provide support, but there appeared to have been no deliberately excavated pit made to receive it. The question arises whether it had had some association with an earlier phase of Room 4, prior to the laying of the floor slabs, or whether it was perhaps associated with Room 10, which lay under Room 4, and which will be discussed below.

A rather complex installation lay beneath the floor between the central firepit and the front bench, and may have been a footdrum or sipapu. This had apparently been a very roughly rectangular hole with slab-lined sides and a clean sandy bottom. Its longer dimension was parallel to the midline of the kiva; it lay slightly off center to the left of that line, and about 95 cm. from the face of the front bench. It had originally measured about 1.00 m. long by about 50 cm. wide and 44 cm. deep. The bottom was covered with clean sand, and vertical stone slabs of varying height were used to line some parts of the sides, particularly the short rear side and the adjoining halves of each of the two longer sides. Another vertical slab stood alone at the opposite short side. Within the slab-lined portion of the hole was emplaced a yellow utility-ware jar, 28 cm. in maximum diameter and 26 cm. high, with a gently inward-sloping neck and orifice 18 cm. in diameter. This jar lay on the sandy bottom and about 8 cm. from the vertical rear slab. Its axis was directed upward and forward at an angle of about 45° to the horizontal. The jar was embedded in adobe mortar which filled the spaces surrounding it within the vertical slabs.

Immediately below the orifice of the jar several small vertical slabs from 6 to 18 cm. in height extended across the box to provide support for the neck of the jar, but they did not rise so high as to encroach upon it. Between these low slabs and the full-height slab that formed the front end of the box were packed numerous large stone blocks, arranged in a series of steps trending upward and forward away from the jar. These blocks were firmly set in adobe mortar supported on a rubble fill, and the uppermost block reached an elevation even with the under surfaces of the floor-paving slabs. The jar contained only sand and undifferentiated debris.

Floor slabs covered the area occupied by the jar, and may also once have covered the other end of the box, above the highest of the stone blocks, although the slabs from that area were missing at the time of excavation. Between these two areas, however, was an opening about 27 cm. wide and perhaps 50 cm. long. A long, narrow ledge surrounded three sides of this area, on which fragments of wood still remained. It thus appeared that a flat board had once covered the area, recessed just enough to place its upper surface flush with that of the paved floor. Since the space beneath the board was hollow, it would have functioned as a footdrum or resonator.

This entire construction can most easily be visualized by reference to the plan in figure 11, the profile in figure 14, and the oblique photograph in figure 13. Reference is made to those illustrations and to the legends that accompany them.

A row of seven holes, each about 4 cm. in diameter, and all from 27 to 36 cm. from the left wall, was drilled through the floor slabs at intervals of from 41 to 75 cm. Two similar holes almost in line with these occurred on top of the rear bench.

The walls of Room 4 were badly broken and had almost completely collapsed at the rear. The front wall and adjoining parts of the side walls stood to about 1.80 m. above the floor but were in poor condition. They had been constructed in the usual unstable manner of irregularly laid slabs and small blocks. All had once been plastered but the only surviving painted areas were a small patch near the left end of the front wall, from which a fragment of one design was recovered, and bits of 12 layers on the right wall. All designs appeared to belong to Layout Group I, which suggested a brief period of occupation fairly late in Pueblo IV. The remnants of these designs are illustrated in Smith (1952a, figs. 57, d, 63, a–f, 73, b, 85, b, 89, d).

A triangular niche, 35 cm. across the base and 19 cm. high, was recessed into the front wall 1.28 m. from the right wall and just above the top of the front bench. It was 32 cm. deep and was lined with many coats of plaster, which were continuous with those on the face of the wall. The niche contained nothing.

The fill of Room 4 contained relatively small quantities of sherds. The assemblage was fairly consistent throughout the four stratigraphic levels, with a heavy predominance of black-on-yellow, small components of Sikyatki Polychrome, and moderate representations of post-Sikyatki types. Collections from the two lower strata approximated Ceramic Group A-3, at about the point where Sikyatki Polychrome was giving way to post-Sikyatki types, while those from the two upper strata approximated Ceramic Groups A-1 or A-2, which would place the date of abandonment and filling toward the end of middle Pueblo IV.

TEST 14, ROOM 4, SHERD COUNT

Depth in cm.	B/W		B/O		Awa. B/Y		Equiv. B/Y		Jed. B/Y		Siky. Poly.		post- Siky.		Totals
	No.	%	No.	%	No.	%	No.	%	No.	%	No.	%	No.	%	
0–50	3	1	11	4	5	2	77	29	92	36	6	2	66	26	260
50–100	12	3	16	4	1	—	117	29	197	48	25	6	41	10	409
100–150	8	1	16	2	3	—	366	52	217	30	49	7	53	8	712
150–180	4	1	13	3	—	—	119	31	142	35	81	21	35	9	394

Five wood or charcoal specimens from the fill were dated 1405, 1411, 1431, 1432, and 1493 (Bannister, Robinson, and Warren 1967, p. 11). The outermost surviving rings on all specimens were an undetermined distance from the bark, but they suggest that the room must have been abandoned and filled perhaps as late as 1500, a date that is reasonably consistent with the inferences drawn from mural paintings and sherds.

Several stone artifacts were found in the fill, including a polished three-quarter-grooved hammerstone, a triangular flat abrader, and two pierced flat pendants (Woodbury 1954, figs. 15, e, 21, s, 31, b, c). Two pecking stones were in the jar beneath the rear bench and a retouched flake in the jar below the footdrum or resonator.

Although Room 4, at the time of excavation and probably for much of its occupational existence, appeared as described above, it had in fact undergone at least two or three minor changes in outline during its lifetime. When first constructed the kiva embraced a large alcove extending outward from its right side. This area was not quite rectangular, but measured 1.05 m. wide

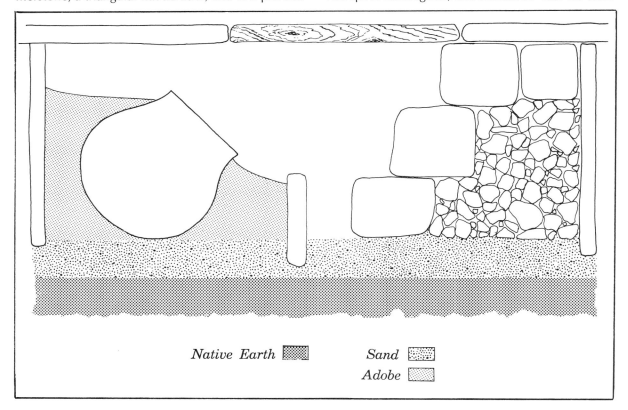

Fig. 14. Longitudinal profile of a pit containing a large utility jar below the floor of Test 14, Room 4, at Awatovi, showing wooden floor slab above the open area of the pit, which may have functioned as a sipapu or footdrum.

at the end nearer to the front of the main room and 1.25 m. wide at the end nearer the rear of the main room. Its length was 2.85 m. at its open side facing the main room, and 2.70 m. at its back. It extended from a point 1.65 m. from the front wall of the main room to a point 1.90 m. from the rear wall of the main room, and just slightly in front of the face of the rear bench. Details of construction are shown in figure 11, to which subsequent remarks are referred.

The three lowest courses of the right wall of the main room were continuous from front to rear, to a height of about 33 cm., but above that level the right wall was continuous along the course A–B–C–D–E–F–G, and bore about 20 continuous layers of plaster, none of them painted. The floor of the alcove was 33 cm. above the floor of the main room, thus providing in effect a recessed bench. If it had ever been paved the slabs had later been removed.

Subsequent to the initial construction the wall D–H–F was constructed, completely isolating the small area D–H–F–E and leaving the area B–C–D–H as a reduced alcove. Additional coats of plaster, none painted, were then applied along the course A–B–C–D–H–F–G. Finally the wall B–H was inserted, completely obscuring the alcove, and more layers of plaster were applied continuously along the now straight wall A–B–H–F–G.

Although the wall abutments and the layers of plaster showed clearly the sequence of events, this chronology was reinforced by the nature of the ceramic debris in the two parts of the abandoned alcove. In the area first sealed off (i.e., D–H–F–E) the fill contained mostly gray corrugated and black-on-orange sherds, suggesting that this area had been abandoned fairly early in Pueblo IV, before the period of dominance by black-on-yellow pottery.

In the area abandoned later, however, the fill contained mostly Jeddito Black-on-yellow and Sikyatki Polychrome, with small components of both gray and yellow utility types but no post-Sikyatki types. This complex seemed to be later than that in the other half of the alcove, but earlier than that in the main room itself.

Doubtless the changes in the main room, evidenced by the successive abandonment of firepits, were related to the changes in the alcove, but there was no way in which they could be correlated.

Two specimens of charcoal, recovered from the alcove, were dated 1401 and 1440 (Bannister, Robinson, and Warren 1967, p. 11), although the outermost surviving rings were an undeterminable distance below the bark. These dates were consistent, however, with those in the fill of the main room.

TEST 14, ROOM 5

Room 5 in Test 14 (figs. 15, 16) was almost perfectly rectangular, as were most kivas at Awatovi, but it was more nearly a square than was any other kiva. And whereas all other kivas in the Test 14 cluster were oriented toward the northwest, this one was at right angles to them, oriented toward the northeast. It measured 4.62 m. across the front, 4.70 m. across the rear, 6.00 m. along the left side, and 5.94 m. along the right side, and was oriented N. 59° E.

This kiva was located immediately southeast of Room 2 and between Rooms 4 and 6. It had been constructed independently of the last two neighbors and its walls were nowhere actually contiguous to theirs. The narrow spaces between were filled with earth and debris. The back wall, however, was so close to the right wall of Room 2 that it was not clear whether they had been built as a unit. They were not quite parallel, which would suggest independent construction, but the interval between the two faces was filled with rubble of small stones rather than undifferentiated debris, and the surface facings would

hardly have been capable of standing alone. Furthermore the unusual ventilator, described below, suggests unitary construction.

Benches existed along all the walls. The one at the rear (fig. 17) was 1.53 m. broad at its right end, 1.65 m. broad at its left end, and 35 to 39 cm. above the floor. The face of this bench was of fairly well laid masonry of five or six courses, and it had once been paved with stone slabs, although only one large evenly rectangular slab remained.

A ventilator tunnel penetrated the bench, about 10 cm. off center toward the right, and penetrated about halfway through the rear wall, which was about 75 cm. thick at this point. Here it intersected a vertical shaft that was contained within the rubble core of the wall. The shaft was 15 to 18 cm. fore-and-aft and 44 cm. wide. It was lined on all sides with vertical stone slabs. The tunnel was from 41 to 44 cm. wide and about 35 cm. high. Its sides were of masonry except at the extreme rear, where one large slab on each side penetrated the rear wall to form the sides of the

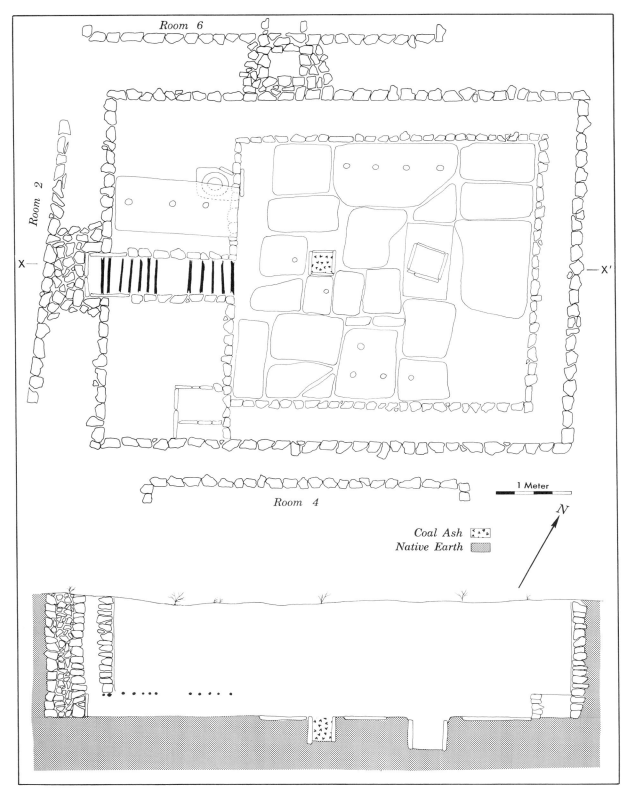

Fig. 15. Plan and profile of Test 14, Room 5, at Awatovi, showing cover beams of the ventilator tunnel, and the ventilator shaft rising within the wall separating Rooms 2 and 5. The ventilator shaft between Rooms 5 and 6 served the latter room. The position of a utility jar beneath the rear bench is indicated.

passage at the point where tunnel and shaft intersected.

The masonry sides of the tunnel rose to a height 2 or 3 cm. below the undersurface of the slabs that paved the top of the bench, and they supported a series of small sticks, 1.5 to 2.5 cm. in diameter, that lay across the tunnel. These sticks in turn supported the paving slabs. Such sticks had probably once been placed closely over the entire length of the tunnel, but only two separated groups of five and six, respectively, remained. Where the tunnel penetrated the rear wall, two wooden poles 4 to 6 cm. in diameter rested upon the vertical side slabs and supported the superimposed masonry of the wall. The floor of the tunnel had apparently not been paved.

The orifice of the tunnel opening into the kiva was somewhat constricted in size by the placement of a block of stone within the left face and of two adobe bricks within the right face, thus reducing the lower half of the opening to 15 cm., while the upper half remained at the full width of 41 cm.

Narrow benches were built against left, right, and front walls, from 35 to 38 cm. high, with masonry faces. The one at the right was 54 to 56 cm. broad, that on the left 56 to 60 cm., and the one in front 49 to 51 cm. No paving slabs were present on these benches at the time of excavation. The two side benches were conterminous with the rear bench.

The floor was fully paved with neatly fitted slabs, most of them large and carefully worked to rectangular form. This floor showed a workmanship superior to that in most other kivas.

An almost square firepit, 26 by 28 cm. and 36 cm. deep, was located exactly on the midline of the kiva and 1.00 m. from the face of the rear

Fig. 16. Test 14, Room 5, from the rear, showing front and side benches, firepit, sipapu, pavement, and loom-anchor holes.

bench. The sides of the firepit were of stone slabs, the bottom was sand, and it was filled with coal ash. No deflector was found.

Another almost square pit was located on the midline of the kiva, its slab-lined sides set at about 45° to the walls. Its two front corners were respectively 1.13 and 1.20 m. from the front wall. Its sides measured 38, 41, 42, and 43 cm., respectively, and it was 41 cm. deep with a hard sand bottom. The fill was undifferentiated debris and there was no sign of burning. A rectangular area much larger than the pit, from above which the paving slabs were missing, extended beyond the pit on all sides, its longer dimension parallel to the shorter dimension of the kiva and not diagonal like the pit itself. Since the vertical slab sides of the pit rose only to a height even with the undersurface of the pavement, it may be assumed that a flat board had once fitted into the space, functioning as a footdrum or sipapu, like those in corresponding positions in many other kivas.

Other floor features were limited to 15 small circular holes drilled through the paving slabs. Four of these seemed to be haphazardly placed, but two straight rows of 4 holes each were set near the left and right walls, respectively; beginning about 1.03 m. from the front bench the holes were placed at intervals of from 39 to 43 cm. and were from 31 to 42 cm. from their respective walls. Another set of 3 similar holes occurred in the single large remaining slab on the rear bench, set in a straight line parallel to the long dimension of the kiva at intervals of 40 to 44 cm.

The most interesting features of Room 5 were two caches containing a variety of objects placed within cists under the respective ends of the rear bench. The one at the right end was the more elaborate, and was contained within a rectangular box measuring 68 by 70 cm., extending vertically from 25 cm. below the floor level of the kiva to the surface of the bench. The right side of the box was formed by the right wall of the kiva, and the front side was the inner masonry face of the front wall of the rear bench itself. This facing wall extended across and beneath the right side bench, which had been built later and abutted against the face of the rear bench.

The rear and left sides of the box were formed by vertical sandstone slabs, extending from the floor upward to the top of the bench. The box had no cover when excavated, but paving slabs

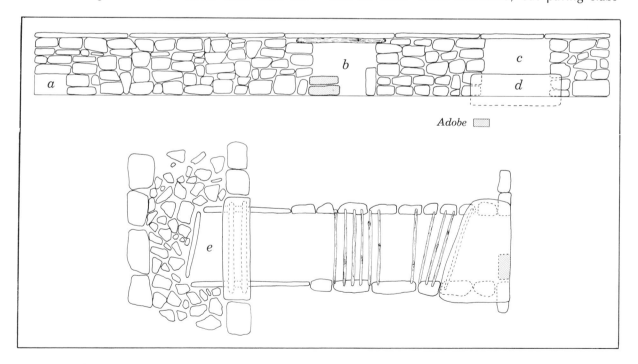

Fig. 17. Elevation of face of the rear bench and plan of ventilator tunnel in Test 14, Room 5, at Awatovi. The mouth of the tunnel (b) was partly closed by two adobe bricks and a stone block, and the tunnel itself was roofed by a series of wooden sticks, of which only a few remained *in situ*. The vertical shaft (e) was irregular in section within the thick rear wall. The small aperture (a) may have provided access to a large storage cist within the bench. The opening (c) gave access to a large utility jar, and was partly restricted by a vertical stone slab (d) set into the floor.

on the surface of the bench had probably once extended across it. Inside, the box was subdivided from front to rear by a partition of three vertical stone slabs set in line 17 cm. from and parallel to the right wall, and about 45 cm. high. The area between this partition and the right wall was solidly filled with adobe.

The bottom of the other part of the box was covered with a layer of coal ash about 15 to 20 cm. thick, its surface approximately level with the floor of the room. Upon the coal ash were haphazardly arranged 34 stone objects. Some were roughly spherical sandstone balls of varying sizes (Woodbury 1954, pp. 171–173, fig. 40, *i*), many were natural concretions, and others were hammerstones of a variety of materials. One was an amorphous chunk of yellow ochre and one was a flake of obsidian.

Sand had been poured on and around these objects, and above the sand was a second layer of similar objects. These were more heterogeneous in character, including several fragments of wood, too fragile for removal, part of a pottery bowl containing black pigment, and the skeletons of several small mammals. There were three irregular but artificially shaped and polished blocks of sandstone, three grooved weights, five pounding or rubbing stones, five stone balls, and several concretions. All had apparently been carefully deposited but without obvious pattern of arrangement.

In the entire cache there were 18 stones that had been used as hammers, as shown by the abrasions on one end, 9 of them of sandstone, 5 of quartzite, 3 of basalt, and 1 of chert. About half were roughly spherical, one or two were ovoid, and the others were of irregular shapes. Two had been grooved but the others appeared not to have been artificially shaped. Lengths varied between 3.5 and 8.5 cm. except for two unusually large specimens that measured respectively 22.7 and 27.3 cm. in length. Deviation from absolute sphericity of these objects generally varied between 2 and 15 percent.

Of 14 natural concretions 8 were almost spherical with deviations generally of less than 5 percent, 2 were of irregular shapes, 2 were double, and 2 were broken.

There were 9 stone balls, 8 of sandstone, 1 of basalt, varying in diameter from 2.0 to 8.4 cm., and mostly deviating from true sphericity by not more than 6 percent.

Museum Catalog numbers of all these objects are: 17022–17034, 17184–17203, 17703–17713.

Above the second level the box extended all the way to the right wall of the kiva, and upon the sand fill were arranged five flat paddlelike wooden artifacts in a generally fore-and-aft orientation, with three transverse sticks beneath them. These artifacts had been carefully carved and some showed evidences of blue, red, and black paint. One had a well-carved handle in the form of four doughnut-shaped rings around a circular shaft. These paddles were not at a uniform level, but lay at depths below the surface varying from 3 to 26 cm. Although they could not be specifically identified, they resembled certain forms of pahos or prayer sticks used today in some Hopi ceremonies.

Means of access to this cache were problematical. A small rectangular aperture, 20 cm. long by 13 cm. high, through the face of the rear bench at its extreme right end and in the corner formed by its junction with the right-side bench, could have provided access to the lower part of the cache box, but above this the masonry wall forming the face of the rear bench was continuous and showed no signs of ever having contained a larger entrance or doorway. Perhaps, though hardly likely, access was had from above, through the top of the bench. Or possibly, the entire cache had been placed in the box and permanently sealed.

Near the opposite end of the rear bench was another cist, which had originally extended from floor level to the top of the bench. It had once been 45 cm. wide by 40 cm. deep and was 36 cm. from the face of the left side bench. It had originally opened into the kiva through the face of the rear bench.

A large yellow corrugated jar, 33 cm. high and 35 cm. in body diameter, stood almost upright within the cist, its orifice just below the slabs that covered the top of the bench. A stick lay horizontally across the jar and the forward extremity of its body was about flush with the outer surface of the masonry face of the bench. The lower part of the opening had been sealed by a large sandstone slab 55 cm. long by 20 cm. high, but about 6 cm. of its height was embedded in the floor. The slab was set snugly against the face of the bench, extending a few centimeters on each side of the opening. Above the slab the upper part of the opening had been plugged with chunks of adobe, and more adobe had been packed over the jar and around its neck and shoulders, so that it was completely sealed from view. The fill beneath the jar and around its body was almost pure coal ash.

Within the jar were a few small mammal bones, 12 flakes of obsidian and flint, a crude hammerstone, an arrow-shaft abrader, 3 pieces of malachite, and 6 pieces of an unidentified white mineral.

The walls of Room 5 were of the usual poorly made masonry of irregularly sized slabs and small blocks. They had largely collapsed before excavation and stood no higher than about 1.65 m. above the floor. A few small fragments of plaster survived, showing between 30 and 40 layers, with occasional bits of paint, although no details were decipherable. A circular niche, lined with plaster, was at the center of the front wall, about 1.00 m. above the floor. The left wall was apparently built integrally with the rear wall of Room 6, since the ventilator shaft of the latter kiva was incorporated within this structure. This left wall, therefore, will

be discussed in connection with Room 6.

The fill within Room 5 was composed of undifferentiated debris, and the ceramic content, which was copious, was dominated by Jeddito Black-on-yellow with roughly half as much Sikyatki Polychrome, and a very large component of post-Sikyatki types, thus placing it within Ceramic Group A-1 or A-2. This kiva must have been occupied for not too long a period during the later but not the latest part of Pueblo IV.

No datable wood was recovered. Several stone artifacts were found in the upper stratum of the fill, including a chert core, a polishing pebble, and a bowl-shaped concretion, perhaps used as a fetish (Woodbury 1954, figs. 27, s, 40, n, y).

TEST 14, ROOM 5, SHERD COUNT

Depth in cm.	B/W		B/O		Awa. B/Y		Equiv. B/Y		Jed. B/Y		Siky. Poly.		post-Siky.		Totals
	No.	%	No.	%	No.	%	No.	%	No.	%	No.	%	No.	%	
0–50	19	1	47	2	14	—	492	20	805	34	352	14	670	29	2399
50–100	42	2	44	2	21	1	606	29	706	32	290	13	442	21	2151
100–165	18	1	41	3	8	—	432	31	356	26	250	18	278	20	1383

TEST 14, ROOM 6

Room 6 in the Test 14 cluster (figs. 18, 19) was a larger than usual kiva, almost perfectly rectangular and situated immediately to the northwest of Room 5 in the same cluster. The rear wall of Room 6 was evidently integral with the left wall of Room 5, suggesting that they were exactly contemporary. The kiva in its final form measured 6.80 m. along its right side, 6.93 m. along its left side, 4.31 m. across its front, and 4.09 m. across its rear. It was oriented N. 28° W. There had once been an earlier left wall, however, about 75 cm. behind the later left wall, so that the kiva was apparently from about 4.85 to 5.05 m. wide as originally constructed.

The usual bench extended across the rear, but this one was broader than most, 1.93 m. at its left side and 1.77 m. at its right. It was 40 cm. high and had probably been fully paved with stone slabs, although only a few slabs were in place at the time of excavation. Its face was of well-coursed masonry.

A ventilator tunnel passed through the bench almost exactly at right angles to its face and off-center to the left only about 7 cm. The tunnel was 38 cm. wide at its mouth and 44 cm. wide

where it pierced the rear wall of the kiva. It was lined with vertical stone slabs and blocks and extended from floor level to the existing surface of the bench. Sticks to support covering slabs may once have been installed, but no trace of either sticks or slabs remained.

Across the top of the ventilator where it pierced the rear wall were two contiguous horizontal beams, each 5 to 7 cm. in diameter, serving as a lintel to support the masonry, and behind the wall a stone-lined vertical shaft rose to the surface. At the bottom the shaft measured about 44 by 34 cm. but tapered inward somewhat toward the top. The shaft was built entirely within the rubble core of the wall separating Rooms 5 and 6 and must have been installed when this wall was built, suggesting contemporaneity of the two rooms. Wedged in the shaft about 50 cm. above the bottom was a post-Sikyatki yellow ladle.

Through the center of the rear wall and about 25 cm. above the top of the bench was a circular hole extending into the ventilator shaft behind the wall. The plaster on the wall surface had been carried around and into the hole to form a smooth lining that tapered slightly toward the rear. Into

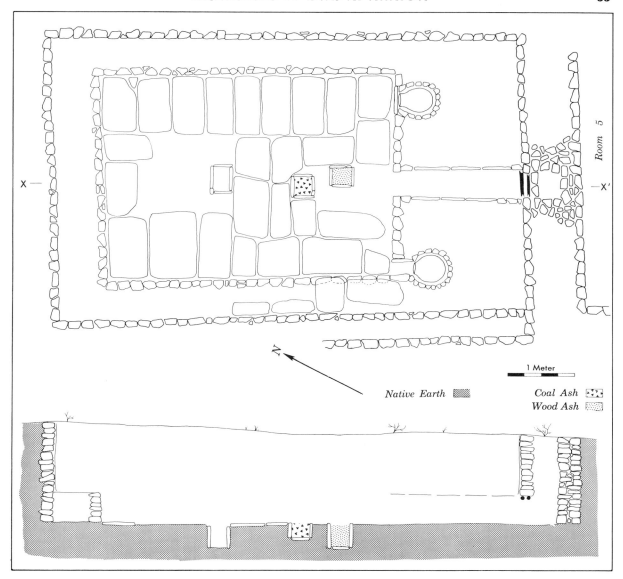

Fig. 18. Plan and profile of Test 14, Room 6, at Awatovi, showing emplacement of two utility jars below the rear bench, two firepits containing respectively wood ash and coal ash, and the ventilator shaft within the wall separating Rooms 5 and 6.

the hole was fitted a circular adobe plug, carefully made in the form of a frustum, about 11 cm. long with a diameter of 10 cm. at its outer face and 7 cm. at its inner. It fitted snugly into the hole, its outer face flush with the surface of the wall, and it could be removed and replaced with the fingers. This device was unique at Awatovi, except for an apparent counterpart in Test 22, Room 10 (p. 69), and so far as known its like has

not been reported elsewhere. Its function was not apparent.

Two cists were let into the rear bench (fig. 20). One, 7 cm. from the right wall of the kiva, was semielliptical in plan, extending from floor level to the top of the bench. The frontal opening was 48 cm. wide, but the lower part had been closed by a vertical slab 25 cm. high, its surface flush with the masonry face of the bench.

Fig. 19. Test 14, Room 6, from the front, showing rear and side benches, firepit, possible sipapu, jars beneath rear bench, pavement, and loom-anchor holes.

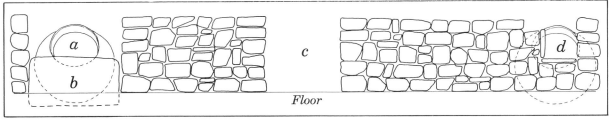

Fig. 20. Elevation of face of the rear bench in Test 14, Room 6, at Awatovi. The mouth of the ventilator tunnel (c) was fully open. A cist containing a utility jar existed beneath each end of the bench. One of these (a) was partly closed at the front by a stone slab (b) set into the floor; access to the other was provided by a small aperture (d) in the masonry.

The sides and back of this cist were lined with a curved masonry wall of small stones, the maximum depth being about 45 cm. Within the cist a large wide-mouth corrugated yellow jar lay on its side, its base set somewhat below floor level and embedded in coal ash and clay. About half of its orifice was above the upper edge of the vertical stone slab, and it was partly covered by a large sherd that had formed about one-third of the body of a similar jar. The jar contained a few small animal bones and some broken sherds.

The cist at the left end of the rear bench was bottle-shaped in plan (fig. 21). Its opening was 18 cm. wide by 20 cm. high, its sill about 15 cm.

above floor level. Right side, sill, and lintel were formed by stone slabs, but the left side was formed by a large block that was part of the masonry face of the left-side bench. This rectangular passageway extended backward 28 cm. and led into a circular chamber about 50 cm. in diameter, fully lined with masonry of small stones. In the circular chamber was a large wide-mouth yellow corrugated jar, embedded in coal ash and clay and inclined outward at about 45°, so that its interior could be reached via the entryway. The jar contained a few small rodent bones, squash stems, and corncobs.

Benches existed along both sides and across the front of the kiva, 36 to 42 cm. high, their surfaces even with that of the rear bench, and their faces constructed of coursed masonry. Those on the sides were from 57 to 60 cm. broad, while that across the front was from 68 to 72 cm. broad. All had probably been paved but a few slabs remained only on the left bench.

The floor of Room 6 was completely paved with large, neatly fitted slabs, nearly all of them rectangular and of about equal size, so that they could be laid in regular rows rather than in the crazy-quilt pattern that was usual in most kivas.

A rectangular firepit, measuring 30 cm. fore-and-aft by 25 cm. transversely and 35 cm. deep, was situated a little to the right of the midline of the kiva, in front of the ventilator opening and 60 cm. from it. Its sides and hearth were formed of stone slabs and it was filled with wood ash. At the time of excavation it was completely obscured by floor pavement, indicating a period of earlier use and abandonment.

A second firepit, also rectangular, was located beyond the first, 1.14 m. from the rear bench and almost exactly in the midline of the kiva. Its sides measured 25 and 28 cm. fore-and-aft by 30 and 33 cm. transversely and it was 21 cm. deep. Its sides and hearth were formed of stone slabs and it was filled with coal ash. It was not covered and must have been in use up to the time of abandonment of the kiva.

A third rectangular pit existed in the floor, very slightly to the right of the midline of the kiva and 1.61 m. from the face of the front bench. This pit measured 24 cm. fore-and-aft by 34 and 37 cm. transversely. It was 42 cm. deep with slab-lined sides and hard sand bottom. There were no paving slabs immediately around it, and it may have been a sipapu or have been covered by a flat board functioning as a footdrum.

Circular holes about 4 cm. in diameter occurred in several areas. A row of five was situated parallel

Fig. 21. Utility jar beneath the rear bench in Test 14, Room 6, with covering slab removed, showing access niche.

to the right wall and 28 cm. from it, at intervals of 37 to 60 cm., the forward hole being 1.34 m. from the front bench. Another row of five occurred parallel to the left wall, and 20 to 25 cm. from it, at intervals of 38 to 84 cm., the forward hole being 50 cm. from the front bench. Four closely grouped holes were from 80 to 90 cm. from the front bench and 65 to 95 cm. from the left bench, but they had been carefully plugged with small sherds ground to fit, an unusual if not unique circumstance, which suggests the possibility that other pottery disks often found in debris may have been made for the same purpose.

The walls of Room 6 were of the usual poorly laid masonry and stood nowhere higher than 1.50 m. above the floor. Some small areas of plaster survived, displaying about 25 layers, some painted, but they were too small to make feasible a study of their designs.

The fill in this kiva contained copious quantities of sherds, more than 12,000 in all. In general the ceramic content was dominated by Jeddito Black-on-yellow, with considerably smaller components of Sikyatki Polychrome and of post-Sikyatki types. But there was a notable change in relative proportions of the two last components between the lower and upper strata. In the two lowest strata taken together Sikyatki Polychrome accounted for 14 percent of the total and the post-Sikyatki examples for only 10 percent; whereas in the uppermost stratum Sikyatki Polychrome had fallen to 9 percent, the post-Sikyatki types had increased to

25 percent. Thus the later part of the fill conformed generally to Ceramic Group A-1 whereas the earlier part fell in Ceramic Group A-2 or A-3.

No datable wood specimens were recovered. Several stone artifacts were found in the fill, including a large, probably two-handed pecking stone, a subcircular flat abrader, and an irregular concretion (Woodbury 1954, figs. 19, *v*, 21, *t*, 40, *j*).

From the architectural evidence of the common wall, Rooms 5 and 6 appeared to have been constructed simultaneously, but the presence of a much smaller proportion of post-Sikyatki types and a larger proportion of Sikyatki Polychrome in the lowest stratum of Room 6 as compared to the lowest stratum in Room 5 suggests a somewhat earlier abandonment of Room 6, perhaps just after middle Pueblo IV. The ceramic character of the upper fill of the two kivas was not significantly different.

TEST 14, ROOM 6, SHERD COUNT

Depth in cm.	B/W		B/O		Awa. B/Y		Equiv. B/Y		Jed. B/Y		Siky. Poly.		post-Siky.		Totals
	No.	%	No.	%	No.	%	No.	%	No.	%	No.	%	No.	%	
0–50	38	1	85	2	24	1	1040	30	1145	32	326	9	873	25	3531
50–100	32	1	62	2	31	1	1241	30	1885	46	462	11	406	9	4119
100–150	12	1	24	2	5	—	326	25	445	35	298	23	166	13	1276

TEST 14, ROOM 10

Directly beneath Room 4 in the Test 14 cluster was an earlier kiva, designated Room 10 (figs. 22, 23), that displayed some interesting features and represented probably the only kiva excavated at Awatovi of the Black-on-orange period. It was thus the oldest kiva recorded at the site. It had been considerably damaged by the building of Room 4 above it, but enough remained to provide the basis for a hypothetical reconstruction.

The complete outline was impossible to define and the position of the floor was indefinite, although the latter could be identified here and there by areas of hard, clean sand, only 6 to 12 cm. above bedrock. In many places around the edges the junction of floor with wall plaster was clearly marked, and it had probably not been paved with slabs.

The surviving walls stood no more than 30 cm. high and had been entirely overlaid by the floor of Room 4, except where the walls of Room 4 had been built directly upon those of Room 10, or, as it may have been, where the walls of Room 10 had been retained and incorporated into Room 4. One or the other of these alternatives seemed to have been the case along the northwest and northeast sides.

Room 10 had had two periods of use between which it was remodeled and its orientation changed. The following postulated history is hypothetical but seems to be justified on the basis of available architectural evidence. For ease of understanding the discussion must be read with reference to figure 22 and the symbols incorporated in it.

Originally the kiva probably extended over the area B–C–F–G, with a rear bench at the southeast end in the area P–B–C–D, the face of which was indicated by the surviving masonry wall running from P to D. The kiva at this period measured approximately 4.35 m. along its left side, approximately 4.00 m. along its right side, 2.57 m. across the rear, and probably about the same across the front, although the exact position of the right-front corner was not determinable. In this phase it was oriented about S. 55° W.

The bench was 1.05 m. broad at its right end and 1.18 m. at its left end, with a masonry face. Its upper part and original surface had been completely removed, however. A ventilator tunnel, 38 cm. wide at its mouth but 35 cm. wide where it pierced the rear wall, passed beneath the bench, but at an unusually sharp angle to the face of the bench and so far off-center toward the left that its rear opening was almost in the corner of the kiva. It had masonry sides, but they were not parallel, the right wall being bowed outward. Originally the tunnel had opened into the kiva, but had later been plugged by the insertion of large stones when the rebuilding of the kiva was undertaken. The tunnel also passed through the rear wall B–C

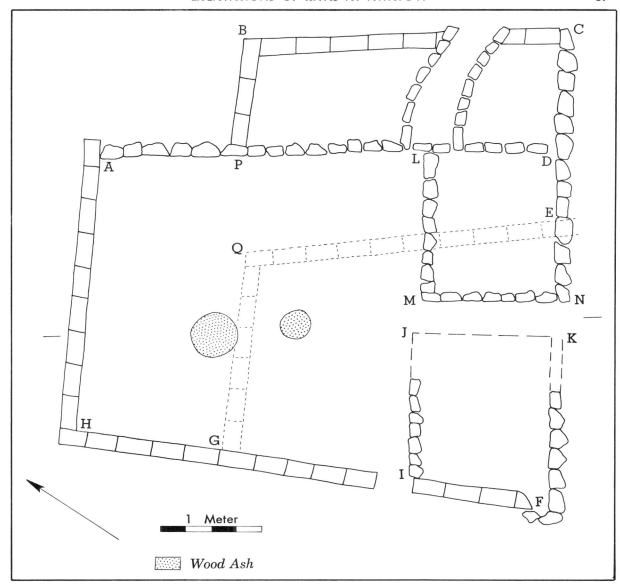

Fig. 22. Plan of Test 14, Room 10, at Awatovi, showing successive revisions. The superimposed letters are explained in the discussion on pages 36–38.

where a rectangular hole smaller than the tunnel itself pierced the masonry. Excavation beyond the wall to discover a vertical shaft was not undertaken.

It may be remarked that the walls enclosing the area of the bench exactly coincided with the walls of the alcove in the superimposed Room 4 (fig. 11), which had evidently been carried upward upon the earlier walls of this part of Room 10. Room 10, thus, may have somehow conditioned

the shape and placement of Room 4, although any supposed relationship may be only a fortuitous illusion.

Later, walls L–M–N and I–J–K were built, thus forming a new bench at the southeastern part of the kiva, which now became its rear portion. In this second phase it measured about 4.50 m. along both its right and left sides, 2.71 m. across the front, and 3.17 m. across the rear. The bench was 1.27 m. broad on its right end and 1.36 m. on its left end, with a masonry face. The upper part and surface of the bench had been destroyed prior to excavation. A ventilator tunnel pierced the bench in the area M–N–K–J. The corner at J was missing, but this was explainable by the fact that it had been torn out during the later installation of one of the firepits in Room 4, all of which extended nearly to bedrock and pierced the floor of Room 10. The tunnel was 23 cm. wide with masonry sides. It was only 8 cm. to the left of center, and pierced the rear wall of the kiva, although no vestige of a vertical shaft remained in or beyond the wall.

At the time the second bench was built the kiva must have been extended forward toward the northwest by the building of walls in the course P–A–H–G–I–F, thus obliterating whatever earlier wall may have existed in prolongation of B–P

toward G. Orientation in this phase was about N. 31° W.

Barely visible and seemingly just at floor level was found an angled wall G–Q–E. The surviving remnant of this wall was made of adobe bricks, and it may have been part of a still earlier room that was razed when Room 10 was constructed. Its alignment had no reasonable relation to either phase of Room 10.

Walls F–H–A of the second phase and walls P–B–C of the early phase were also made of adobe bricks, while all other walls were of stone masonry. The difference between two masonry styles, therefore, does not represent a time criterion, since both styles occurred in each phase.

Two vaguely basin-shaped firepits were found in the floor of Room 10, almost certainly belonging to its second phase. One was 1.00 m. directly

Fig. 23. Test 14, Room 10, showing early rear bench and ventilator tunnel at the left, with later bench and ventilator tunnel at the right. Covering slabs of both benches, if any ever existed, were missing at the time of excavation.

in front of the later ventilator opening and contained coal ash. It was 35 cm. in diameter and 9 cm. deep to bedrock. The other was located 1.07 m. from the front wall, 92 cm. from the left wall, and 1.45 m. from the right wall. It was 45 cm. in diameter and 15 cm. deep to bedrock. Both firepits were lined with clay.

The front, right, and left walls of the second phase showed remnants of 15 coats of plaster, some with possible bits of paint, although this was not certain.

The shallow fill of Room 10 below the floor of Room 4 contained a moderate quantity of sherds, characterized by a dominance of Jeddito Black-on-orange, smaller quantities of Awatovi Black-on-yellow and Jeddito Black-on-yellow, and a very few sherds of either Sikyatki Polychrome or post-Sikyatki types. The complex thus represented Ceramic Group B-5 or C-6. Utility sherds were almost entirely gray.

No datable wood specimens were recovered from Room 10.

TEST 14, ROOM 10, SHERD COUNT

Depth	B/W		B/O		Awa. B/Y		Equiv. B/Y		Jed. B/Y		Siky. Poly.		post-Siky.		Totals
	No.	%	No.	%	No.	%	No.	%	No.	%	No.	%	No.	%	
0–floor	29	9	100	33	46	15	39	13	73	24	6	2	10	3	303

The pottery complex indicated an early Pueblo IV date of occupation of this kiva, perhaps in the 14th or early 15th century. It was certainly the earliest kiva excavated at Awatovi.

TEST 19, ROOM 3

Test 19 was situated about 16 meters northwesterly from Room 6 of Test 14 in a part of the village that was not otherwise excavated. The mound at this point stood more than 3.00 m. deep and contained the ruins of other structures completely surrounding Test 19, but no examination of them was made. It is impossible to say, therefore, whether Room 3 was only one in a cluster of kivas, like those in Test 14, or whether it stood alone among domestic apartments.

The kiva (fig. 24) was nearly rectangular and measured 5.85 m. along its right wall, 4.50 m. across the front, approximately 6.10 m. along the left, and approximately 4.45 m. across the rear. The reason for doubt as to the exact dimensions of the latter two sides was because the walls at the left-rear corner had partly collapsed, making the precise location of this corner impossible to determine. The floor lay just above bedrock and about 3.10 m. below the surface. The kiva was oriented N. 25° W.

A bench extended across the rear, 1.50 m. broad at its right end, 1.30 m. broad at its left, and 36 to 40 cm. high. A ventilator tunnel passed beneath the bench and through the rear wall. It lay about 5 cm. to the left of the midline of the kiva, and was 44 cm. wide at its mouth, decreasing to about 30 cm. where it penetrated the rear wall. A rectangular vertical shaft rose immediately beyond the rear wall, formed of masonry on all sides.

It measured 40 cm. fore-and-aft by 25 cm., transversely. The rear bench was entirely covered with fitted slabs, mostly of irregular shapes, although three large rectangular ones lay across the ventilator tunnel resting firmly on each side and without support from underlying wooden beams. The face of the bench was of coursed masonry.

Benches with masonry faces also existed along both sides and the front of the kiva, rising to the same height as the rear bench. That on the right side was 62 cm. broad at its front end and 75 cm. at its rear. That on the left was 53 cm. broad at its front end and 58 cm. at its rear. The front bench varied in breadth from 71 cm. at its right end to 96 cm. at its left. The area of the floor between the benches was thus trapeziform, its outlines somewhat skewed from those formed by the walls.

The floor had probably once been fully paved but slabs remained on only about one-third of the area at the time of excavation.

A rectangular firepit measuring 31 cm. fore-and-aft by 33 cm. transversely and 35 cm. deep was located almost directly in front of the ventilator opening and 1.05 m. from it. Its sides and hearth were formed of stone slabs and it was filled with coal ash. A deflector, consisting of an upright slab 2.5 to 3 cm. thick, 56 cm. long, and 16 cm. high, stood 37 cm. from the ventilator opening.

The surviving walls were of poorly constructed

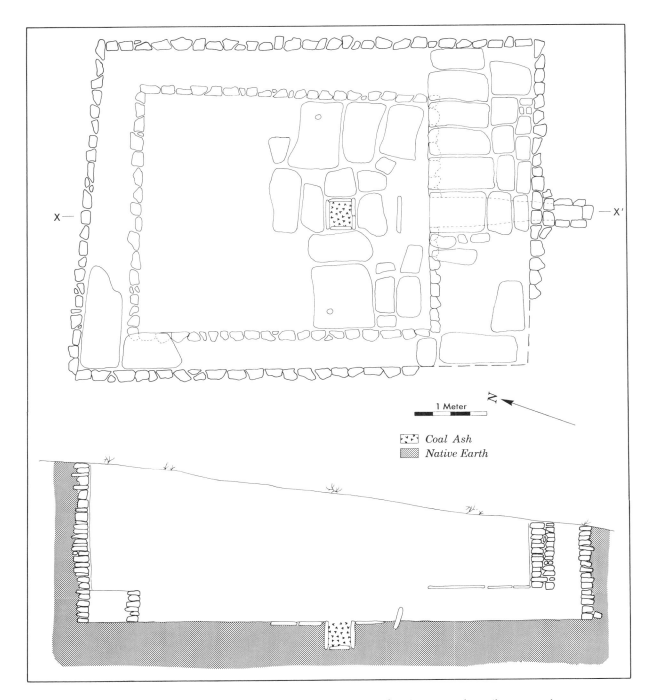

Fig. 24. Plan and profile of Test 19, Room 3, at Awatovi, showing tapered ventilator tunnel.

masonry and stood from 1.80 to 2.30 m. above the floor, except the left wall and the left portion of the rear wall, both of which had almost entirely collapsed.

Along the right wall and the surviving portion of the left wall, and extending upward from 15 to 50 cm. from the surface of the bench were clear impressions of twilled matting in the coating of adobe mortar that still adhered to the masonry. Although no actual fragments of the matting itself survived, the impressions showed that it had been formed of groups of four or five parallel round reeds, each about 1.5 to 2.5 mm. in diameter, woven in a two-over-two-under twill, and crossing each other almost at right angles. The mat was fixed against the wall in a position such that the longitudinal directions of the reeds lay at approximately 45° to the horizontal (fig. 69, a; Smith 1952a, pp. 14–15; figs. 5, 34, b). Above the upper edge of the matting, adobe mortar continued without reinforcement to an additional height of 50 to 60 cm., above which no mortar remained at the time of excavation. The matting was almost identical with that used in Room 788. Almost certainly a second coating of adobe had been applied over the matting and upon this surface were then applied successive layers of finish plaster.

In several small areas on each wall, remnants of plaster up to 20 layers in thickness had survived. At least 6 layers on the front wall and 7 on the left wall had been painted, and in 9 instances enough remained for identification of the general character of the designs, although only 3 warranted reproduction (Smith 1952a, figs. 64, b, 74, b, 90, c). All were classified with Layout Group I, except for the earliest design on the left wall which belonged to Layout Group III.

The fill in this kiva had accumulated to a depth of 3.00 m. above the floor, a level at least 80 cm. above the maximum height of the walls, no parts of which were visible on the surface. Although no evidence of the roof structure was found, it could have existed at the level of the highest surviving walls, which stood 2.30 m. above the floor, a height quite sufficient for clearance. In Room 788, where the entire roof was found *in situ*, the clearance was only 1.90 m. The roof beams from Room 3 were probably removed after its abandonment, and it was then filled, perhaps deliberately. Some kind of masonry structure had subsequently been built above the filled kiva, for the remnants of walls of two or three rooms were evident on the surface. They were so indeterminate, however, that no detailed plan was made.

The fill itself was composed of large components of ash, bones, and cultural debris mixed with sand, and it appeared to have been thrown or washed in from the southwesterly corner. The ceramic content was unusually copious, especially in the second, third, and bottom strata. Jeddito Black-on-yellow was dominant throughout; Sikyatki Polychrome accounted for 24 percent in the lower and middle strata but fell to 13 percent in the upper, whereas post-Sikyatki types rose from 7 percent in the three lower strata to 21 percent in the uppermost. This situation reflected a placement in Ceramic Group A-1 or A-2 and indicated the time of abandonment during late Pueblo IV when the post-Sikyatki types were increasing but Sikyatki Polychrome was still dominant.

In addition to the usual stone, bone, and sherd material, a few specific items in the fill deserve mention. At a depth of 2.60 m. was found a cache of bone beads, apparently once contained in a small bag or basket, although only minute traces of the container remained. On the surface of the right bench lay part of a human skull case. Two stone mortars and a shaft smoother (Woodbury 1954, fig. 22, d) were just above the floor. No datable wood or charcoal was recovered.

All things considered, it may be inferred from the evidence of mural paintings and ceramic debris that this kiva was probably built and occupied a little later than Rooms 2 and 3 of Test 14, but a little earlier than Rooms 4, 5, and 6 of Test 14, during middle or late Pueblo IV, probably during the 15th century.

TEST 19, ROOM 3, SHERD COUNT

Depth in cm.	B/W		B/O		Awa. B/Y		Equiv. B/Y		Jed. B/Y		Siky. Poly.		post-Siky.		Totals
	No.	%	No.	%	No.	%	No.	%	No.	%	No.	%	No.	%	
0–50	12	1	29	2	7	—	595	35	471	28	239	13	357	21	1710
50–150	54	2	52	2	21	1	1185	29	1405	35	528	13	726	18	3971
150–200	22	1	27	1	4	—	1126	35	1054	33	765	24	157	5	3155
200–250	24	1	49	2	11	—	697	33	870	41	373	18	81	4	2105
250–300	13	—	15	—	7	—	991	31	1087	34	815	24	346	10	3274

KIVA A

The room designated Kiva A (figs. 25, 26) was the first kiva discovered in the excavation of Awatovi, and came to light during the digging of an exploratory trench in the autumn of 1935. It was situated about 22 meters west of Room 528 and about 72 meters northeast of Test 14 in an area that had apparently been near the southwesterly edge of the village as it existed during the century

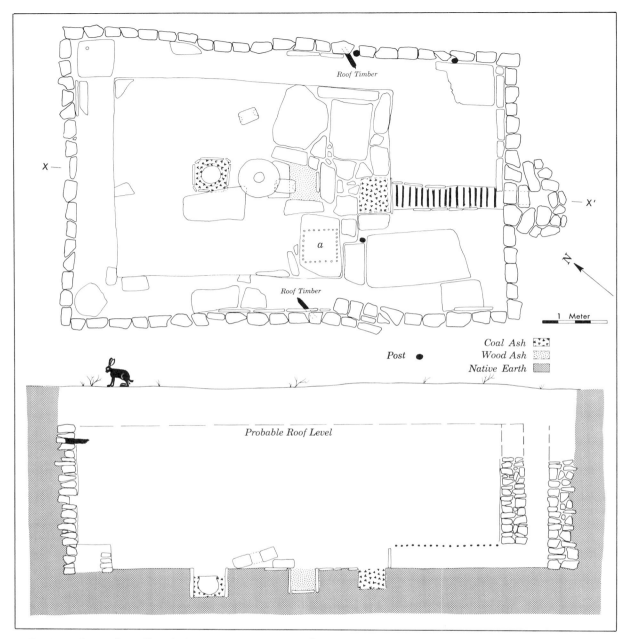

Fig. 25. Plan and profile of Kiva A at Awatovi. Two firepits containing respectively wood ash and coal ash are shown, as well as a possible sipapu and a circular stone collar that presumably had served as its cover. The charred stubs of three beams remained *in situ* in the wall, indicative of the original roof level. A pattern composed of small cup-shaped incisions arranged in the form of a hollow square appeared in one of the floor-paving slabs. See a similar device in Room 529 (fig. 32).

or so before the arrival of the Spaniards. This general area was not fully excavated but was fairly extensively tested, and at least four kivas (A, C, D, and E) were found close together, within what had clearly been a solidly built-up house block. The floor of Kiva A was about 3.00 m. below the

modern surface of the mound, and its walls, which had in part collapsed, stood to a maximum height of about 2.25 m.

Kiva A was roughly rectangular, 6.60 m. long by 4.30 m. wide along its front wall and 3.70 m. along its rear wall. The shorter walls were comparatively straight, but both side walls were exceedingly irregular and bulged inward in some places as much as 35 cm. from true alignment. The room was oriented about N. 40° W.

Across the rear (southeast) end of the room was a bench that varied in breadth from 1.70 m. at its right end to 2.40 m. at its left end. These differences in breadth do not, however, indicate a diagonal face. The face along the right side, though somewhat uneven, was generally parallel to the rear wall up to a point 2.40 m. from the right wall and just to the left of the ventilator tunnel, which will be discussed below. At this point the face of the bench extended forward at a right angle about 50 cm., then toward the left about 50 cm., then forward again about 25 cm., and finally toward the left until it intersected a narrow bench against the left wall. This double offset was unique among the kivas in the Jeddito sites.

The rear bench was about 35 cm. high and had been paved with large slabs of sandstone, most of which had been removed prior to the time of excavation. The face was supported by crude masonry which was in turn covered with vertical sandstone slabs.

Almost exactly midway between the right and left walls was a ventilator tunnel, about 30 cm. wide, extending from the face of the bench directly back through the rear wall, where it intersected a vertical shaft. Although the tunnel had partly collapsed, it had originally been lined with vertical slabs along both sides but its floor was unpaved. Across the tunnel had extended a series of horizontal poles or sticks, apparently about 17

Fig. 26. Kiva A from the front, showing rear bench and ventilator tunnel, with perforated deflector slab, firepit, and sipapu. The doughnut-shaped stone was originally placed over the utility jar within the sipapu.

in number, and upon them or perhaps on a mat above them had rested the paving slabs of the bench surface. The vertical shaft was approximately square in section, 24 by 20 cm., and it extended upward against the outer surface of the wall of the kiva. Its other three sides were formed by substantial double-coursed masonry.

The mouth of the ventilator tunnel was closed by a single large slab, roughly chipped to fit snugly into the aperture, but a small arched hole penetrated the slab just at floor level, very much as was the case in Room 788, and in Test 31, Room 1. No deflector was found, and was probably made unnecessary by the placement of the slab.

Narrow benches of the same height as the broad rear bench extended along the left, front, and right walls. They varied in breadth because both their faces and the main walls behind them were irregular. The front bench, which was most nearly uniform, varied between 55 and 65 cm. and the left and right benches, between 35 and 65 cm. All benches had evidently been originally paved with stone slabs, but only a few of the latter remained in position. The faces of side and front benches were constructed of fairly even courses of sandstone masonry, but there was no evidence of vertical facing slabs, which may or may not have originally been present. Along one part of the surface of the left bench four or five stone slabs leaned against the main wall of the room.

The floor of the kiva had probably been entirely paved with stone slabs, and those in the rear half of the area still remained *in situ*. Elsewhere they had mostly been removed. The slabs lay upon a thin layer of coal ash and sand, which in turn was spread over a reddish earth fill.

Immediately in front of the slab that closed the mouth of the ventilator tunnel was a large firepit filled with coal ash. It was roughly rectangular, measuring about 50 cm. longitudinally by about 60 cm. transversely, and was neither lined nor paved with stone. Its depth was not recorded. Another firepit, also roughly rectangular, was situated along the midline of the room, 1.20 m. in front of the face of the rear bench. It measured about 35 cm. longitudinally by about 40 cm. transversely by 40 cm. in depth, with slabbed sides and slab bottom, and was filled with wood ash.

Also on the midline of the room, 1.20 m. from the front wall and 2.40 m. from the face of the rear bench, was another pit about 50 cm. square, entirely slab-lined but not paved. Within it stood upright a large-mouth globular yellow corrugated jar about 40 cm. in maximum diameter and 27 cm. in height. Its rim, which was sharply outflaring, was 32 to 34 cm. in diameter and 12 cm. below the level of the floor. Coal ash and sand had been packed around the vessel, which also contained coal ash and sand when excavated, but this had probably drifted in after abandonment. It had no other contents.

Immediately between this pit and the wood-ash firepit lay a large doughnut-shaped stone collar. It was 60 cm. in maximum diameter and about 12 cm. thick, with a center hole 15 cm. in diameter. The stone was fairly accurate in form but was crudely finished. Hypothetically it had originally covered the subfloor jar just described and the whole assemblage might thus have fulfilled the function of a sipapu or a footdrum, like that in several other kivas (fig. 27).

On the floor of the kiva lay two sandstone blocks that had probably once served as loomblocks. Both were carefully formed and smoothly ground on all surfaces. One measured about 30 by 25 by 15 cm. and had a small finger socket in each end. The other was similar but was slightly longer and narrower. (*See* Woodbury 1954, fig. 33, a.)

Five paving slabs (two on the floor and three on the rear bench) were pierced with circular holes about 5 to 8 cm. in diameter, which had probably served for the insertion of loom anchors. Their positions bore no recognizable pattern toward one another, and the stones that contained them had probably been used originally elsewhere.

The very large slab in the left-rear corner of the floor contiguous to the face of the rear bench was engraved with a pattern of small cup-shaped holes arranged parallel to the edges of the slab and forming a hollow rectangle about 60 by 55 cm. with 9 or 10 holes on each side. The holes had been circularly ground into the slab and penetrated about half its thickness. These devices resembled those in Room 529 (figs. 32, 33), but lacked the "tails" appended to the latter. Their significance is not known.

The walls of Kiva A had been constructed of fairly well-shaped sandstone blocks and slabs but were in general of the rather degenerate "late" style (figs. 67, 68). The front and rear walls remained in approximately their original positions, but both the left and right walls had slumped inward in an uneven manner, which accounted for the irregular outline of the room. Doubtless these walls had originally been much more nearly straight than they were when excavated.

Fig. 27. Detail of sipapu in the floor of Kiva A, with doughnut-shaped covering stone removed. A skeleton of a sheep lies on the floor at the right and a loom weight at the upper left.

Mud mortar had covered all walls and was still intact on large areas, especially on the rear wall. A reinforcing material was laid within the mortar in the form of bundles or mats of reeds arranged horizontally. Contiguous bundles extended the entire length of the front wall to a height of about 35 cm. above the bench. Along the left and right walls the mats extended from the front corners backward about 1.75 and 1.10 m., respectively. On one portion of the right wall there was evidence that vertical reeds had overlaid the horizontal ones (Smith 1952a, pp. 14–15, fig. 34, d). No mat was recorded along the rear wall, but it seems likely that one had existed there. Rotted fragments of reeds survived but were not preservable.

Only one niche was discovered, exactly midway in the front wall, and 98 cm. above the floor. It had originally been 19 cm. wide by 13 cm. high by 16 cm. deep, but had become rounded and smaller by having been lined with plaster. It con-tained no sill or lintel, and its floor sloped down-ward toward the rear. Nothing was found in it.

No evidence of finish plaster was found on any of the walls, and consequently no remnant of mural decoration.

The roof had probably been supported by two or more main beams across the narrow dimension of the room, but the right and left walls had col-lapsed to a level below that of probable sockets. A row of eight sockets in the front wall, however, indicated that smaller beams had once extended from that wall parallel to the long dimension of the room, their distal ends probably resting on one of the main beams, as in Room 788 (figs. 40, 41). These sockets were between 1.92 and 2.05 m. above the floor and were placed at horizontal intervals of from 30 to 50 cm.

The fill within Kiva A was not excavated in stratigraphic levels and no precise record was made of the ceramic contents beyond the fact that the sherds consisted mostly of black-on-yellow and Sikyatki Polychrome types, placing the complex within Ceramic Group A-1 or A-2.

On the bench were found several "pipes and other artifacts." And on the floor, immediately to the left (west) of the large stone collar were found bones and a skull, subsequently identified as those of a domestic sheep.

In the fill, 50 cm. below the surface, was a small piece of charcoal that was dated 1504±x, but its location was such as to preclude any reliability as a dating fossil for the room itself. All that can be said of the probable date of construction is that the room must have been built after the inception of Sikyatki Polychrome, which seems to have occurred in the early 15th century.

The sheep bones must have been deposited after the coming of the Spanish fathers, and their presence on the floor establishes occupancy of the kiva at that period.

KIVA B

A small room designated Kiva B contained few of the usual criteria of a kiva and may not actually have functioned as such (fig. 28). It did, however, have some unusual, perhaps unique, features, and at the time of excavation was regarded as a kiva. It has been included in this report without certainty as to its functional classification. (For a discussion of "when is a kiva," see Smith 1952b, pp. 154–165.)

The room was situated about 21 meters southerly from Kiva A and like it was discovered during the digging of the exploratory trench in 1935. It was apparently integral with the same large house block that also contained Kivas A, C, and D, and must have been built and used at about the same time.

In shape Kiva B was very nearly a perfect rectangle, its longer dimension oriented N. 60° E., with its rear wall at the southwest end. The length of the rear wall was 1.60 m., front wall 1.50 m., left wall 2.50 m., and right wall 2.60 m. The area of the room was thus only about five square meters, less than one-fourth that of most kivas at Awatovi.

The surviving field notes are meagre, but the plan and position of the room were carefully drawn on the field map, and one photograph was taken showing details of the southerly corner. It is from these data that the following description has been drawn.

Whether a raised bench existed across the rear or southwesterly end is not certain although the surface across the rear part of the room was about 15 cm. higher than elsewhere, as indicated on the field plan, but such a feature is not mentioned in the notes, nor is it evident in the photograph. The floor was paved with large stone slabs and lay about 15 cm. above bedrock.

The only floor features recorded were a rectangular firepit and an upright stone block between it and the opening of a shaft that will be discussed below. The firepit measured about 30 cm. longitudinally by 22 cm. transversely by 12 cm. in depth. Its position was abnormal, being about 1.25 m. from the rear wall and only about 15 cm. from the right wall. The upright stone was set into the slabbed floor almost exactly midway between the firepit and the rear wall. It was about 50 cm. long by about 17 cm. high and was set snugly against the right wall and at right angles to it. Its thickness was not recorded, but it can be described as a block rather than a slab.

The walls of the room were evidently built of crudely shaped blocks and slabs laid up in the rather irregular manner characteristic of the late prehistoric period of the village. At the time of excavation they stood from 1.40 to 1.60 m. above the floor. For the most part they were of single-course thickness, but the rear (southwesterly) half of the right wall had been at least doubled in thickness by the erection of a second wall outside the main wall and apparently not quite in contact with it.

The space between these walls was filled with rubble except for an area at the extreme rear (southwesterly) end about 60 cm. long by about 20 cm. wide. This open space extended vertically downward in the form of a shaft that may have been the upper portion of a ventilator. At a level 75 cm. above the floor this shaft opened into the room through the inner face of the right wall, but here an additional feature had been constructed to form another shaft of similar shape and dimensions extending downward to floor level.

This lower or inner shaft was contained within a kind of box, built into the corner of the room and formed by a large slab extending outward from the right wall, parallel to the rear wall and about 18 cm. from it. Between the outer edge of this slab and the rear wall a column of small rocks formed the end of the box, and from this point a secondary wall had been built up to the height

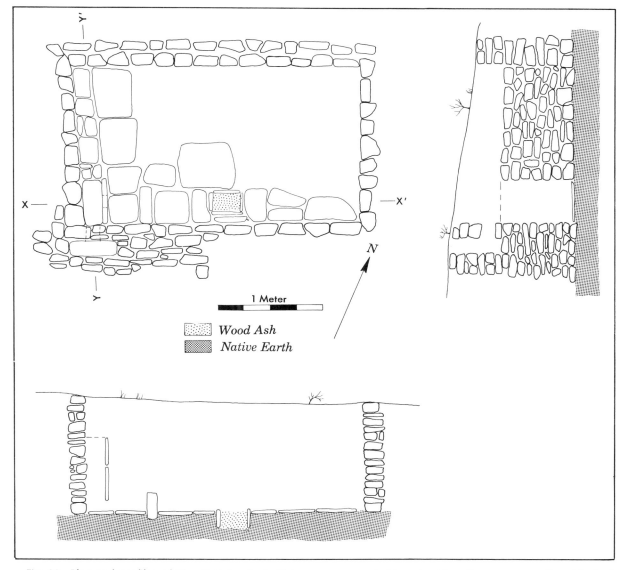

Fig. 28. Plan and profiles of Kiva B at Awatovi. This room was probably not a kiva; it was very small and lacked a bench. But it did have an unusual double rear wall and a peculiar ventilating system, which is illustrated above and described on pages 46–47.

of the box, snugly against the rear wall and extending across the room. It was not more than 20 cm. thick and can hardly be called a bench.

At floor level a small rectangular opening led from the bottom of the box into the room itself. Whether the box had originally been covered was not apparent, but if it was to function as a ventilator it must have been sealed in some way. The vertical block set in the floor midway between the ventilator opening and the firepit could have served as a deflector.

As already indicated, the ascription of kivahood to this room is dubious at best, but the construction and location of the firepit and shaft, though rare, were not unique. The corner position of the latter suggests an analogy to the similar placement of many Spanish fireplaces, but it hardly seems possible that the box and shaft in Kiva B could have served as a stove with a flue. Even if it did so, corner fireplaces were not unknown in Anasazi architecture, and this position does not necessarily point to Spanish influence.

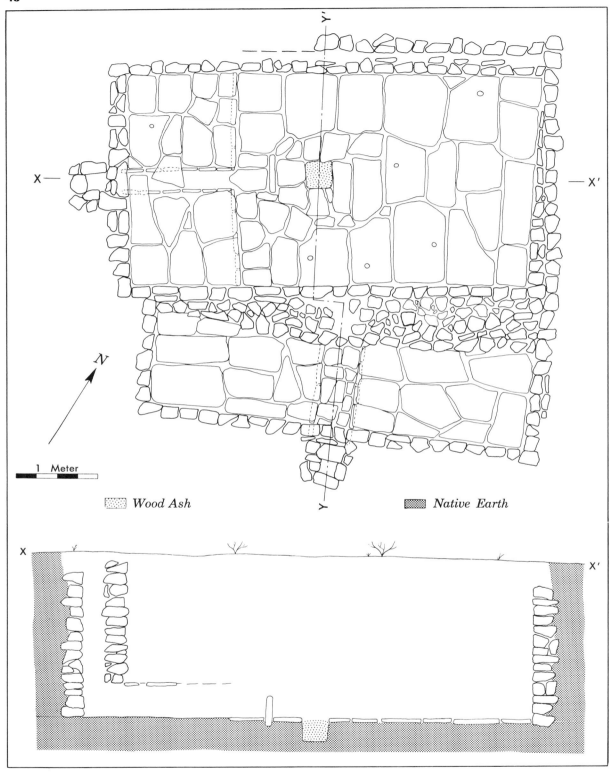

Fig. 29, *a*. Plan of Kivas C and D and profile through X–X' of Kiva C at Awatovi, showing how the building of Kiva C had partly destroyed Kiva D. A transverse profile through Y–Y' is illustrated in figure 29, *b*.

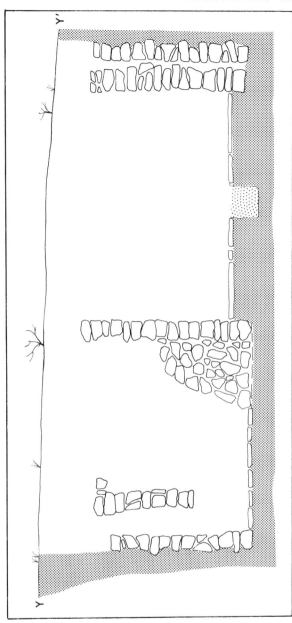

Fig. 29, *b*. Profile through Y–Y' of Kivas C and D at Awatovi, a plan of which is shown in figure 29, *a*.

This puzzling feature suggests an unusual construction that was found by Dr. Hodge at Hawikuh, and while it may not actually have been an analog of the latter, the similarity is provocative. The structure at Hawikuh was identified by Hodge as a grain bin that he supposed had functioned somewhat like a silo. It will not be described here, but

is fully discussed in Smith, Woodbury, and Woodbury (1966, pp. 32–34; pls. 14, *a*, 15, *a*, *c*).

The interior surfaces of the walls of Kiva B were very roughly plastered, without evidence of paint.

No data were recorded on the nature of the fill or the ceramic remains with it, except that the fragments of a restorable Sikyatki Polychrome jar were recovered. The date of construction and occupancy can only be conjectured; it must have been during the early 16th century, in the pre-Spanish period, but after the inception of Sikyatki Polychrome.

KIVA C

The building of Kiva C had caused the partial destruction of an earlier kiva, D, which had previously existed in very nearly the same location. Kiva C in fact had been formed by utilizing parts of the right and front walls of Kiva D, but it was oriented at almost 90° from its predecessor (figs. 29, 30). Its left-front corner thus became what had been the right-front corner of Kiva D, and part of its left wall had been the front wall of Kiva D. Its right and rear walls were entirely new, however, the former being constructed across Kiva D at about the position of the face of the rear bench of the latter.

Kiva C was almost a perfect rectangle, the lengths of its walls being as follows: rear 2.65 m., front 2.60 m., left 4.60 m., right 4.85 m. Its orientation was approximately N. 63° E.

Kiva C had a bench entirely across its rear end, 1.25 m. broad and varying in height from 35 to 42 cm. above the floor. Almost exactly along its midline was a ventilator tunnel 25 cm. wide, its bottom at floor level. The sides of the tunnel had been lined with slabs as had the bottom, but there was no surviving remnant of a roof. The surface of the bench was completely paved with large stone slabs, but only two of those remaining *in situ* extended across the tunnel. The face of the bench was supported by vertical slabs. No side benches existed.

The floor of the kiva was about 75 cm. above bedrock, and thus slightly but not significantly higher than the floors of Kivas A, B, and D. It was fully paved with large, neatly fitted slabs. A nearly rectangular firepit, measuring 30 cm. longitudinally by 35 cm. transversely by 34 cm. in depth, was located about 85 cm. out from the opening of the ventilator tunnel, 1.25 m. from the right wall and 1.00 m. from the left. A vertical slab 25 cm. high stood about midway between the firepit and the ventilator opening, serving as a deflector.

No other floor features were noted, except five circular holes drilled through some of the floor slabs. The positions of these seemed fortuitous, and the slabs in which they occurred had probably been taken for reuse from an abandoned kiva elsewhere. One similar hole also existed in a bench paving slab.

Walls were fairly evenly and substantially laid and had been coated with an undetermined number of layers of plaster. At various places on the rear wall some indecipherable remnants of paint were seen but were not sufficiently definable to warrant preservation. After the original excavation, however, it was noted that the exposed right wall stood immediately in front of an earlier wall, and further investigation revealed surviving patches of painted plaster upon it. One area about 90 cm. long by 1.10 m. high at the extreme right end of

this wall displayed at least seven layers of painted decoration, five of which were recorded. They are illustrated in Smith (1952a, figs. 46, b, d, 50, e, 51, a, 62, b) and represented Layout Groups I, II, and III (2), suggesting a fairly long period of occupation even before the secondary wall was constructed.

It was the discovery of painted fragments on the wall plaster of this kiva that first alerted the members of the expedition to the presence at Awatovi of ceremonial kiva mural paintings, which were later so abundantly found.

The ceramic content of the fill was copious and homogenous from bottom to top, with a large component of Sikyatki Polychrome, of Ceramic Group A-1 or A-2, from middle Pueblo IV.

In the absence of datable wood or charcoal, the period of occupancy of the room can be ascribed, on the basis of the murals as well as the ceramic fill, to sometime in the 15th century.

KIVA D

A short distance south of Kiva A there had been constructed another kiva whch in the field notes was called Kiva D, but it had been partly destroyed before excavation by the later construction within it of Kiva C. The original dimensions could not be determined exactly, for only the rear (southeast) wall, 3.70 m. long, had survived. Right and left walls extended forward almost exactly at right angles to the rear wall, but had been cut off by the later construction of Kiva C at points 1.50 and 1.30 m., respectively, from the rear wall, and by an irregular pile of boulder rubble that had been heaped against and beneath the right wall of Kiva C for support. It was oriented approximately the same as Kiva A, at about N. 20° W.

The surviving slabs of a pavement within Kiva D probably represented the surface of what had been a rear bench 70 cm. above bedrock. A trench extended across this area and through the rear

wall, representing the unroofed horizontal tunnel of a ventilator; it was 55 cm. wide, 60 cm. deep, and paved and lined with stone slabs. The tunnel was situated 2.00 m. from the right wall and 1.90 m. from the left and ran forward slightly to the right of the midline of the room. Contiguous to the outer face of the rear wall a roughly circular, stone-lined shaft, about 25 cm. in diameter, rose to the surface of the ground, which at the time of excavation was about 3.00 m. above the floor of the tunnel.

No record was made of the ceramic content of the fill and no datable wood was recovered. Because of the partial destruction no additional features could be recorded. No evidence of painted plaster was noted. The date of construction can be only conjectural, but it was clearly earlier than that of Kiva C, and perhaps about contemporary with Kiva A, sometime in the 15th century.

KIVA E

Kiva E was situated directly northeast of Kiva A, its southerly (left-rear) corner being almost contiguous to the northerly (right-front) corner of Kiva A. Its floor lay at about the same level as that of Kiva A, but it appeared to be structurally unrelated to it (fig. 31).

The room, as usual, was approximately rectangular, although its exact dimensions were not deter-

mined, since the rear wall lay beyond the limits of our excavation, which were restricted by rapidly expiring time and resources. The width across the front was 3.60 m. and probably about 4.00 m. across the rear. The length was slightly longer than 4.90 m. Orientation was approximately N. 20° W.

A bench extended across the rear of the room;

Fig. 30. Kiva C from the front, showing rear bench, ventilator tunnel, pavement, firepit, and deflector. The workman stands in Kiva D.

although its length was not determined, this must have been about 4.00 m., and it was more than 1.35 m. broad. Its face, which was of crude masonry, was not quite parallel to the front wall of the room, so that the floor area measured as follows: front 3.60 m., face of rear bench 3.90 m., right side 3.55 m., left side 3.30 m.

The top of the bench was from 38 to 43 cm. above the floor and was paved with neatly fitted slabs which also covered a ventilator tunnel that extended beneath the bench a little to the right of its midline. The face of the bench consisted of a masonry wall through which a small rectangular opening led into the tunnel, considerably smaller in height than the tunnel itself, though of about the same width. The interior character of the tunnel was not recorded, and the vertical shaft of the ventilator was not excavated.

The floor lay just above bedrock, at very nearly the same level as the floors of Kivas A and B, but slightly lower than those of Kivas C and D. It was completely paved with carefully fitted stone slabs. Close to the center was a rectangular firepit measuring 24 by 23 cm. and 18 cm. deep, 1.74 m.

from the right wall, 1.72 m. from the left wall, 1.15 m. from the face of the bench, and 2.05 m. from the front wall. The firepit was paved and lined with stone slabs.

Between the firepit and the bench and 43 cm. in front of the latter was set an upright slab functioning as a deflector. It was 54 cm. long and about 21 cm. high, with a broken top, suggesting a greater original height.

Between the firepit and the front wall and 94 cm. from the latter, a large rectangular aperture measuring 44 by 22 cm. had been let into the floor, its longer dimension transverse to the length of the room. It was 24 cm. deep and contained no artifacts or other features except vertical slabs against the longer faces. In all probability this pit had been the sipapu, covered by a stone or wood slab serving as a resonator or footdrum as in several other kivas at Awatovi.

The walls of Kiva E were fairly substantial and still stood to heights of slightly more than 2.00 m. above the floor, their tops about 1.75 m. below the modern surface. That these walls stood at about their original height is indicated by a hori-

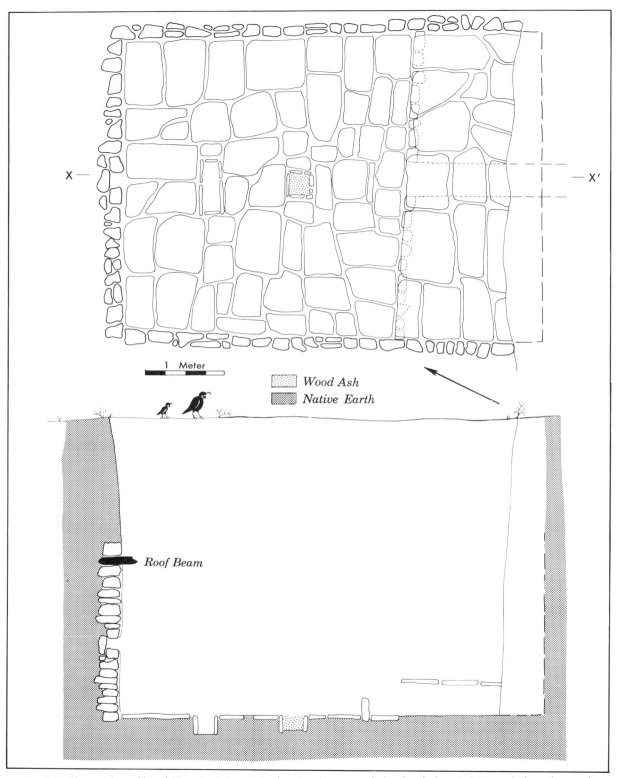

Fig. 31. Plan and profile of Kiva E at Awatovi, showing its unusual depth of almost 4.00 m. below the modern surface. The butt of a charred beam *in situ* in the front wall indicated the height of the roof, about 2.00 m. above the floor.

zontal row of small secondary beam sockets across the upper portion of the front wall. These sockets ranged in height from 1.92 m. at the right end to 2.05 m. at the left. Intervals between them varied from 30 to 80 cm.

Exactly at the midline of the front wall occurred a rectangular niche, 19 cm. wide, 13 cm. high, and 16 cm. deep. It slanted downward slightly toward the back, and had been somewhat rounded and reduced in size by having been lined with several thicknesses of plaster. The walls of the room had probably once been plastered but no remnants remained.

The fill of Kiva E contained nothing of note beyond scattered sherd material, which indicated a date roughly in the middle of Pueblo IV.

Kivas A, B, D (later C), and E (if indeed B was a kiva) were in close proximity to one another and appeared to have formed a cluster, all nearly contemporaneous and at an almost uniform level, within the large house block that surrounded them. Such clustering seems to have been characteristic of Pueblo IV sites in the Jeddito, as exemplified, for instance, by the kivas in Test 14 at Awatovi and in Tests 4 and 5 at Kawaika-a.

ROOM 528

Room 528 lay about 1.00 m. east of Room 529, and although it had clearly been a kiva, only the northerly part of it was excavated. This exposed the front wall and a small part of the left wall, both of which were in an unstable condition and had partly collapsed. The room was about 3.40 m. wide across the front but no other dimensions were obtained.

Orientation was about N. 30° W. No benches were observed against either of the walls exposed.

Within the enclosed area of Room 528, at a depth of 2.30 m. below the surface and about 1.30 m. above the floor level of the adjacent Room 529, there occurred a thin but uniform layer of coal ash, such as was frequently used in other kivas as a bedding for floor-paving slabs. Although no slabs were found, the ash layer probably marked the original floor level.

Numerous coats of plaster had been applied to both the front and left walls, but only fragmentary patches survived. There were 3 painted coats on

the front wall and at least 18 on the left wall. Of the designs, 12 were too fragmentary for classification, but the other 9 all belonged to Layout Group I, suggesting a relatively late date for the entire period of occupation and use of the kiva. They are illustrated in Smith (1952a, figs. 37 d, 68, a, c, d, 69, a, b, c, d, f, 76, b, and 91, c).

The fill in Room 528, at least the lower two-thirds of it, was composed mostly of clean sand, with several thin lenses of ash. The quantity of sherds was meagre, and the ceramic complex was dominated by black-on-yellows, with some Sikyatki Polychrome and a fairly large component of post-Sikyatki types, being thus representative of Ceramic Group A-1 or A-2. No wood or charcoal specimens were recovered.

The clean sand and the relatively late pottery suggested the possibility that the room had perhaps been deliberately and quickly filled, like Rooms 529 and 788, soon after the Spanish occupation.

ROOM 528, SHERD COUNT

Depth in cm.	B/W		B/O		Awa. B/Y		Equiv. B/Y		Jed. B/Y		Siky. Poly.		post-Siky.		Totals
	No.	%	No.	%	No.	%	No.	%	No.	%	No.	%	No.	%	
0–50	—	—	—	—	—	—	—	—	5	15	—	—	29	85	34
50–100	—	—	—	—	—	—	55*	32	63	37	18	13	33	18	169
100–200	2	—	—	—	—	—	71*	29	62	26	37	15	74	30	244
200–230	—	—	—	—	—	—	6*	30	6	30	1	5	7	35	20

* Awatovi Black-on-yellow and Equivocal Black-on-yellow consolidated.

ROOM 529

Room 529 was situated within a block of rooms in what had been the westerly portion of the village during the period shortly prior to the beginning of the Spanish occupation (fig. 32). It was

about 92 meters northeast of the kivas in Test 14, about 42 meters west of the westerly corner of the Franciscan convento, and near the eastern bank of a shallow swale that drained the higher

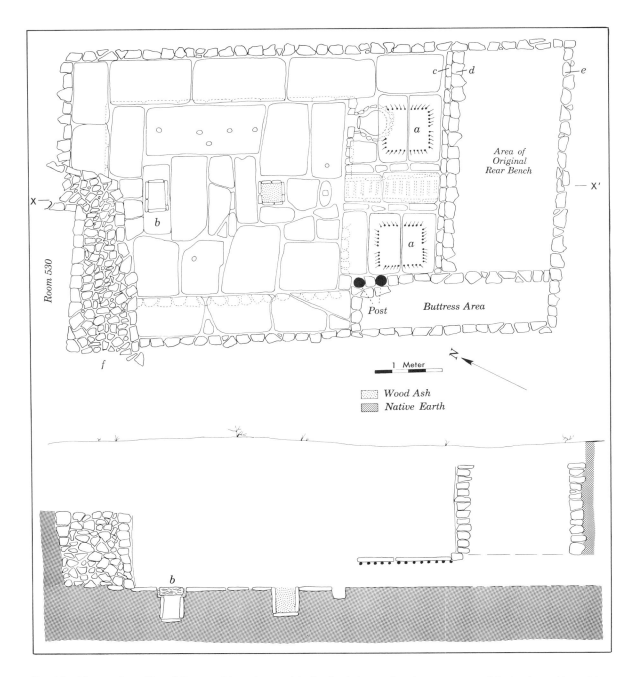

Fig. 32. Plan and profile of Room 529 at Awatovi in its final form, showing two sets of incised markings (a) on the surface slabs of the rear bench, similar to those in Kiva A (fig. 25), the probable sipapu (b), which had once been covered by a wooden plank, and the utility jar beneath the rear bench. Originally the kiva had been longer, its early rear wall (e) about 1.60 m. behind the ultimate rear wall (d). Remains of the masonry face of an early bench existed at c, just in front of the later rear wall (d). After the abandonment of Room 529 a rubble fill (f) was placed in its left-hand front corner to support the wall of a subsequently constructed kiva, Room 530, which was not excavated.

area to the north toward the southerly escarpment of the mesa. This kiva and the rooms adjacent to it had been dug into the natural soil but did not reach downward to caprock, and it was impossible to ascertain whether they had originally been completely subterranean.

The kiva was originally built in a roughly rectangular form, measuring 4.25 m. across the front,

4.10 m. across the rear, 7.15 m. along the right side, and 7.00 m. along the left, thus making it possibly the largest non-Spanish chamber excavated at Awatovi. It was oriented about N. 30° W. A bench 1.70 m. broad and about 30 cm. high was constructed across the rear of the kiva and was covered with very large sandstone slabs.

Subsequently a masonry pier was constructed in the left-rear corner, protruding inward to form a buttress about 80 cm. wide and about 2.90 m. long. Two vertical wooden posts had been set into the masonry of this pier, one at its interior angle, and the other about 15 cm. from it. Two large roof beams, each about 23 cm. in maximum diameter, had been inserted into sockets in the wall and were further supported on the two vertical wooden posts. The beams had originally extended across the kiva parallel to its shorter dimension, but the easterly portions had rotted away. One was of Douglas fir, with charred exterior, the other was of pinyon or juniper, almost entirely rotted away. Other fragments of the same beams were found in the debris about midway across the kiva. The height of the beams above the floor was approximately 2.00 m. Immediately above the fallen beam fragments lay a jumble of large stones, suggesting the existence of a parapet that had once been constructed around a hatchway in the roof above this point.

At a still later period further alterations were made in the kiva. A new wall was built across the rear about 1.60 m. inward from the original rear wall, thus shortening the kiva and obscuring the rear parts of the right and left walls by that amount. It was constructed slightly behind the masonry that composed the face of the original bench. The kiva may have been abandoned for a brief time as suggested by the fact that about 30 cm. of fill had accumulated, and upon this a new floor was laid at about the level of the top of the original bench. Within the shortened area a new bench was constructed across the rear, 1.48 m. broad, and from 42 to 45 cm. high; and apparently at the same time narrow benches of similar height were also built along the other three sides, varying in breadth from 55 to 67 cm. Side and front benches had apparently not existed in the kiva as originally built.

The new rear bench was fully covered with very large, rectangularly formed, sandstone slabs and its face was of coursed masonry covered with five or six coats of plaster. A ventilator tunnel, 25 cm. wide at its orifice but increasing to 40 cm. toward the rear, existed beneath the bench; it was a little off-center, 1.18 m. from the right wall and 1.45 m. from the left. The sides were formed of upright sandstone slabs, but the floor was not paved. Across the top of the tunnel a series of small wooden sticks, 2.5 to 4 cm. in diameter and 4 to 5 cm. apart, rested upon the upright slabs. A matting of reeds or rushes lay over the sticks. It had been woven in a two-over-two-under twill with bundles of four stems each. Over the matting lay a thin coating of adobe on which rested the paving slabs that formed the surface of the bench. This arrangement appeared also in other kivas, notably in Room 788.

The paving used on top of the bench was unique among the kivas at Awatovi. Directly over the tunnel lay two large rectangular slabs, only slightly wider than the tunnel itself; and in areas about 20 cm. wide on each side of these central slabs were set strips of small, irregularly shaped slabs. Between each of these strips and the respective side walls of the room, were three still larger, carefully formed, rectangular slabs, each measuring from 40 to 50 cm. in width by about 95 cm. in length on the left side of the tunnel and about 1.00 m. in length on its right side. The two outer slabs that covered the forepart of the bench were unembellished, but the other four had been decorated with rows of incised figures, each formed of a circular basin-shaped "head" that had been drilled into the slab to a depth of about 2 cm., and a long straight "tail" varying in length from 8 to 18 cm. They were about 1 to 2 mm. deep and might be said to resemble "pollywogs." They were arranged in groups of five each, the heads toward the center and the tails radiating outward, two sets of five forming one side of a hollow square that extended over most of the surface area of the two contiguous slabs (figs. 32, 33). The purpose and significance of these incisings has not been elucidated (see also fig. 25).

Through the masonry face of the bench, between the right wall and the ventilator tunnel, was a rounded rectangular hole, 20 cm. wide by 18 cm. high, 18 cm. above the floor, and 24 cm. from the right wall, that led into a larger cist, within which had been embedded a large-mouth, yellow corrugated jar, placed so that its orifice pointed outward and upward at about 45° from the horizontal (fig. 34). The upper part of its rim touched the paving slab immediately above it at a point 38 cm. inward from the face of the bench. The jar was 35 cm. deep with mouth 32 cm. in diameter, and the hollowed-out cist within which it was placed had been lined with small stones. The jar

Fig. 33. Incised pattern in paving slabs on rear bench of Room 529. See also figure 25.

contained a clay pipe, a fragment of antler, a ball of yellow pigment, some unworked chips of chert and obsidian, and some unidentified vegetal matter.

The narrow benches along the other three sides of the room differed somewhat in construction. All were surfaced with large, carefully shaped, sandstone slabs, and the faces of those along the front and right walls were also formed of slabs; the face of the left-wall bench, however, was of masonry. Apparently all faces had once been coated with plaster, but this had almost completely fallen except along a part of the right-wall bench, where some fragments of paint were evident, the only example recorded at Awatovi of paint on the face of a bench.

The floor of this kiva was fully paved with fitted sandstone slabs, most of them large and rectangular. A firepit lined and paved with slabs was situated just to the right of the midline of the room, but directly in front of and about 90 cm. from the entrance of the ventilator tunnel. It was about 34 cm. square, 42 cm. deep, and filled with wood ash. No deflector was discovered. Immediately in

front of the tunnel mouth was an open oval area with a small square stone in its center, perhaps the rest for a pole ladder.

Near the front of the room was a rather complex structure that was apparently a sipapu in the form of a footdrum or resonator. It consisted of a rectangular pit, 35 cm. long by 25 cm. wide and 45 cm. deep, paved and lined with sandstone slabs. The vertical slabs extended upward to a level just beneath that of the floor pavement, which had been carefully laid to leave rectangular unpaved areas extending outward from the pit on each end for distances of 26 and 35 cm., respectively. This formed a countersunk ledge 1.03 m. long by 30 cm. wide into which a flat plank could have been placed, its upper surface level with that of the stone pavement. The empty hollow beneath would have provided resonance for a man stamping upon the covering board during a ceremonial dance.

Small circular holes drilled through the paving slabs occurred in various locations in the floor for loom anchors, but their random arrangement suggested that the slabs had originally been used elsewhere and later reused in this kiva.

At some time, probably soon after the abandonment of this kiva, another kiva (Room 530) was constructed immediately to the northwest, part of it extending slightly into the left-front area of Room 529. The floor of the new kiva was slightly

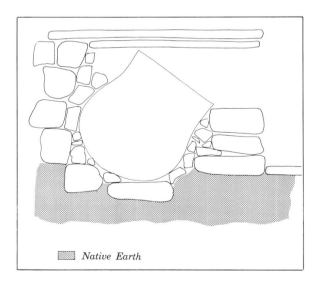

Native Earth

Fig. 34. Profile of utility jar emplaced beneath the right-hand side of the rear bench in Room 529 at Awatovi.

higher than that of Room 529, and in order to support it and the adjacent walls a rock fill had been emplaced that destroyed the left-front corner of Room 529. Room 530 was not excavated.

The walls of Room 529 were all of the usual single-faced type, with crudely laid and unshaped slabs of sandstone in abundant mortar. The surviving portion of the front wall stood to a height of about 2.50 m., as did the right and rear walls, and the pier in the left-rear corner. The left wall had almost entirely collapsed.

All walls had been coated with from 15 to 20 coats of plaster, which survived to varying heights: 1.40 m. on the front wall, 1.60 m. on the rear wall, 1.40 m. on both faces of the pier, and from 70 cm. to 1.70 m. on the right wall. In most areas the plaster was applied either directly to the masonry, or to rough mud mortar, the latter having been used to minimize the unevenness of the masonry surface. At one point on the front wall, however, the imprint of a twilled matting of grass or reeds was found between the mortar and the first layer of plaster (fig. 69). This method of reinforcement was evident in several other instances, for example in Room 788 and in Test 19, Room 3, although no fragments of the actual matting had survived (Smith 1952a, pp. 14–15, figs. 5, 34, b).

Remnants of painted decoration occurred on all surviving walls, but were much more numerous on the right wall, where at least 15 separate designs were identified. Only 3 were found on the front wall, 2 on the secondary rear wall, and 3 on each face of the pier. The earlier designs on the right wall were classified with Layout Groups II and III, those on the pier and the rear and front walls with Layout Group II, and the later designs on the right wall with Layout Group I, which suggested a fairly long period of occupation. These designs have been fully discussed and reproduced in Smith (ibid., figs. 38, c, 47, b, c, 49, b, 53, b, 57, b, 58, c, 61, a, b, 72, b, c, 73, c, 76, d, 90, a, b, d; plate A).

When the secondary rear wall was removed, it was found that the portion of the right wall that extended behind it and had belonged to the room in its original period bore four painted layers, all classified with Layout Group II (ibid., figs. 50, a, c, 51, b, c). These were individually unrelated to any of the decorations on that part of the right wall that continued in use after the remodeling, although they were stylistically consistent with the earlier examples on the latter. There was no painted decoration on the original rear wall, but it did have an incised design of a human figure (ibid., fig. 92, a).

The fill of Room 529 was removed in five strata, each 50 cm. deep, but the ceramic complexes were almost identical in all of them, suggesting a fairly rapid filling after abandonment. Black-on-yellows were heavily dominant, with small but insignificant quantities of Sikyatki Polychrome and large quantities of post-Sikyatki types. The presence of the latter, which were almost completely absent from the rooms in the Western Mound and in the intervening areas of Tests 14 and 19, suggested the possibility that this kiva had been occupied up to the Spanish arrival, and had been quickly filled soon thereafter. The complex corresponded to Ceramic Group A-1 or A-2. In the upper stratum of the fill were part of a tubular stone pipe and a small side-notched point (Woodbury 1954, figs. 26, g, 36, e).

ROOM 529, SHERD COUNT

Depth in cm.	B/W		B/O		Awa. B/Y		Equiv. B/Y		Jed. B/Y		Siky. Poly.		post-Siky.		Totals
	No.	%	No.	%	No.	%	No.	%	No.	%	No.	%	No.	%	
0–50	4	—	2	—	*	—	162*	21	212	28	117	15	274	35	771
50–100	2	—	—	—	4	—	172	17	232	22	88	9	524	51	1022
100–150	3	—	—	—	*	—	130*	20	150	23	73	12	280	44	636
150–200	—	—	—	—	1	—	169	35	148	30	50	11	114	24	482
200–250	1	—	—	—	*	—	70*	20	111	33	21	7	133	39	336
Between South Walls	—	—	1	—	*	—	25*	12	98	49	57	28	22	11	203

* Awatovi Black-on-yellow and Equivocal Black-on-yellow combined.

The only tree-ring date from this kiva was provided by the charred Douglas fir beam already referred to. Four different fragments of it were dated between 1375 and 1432, none of which was from an outside ring (Bannister, Robinson, and Warren 1967, p. 9). These dates are considerably

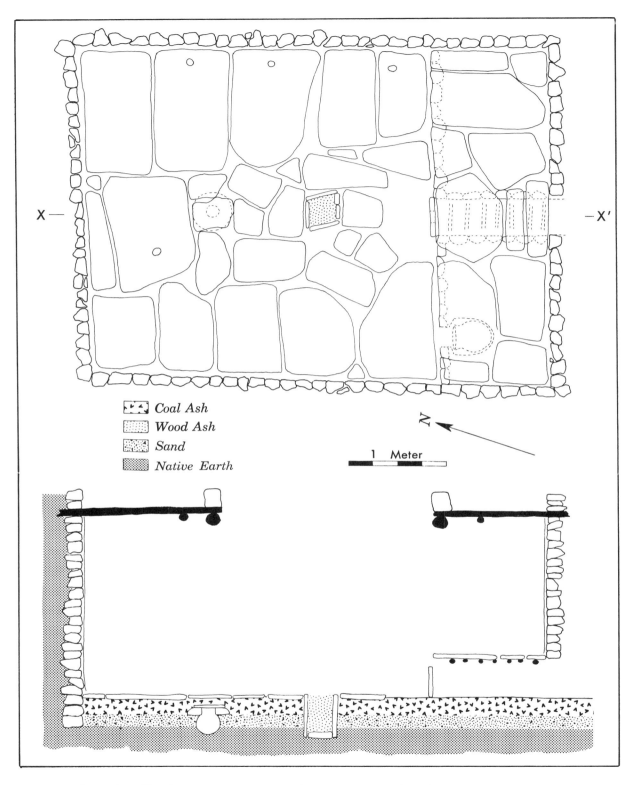

N

1 Meter

Fig. 35. Plan and profile of Room 788 at Awatovi, showing positions of a utility jar beneath the left-hand side of the rear bench, and a jar-shaped pit (sipapu?) below the floor near the front wall. The positions of the roof beams and hatchway coping are also indicated.

earlier than the date of abandonment indicated by the ceramic complex in the fill, but since they were not cutting dates, and since the beam may have been reused, they are consistent with a hypothesis that the kiva could have been built as late as the 16th century.

ROOM 788

The kiva designated Room 788 (fig. 35) was the most exciting and revealing among those excavated at Awatovi and Kawaika-a. Its very location was provocative, situated as it was directly beneath parts of the sanctuary and sacristy of the mission Church of San Bernardo. Before discussing the significance of this fact, however, we shall describe the kiva objectively.

Room 788 was almost precisely rectangular, and was thus more nearly accurate in shape than were most rooms or kivas at Awatovi. It measured 3.40 m. across the front wall, 3.55 m. across the rear, 4.65 m. along the left, and 4.75 m. along the right, and was oriented about N. 20° W. The left-front and right-rear corners were very slightly more than right angles, the other corners slightly less. The floor was 3.15 m. below the floor of the predella in the sanctuary of the superimposed church, and 2.50 m. below the floor of the nave (fig. 42). About 1.90 m. above the floor of the kiva and well below that of the church was the kiva roof, which had survived almost intact, and which will be discussed later.

Across the rear (southeast) end of the kiva was a bench from 1.10 m. to 1.20 m. broad and 37 cm. high (fig. 36). The face of this bench was made of fairly substantial masonry composed of sandstone blocks of varying sizes, but mostly rectangular and carefully laid in a manner approaching regular courses. The surface of the bench was completely paved with large sandstone slabs of irregular shape and varying size, but their generous dimen-

sions are indicated by the statement that only 12 slabs served to cover the entire area (fig. 35).

Transversely beneath the bench and exactly along the midline ran a ventilator tunnel 36 cm. wide and about 25 cm. high. Its sides were formed of irregular masonry, and its floor was not paved. The tunnel extended through the rear wall beyond which rose a vertical shaft, the details of which were not precisely recorded.

Across the mouth of the tunnel and snugly against the face of the bench was set a rectangular slab of stone about 38 cm. wide by about 20 cm. high with a rounded rectangular hole through its lower portion about 12 cm. high by about 15 cm. wide, very closely similar to the analogous arrangement in Kiva A. The effect was to reduce the size of the opening and thereby also to reduce the volume of air admitted through it (fig. 36).

Within the tunnel were eight accurately ground stone balls. Similar collections occurred in the ventilator tunnel of Test 31, Room 1, and in the jar that was set under the rear bench in Test 14, Room 5. Their possible significance and use are discussed by Woodbury (1954, pp. 171–173). The tunnel was roofed by seven wooden beams set irregularly across it and supported by its masonry side walls (fig. 37), and directly upon the beams lay a mat of rushes woven in a twilled pattern exactly like other mats that were sometimes used on walls to support the overlying plaster (figs. 68, e, 69). These mats will be discussed below. Over the mat was a coating of adobe from 2 to 5 cm.

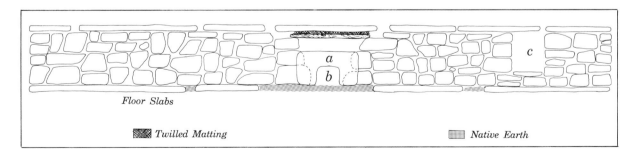

Floor Slabs

Twilled Matting   Native Earth

Fig. 36. Elevation of the rear bench in Room 788 at Awatovi. The mouth of the ventilator tunnel was partly closed by a vertical stone slab (a), which was pierced by a rectangular hole (b). A twilled mat of rushes lay upon the roof beams of the tunnel. Access to a cist beneath the bench was provided by the opening (c).

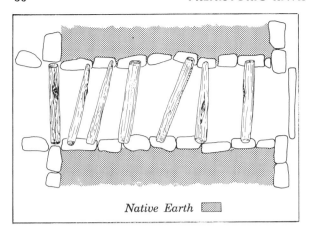

Fig. 37. Plan of roof structure of ventilator tunnel through the rear bench of Room 788 at Awatovi.

mentioned, across the mouth of the tunnel, partially blocking the inflow of air.

Below the floor toward the front of the room, 1.10 m. from the front wall and midway between the right and left walls, was a construction that must have represented a sipapu. At first this was not discovered because it was completely obscured by the paving slabs of the floor. On subsequent investigation, however, one such slab was removed, and a few centimeters beneath it was found a thin triangular slab measuring between 40 and 50 cm. on each edge, and only about 1 cm. thick. This thin slab lay directly upon a circular collar of modeled but unbaked clay, flat on its lower surface but rounded on its outer and upper surfaces, exactly like the upper half of a doughnut. This collar was about 40 cm. in outer diameter by about 8 cm. high. The orifice was almost circular, 14 to 15 cm. in diameter. Below the orifice a

thick, and upon this rested the surface paving slabs. This arrangement was used also in the other kivas, notably in Room 529.

A cist penetrated the left (or southwest) half of the face of the bench, about 40 cm. from its left end, and about 20 cm. wide by 25 cm. high (fig. 38). Its sill was formed of a thin slab of sandstone and the paving slabs on top of the bench formed its cover. Behind this cist was emplaced a large globular yellow corrugated jar, 32 cm. deep with a mouth 30 cm. in diameter. It was set at an angle of about 45° to the horizontal, upper and lower points of the rim being in contact with the sill and roof of the cist. It contained only a few seeds, apparently squash. This feature was homologous to similar arrangements in several other kivas (figs. 12, 34, 52, 56). No benches existed along the left, right, or front walls.

The entire floor of the kiva was paved with large slabs of sandstone, neatly fitted, most of them roughly rectangular. About 1.00 m. from the mouth of the ventilator tunnel, and midway between the right and left walls, a firepit was let into the floor. This pit was a rhombus in plan, each side measuring about 28 cm. long. Each of three sides was formed by a single, upright slab, but the north side consisted of two adjacent slabs. The pit was 44 cm. deep, paved with a single slab, and filled with wood ash and charcoal. A tubular clay pipe with an incised decoration was found in the fill.

No deflector was found between the firepit and the ventilator tunnel, but its function was probably served by the slab that was placed, as already

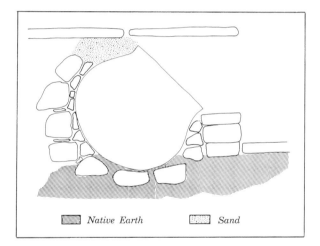

Fig. 38. Profile of a cist containing a globular utility jar under the rear bench in Room 788 at Awatovi.

globular pocket had been excavated into the underlying strata, its profile closely approximating that of a large-mouth jar, although no actual jar had been emplaced.

The rounded bottom of the pocket had been dug into pure native clay to a depth of about 12 cm. Over the clay was a thin stratum of clean sand about 2 cm. thick, above this a layer of mixed sand and black coal ash about 6 cm. thick, then a second stratum of clean sand about 4 cm. thick, and finally about 16 cm. of red coal ash. The floor slabs of the kiva lay directly upon this uppermost ash layer, and the clay doughnut and its cover slab

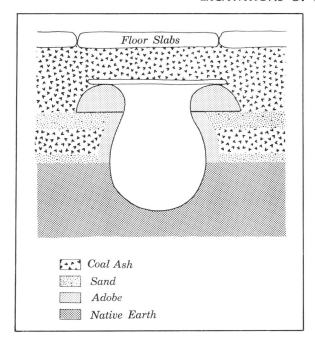

Fig. 39. Profile of probable sipapu beneath the floor of Room 788 at Awatovi, showing a jar-shaped pocket and doughnut-shaped clay ring forming its neck.

were surrounded by it. Below the doughnut, where the excavation penetrated the successive layers of sand and ash, a clay lining or facing had been modeled to support the loose surrounding material and prevent its collapse into the pocket. No supporting lining was necessary in the underlying clay bed. The height of the pocket was about 26 cm. and its maximum diameter, which occurred at the contact between the clay bed and the immediately overlying sand, about 22 cm. This sipapu, if indeed it was one, is illustrated in profile in figure 39. It contained nothing. The whole thing was puzzling because it had been completely covered by the uppermost ash layer and sealed by the floor-paving slabs, periodic removal of which had clearly not been intended. Nor was there surviving evidence of an earlier floor, flush with the orifice of the sipapu, although such a floor might once have existed and have been entirely removed before the installation of the surviving floor found at the time of excavation.

Numerous circular holes were drilled through the slabs of the floor and of the surface of the bench. These had probably been for the purpose of inserting loom anchors. Five were arranged in a straight row about 25 cm. from the left wall, at intervals of between 20 and 30 cm. Three holes

were in a similar row about 15 to 25 cm. from the right wall, spaced about 70 cm. and 1.00 m. apart, respectively. Other holes were randomly placed and probably had been drilled when the slabs in which they occurred had been in use in another room, from which they had been robbed for placement in Room 788. On the floor was found a small fragment of turquoise.

The walls of this kiva were of the usual rather slovenly masonry characteristic of all the late pre-Spanish rooms of the village, but they were rather more nearly straight and vertical than most. This condition was probably due to the fact that the roof remained almost intact, and the walls beneath it had not collapsed.

The walls on all interior faces had been heavily plastered, and although the extreme upper areas of plaster had fallen in irregular patches and a few centimeters along the base had eroded away, this room exhibited by far the most extensively preserved mural coverings and painted decorations that were found at Awatovi or Kawaika-a. The method of construction by which plaster was applied and supported was perfectly exemplified here. Directly over the masonry surface had been applied a thin coating of gray adobe mortar of variable thickness to produce a fairly even surface over the irregular stones of the masonry. Into this mortar was pressed a mass of grass and reeds, arranged horizontally and composed mostly of reeds from 2 or 3 mm. to 6 or 7 mm. in diameter. More adobe was then applied over the reeds and grass and firmly consolidated with the underlying material.

After application of the outer coatings of adobe, long sections of roots or vines up to 1.50 m. long and from 5 to 15 mm. in diameter were pressed into the fresh adobe in a generally vertical position. These roots or vines were usually laid in pairs, not twined but snugly parallel, or sometimes singly, and extended from floor to roof, at horizontal intervals of from 25 to 35 cm. Over this reinforced undercoat was then applied the reddish sandy plaster that was used generally on all kivas as a finish coat for the application of painted designs. Similar reinforcement was used in Kiva A, Test 22, Room 10, and other kivas (fig. 68, f).

In the corner areas, where two contiguous walls intersected, a different sort of reinforcement was used. Here were strips of matting woven in a rectangular twill in a two-over-two-under pattern, apparently to provide a strong and continuous backing for the plaster as it rounded the corner.

The fabric was formed of groups of four or five parallel reeds, each about 1.5 to 2.5 mm. in diameter (fig. 69, a). Similar mats had been used on the walls of Kiva A, Room 529, and Test 19, Room 3, but the elements of the fabric in those kivas lay diagonally with relation to one another. Furthermore in Test 19, Room 3, the mats were used not only in corners but along the entire lower parts of the right and left walls to a height of from 15 to 20 cm. above the floor. Bundles of reeds had been used also in Test 22, Room 10.

No vestige of the underlying reinforcement of grass and reeds nor of the twilled matting had survived in any case, but clear impressions of both occurred in many places (fig. 68, e; see also Smith 1952a, pp. 14–15, figs. 5, 34, b, d). Some of the vertical vines or roots, however, were preserved, but have not been botanically identified.

Numerous coats of finish plaster covered each wall and, although the total number was not exactly determined, those that had carried painted decoration were recorded and numbered. Of these, there were 14 on the left wall, 9 on the right wall, 1 on the front wall, and 2 on the rear wall. Of those that were sufficiently well preserved for classification, all belonged to Layout Group I. They were among the most nearly complete and complex designs found in any kiva and have been fully discussed and reproduced in Smith (ibid., figs. 35, a–d, 38, a, b, 39, a, 67, a, 71, b, 76, c, 77, a, 78, a, b, 79, a, b, 80, a, b, 81, a, 82, a, 85, d, 86, c, 87, b, 89, a, c, 90, f, 92, b–d; plates B, F, I).

After the excavation of the sanctuary of the Franciscan Church of San Bernardo, it was suggested by Mr. Ross G. Montgomery, who was acting as consultant on the ecclesiastical structures of the village, that it had often been the custom of the Spanish missionaries to build the altars of their churches above or upon the sacred fanes of the pagan tribes whose conversion to the Faith they sought to accomplish. In order to test this thesis, a small pit was dug through the floor of the sanctuary near the steps that led up to the predella, and at a depth of about 1.25 m. below that level there came to light the top of a masonry wall with the butt of a wooden beam emplaced in a socket extending through it. Realizing that the structure was probably the kiva that we sought, we removed the altar of the church and the north wall of the sanctuary in order to permit its complete excavation.

Gradually the entire roof structure was exposed and, although the central area had subsided about 30 to 40 cm. from its original position, the method of its construction was apparent (fig. 40). The major support consisted of two heavy main beams that had been emplaced across the shorter dimension of the room, resting in sockets in the left and right walls, with their ends extending through and somewhat beyond the exterior faces of the walls. The front (northwest) beam was about 1.10 m. from the front wall, the rear (southeast) beam about 1.20 m. from the rear wall. That portion of the left (southwest) wall, in which the rear (southeast) beam had been socketed, had been destroyed by the Spaniards to provide a footing for the north wall of the sanctuary, thus also destroying a portion of the beam itself, but in no other respect had the construction of the church significantly damaged the kiva roof or walls.

The diameters of the two main beams were not recorded, but the interval between them was about 2.25 m., although this varied slightly because they were neither perfectly straight nor exactly parallel. These beams were about 1.90 m. above the floor.

The secondary roof component consisted of several smaller beams or stringers. Two of these were placed approximately parallel to the main beams and each lay between one main beam and its nearest parallel wall. They were perhaps one-third the diameter of the main beams and like the latter extended fully across the kiva, their ends resting in sockets in the side walls. Spanning the interval between the two main beams, lying upon them at right angles but not extending beyond them, were five other secondary beams or stringers, each about 2.70 m. in length and irregularly spaced between the right and left walls of the kiva. The central pair were about equidistant (approximately 1.00 m.) from and parallel to the left and right walls, respectively, and were almost as thick as the main beams themselves. Between them and the side walls lay three other and thinner secondary beams or stringers, one on the right side, two on the left.

The intersections of the two main beams and the central pair of secondary beams embraced a rectangular aperture about 2.40 m. long by 1.10 m. wide, which formed a hatchway for access to the interior of the kiva. Surrounding the hatchway and directly upon the framing beams had been erected a masonry parapet (figs. 40, 41). This structure was about 30 to 35 cm. high by about 20 to 25 cm. thick and was formed of small, irregularly shaped stones set in a matrix of copious adobe mortar.

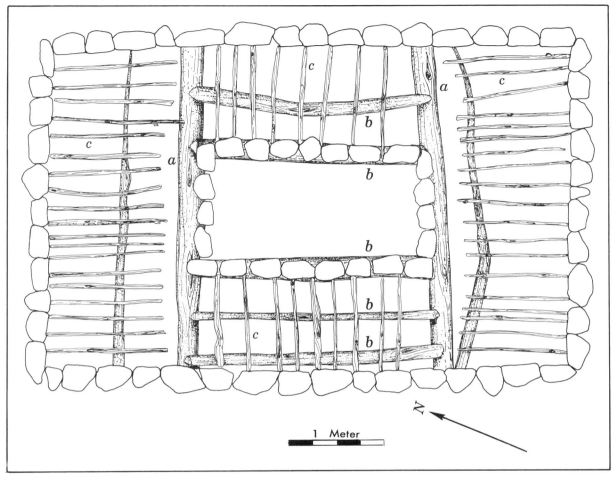

Fig. 40. Plan of roof construction for Room 788, beneath the sanctuary of Church 2 at Awatovi. The frame consisted of two main and two secondary transverse beams (*a*), at right angles to which and across the two main beams lay five secondary longitudinal beams (*b*). The main beams and two central secondary beams supported a masonry parapet framing a hatchway, and numerous close-set *savinos* (*c*) spanned the areas on all sides of the central opening. Although this roof had sagged considerably from its original level, its members remained intact and in proper relation to one another.

A third component of the roof skeleton consisted of a series of closely spaced sticks or poles arranged in parallel sequences along each side of the structure. The butt ends of these members were socketed into interstices between the stones of the masonry walls, and they extended outward at right angles to the walls toward the main and secondary beams that supported the parapet. In most cases, however, they did not quite reach these beams, but were actually supported by the secondary stringers that have been mentioned above as lying outside but parallel to the heavy beams that supported the parapet. There were 20 poles along the front sector of the roof and 19 along the rear, both groups extending from wall to wall. The sets of poles along the right and left sides were shorter, since they filled only the areas between the two main beams. There were 8 on the right side and perhaps a few more on the left, although some of the latter had been destroyed by the construction of the footings for the wall of the sanctuary.

All members of this roof structure were found in their original relation to one another, but the entire fabric had slumped downward about 30 to 40 cm. below its original level and rested upon the debris that filled the kiva (fig. 41). The roof skeleton had probably been covered with grass and brush topped off with earth, but no evidence of such material was found.

The fill of the kiva below as well as above the level of the roof was composed of almost pure sand. That below the roof appeared to have been poured through the hatchway, since its strata sloped downwards in all directions from the center. There were very few potsherds, stones, or other material within the sand and the inference was very strong that the kiva had been deliberately and rapidly filled by human agency. If this was so, it may be explained by consideration of certain practices known to have been frequently followed by Spanish missionaries.

In Mexico and elsewhere in the New World, one of the first actions of the religious was to erect an altar to their Christian Faith. Usually this was done in a native village within which was a shrine or holy place that was already venerated by the inhabitants. The Christians wished to obliterate the pagan shrine and in its stead to erect their own. It was reasonable to accomplish both purposes by superimposing the Christian fane upon the pagan counterpart, thus demonstrating the dominance of the new Faith over the old, and at the same time perhaps translating the established sanctity of the particular locale into the substitutional structure.

This was apparently done at Awatovi (fig. 42). Of the many kivas that were excavated there and at other villages in the vicinity, only two still retained their roofs intact. These were Rooms 788 and 908, which adjoined each other, and both of which lay beneath the sanctuary and sacristy of the mission church. Generally in the Pueblo Southwest, roof timbers were removed from abandoned rooms for use elsewhere, for they were too precious to be left behind. Rarely, except in cases of fire or when the entire village was abandoned, have such timbers been found still *in situ*. The two exceptions at Awatovi argue strongly for the hypothesis that the missionaries sought to supplant the kivas as foci for religious observances but not to destroy them, and thereby to identify their new sanctuary with the old. This subject has been more

Fig. 41. Roof of Room 788, beneath the sanctuary and sacristy of the second Franciscan church. In the center is part of the masonry coping surrounding the hatchway, the remainder of which had been destroyed by the building of the north wall of the sanctuary, the end of which appears at the upper left.

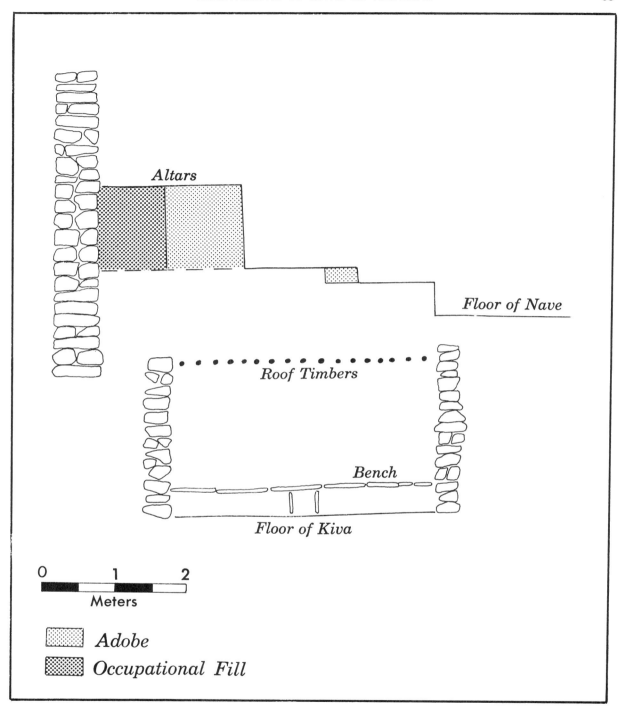

Fig. 42. Profile showing Room 788 in relation to the altar and sanctuary of Church 2 at Awatovi. The section is along the longitudinal dimension of the church and the transverse dimension of the kiva, and indicates the depth of the latter beneath the superimposed Franciscan structure. (See Montgomery, Smith and Brew, 1949, pp. 62–67.)

fully discussed in Montgomery, Smith, and Brew (1949, pp. 65–67, 134–136, fig. 10).

Certain other objects found in the fill included scattered small fragments of charcoal, a three-quarter-grooved axe a chert blade, two polishing pebbles (Woodbury 1954, figs. 14, *k*, 27, *a*, 40, *l*, *o*), four pecking stones, two stone loomblocks, a human femur, fragments of six painted wooden pahos, or prayer sticks, and two fragmentary animal skulls with straight tapering horns that may have belonged to goats. If so, they had certainly arrived with the Spaniards.

The sherds within the fill of Room 788 were mostly of post-Sikyatki types with small components of Jeddito Black-on-yellow and Sikyatki Polychrome, characteristic of the late phase of Ceramic Group A-1.

Four of the roof timbers were dated by Hall at 1382±5, 1502±5, 1504+x, and 1564+x, and by the Laboratory of Tree-Ring Research at 1385vv, 1412vv, 1498vv, and 1503vv (Bannister, Robinson, and Warren 1967, p. 11). The outer ring of each specimen was an undeterminable distance from the bark, but we may reasonably infer from them collectively that the kiva may have been built well after the beginning of the 16th century. From other considerations discussed above we may also infer with confidence that it was abandoned very shortly after 1630, when the missionaries arrived.

If these inferences are correct, the kiva would have been in use for a period of between 70 and 100 years, but the presence of only 14 coats of painted wall plaster would account for ceremonial renewals at intervals of roughly every 5 to 7 years, which seems too long between drinks. It may thus be warrantable to hypothesize a later date of construction, say about 1580 or so, on the supposition that the beam dated 1564+x was nearer to the actual date than were the others, and that the latter had been taken from earlier structures for reuse here. It is also possible but not very convincing to suppose that the surviving mural paintings were all executed during the latest years of occupancy, perhaps following a renovation and removal of possible earlier ones.

ROOM 788, SHERD COUNT

Depth	B/W		B/O		Awa. B/Y		Equiv. B/Y		Jed. B/Y		Siky. Poly.		post-Siky.		Totals
	No.	%	No.	%	No.	%	No.	%	No.	%	No.	%	No.	%	
Above Roof	2	1	—	—	—	—	*42	13	36	12	32	10	194	64	306
Roof to Floor	2	—	—	—	—	—	*33	4	27	3	43	5	696	88	801

* Awatovi Black-on-yellow and Equivocal Black-on-yellow combined.

ROOM 908

Room 908 was another kiva that lay directly west of Room 788 and shared with it a common wall, which was therefore finished on both faces. The two rooms were probably built at the same time and occupied contemporaneously. Like Room 788, parts of this kiva were directly beneath the sanctuary and sacristy of the Franciscan Church of San Bernardo, while other parts lay beneath Rooms 464 and 727 of the convento. This situation made complete excavation unfeasible, since removal of the overlying Spanish structures would have entailed extensive destruction as well as a great amount of time and labor. Only two small test pits were sunk against the east and north walls of the kiva where circumstances permitted.

At a level just below the footings of the west wall of the sacristy there was found a roof structure, apparently still intact and similar in construction to that of Room 788 (figs. 40, 41). The main beams extended from east to west, indicating that this had been the shorter dimension of the kiva, which was thus oriented in the same direction as Room 788, about N. 20° W. These beams were socketed into the masonry walls and some of them penetrated the right (northeast) wall, where their extremities protruded into the area of

Room 788, slightly above the level of the main beams of that kiva. Smaller beams ran at right angles above the main beams and were also socketed into the masonry. Samples of six beams were removed, one 23 cm. in diameter, another 30 cm. in diameter. They were of cottonwood, juniper, and Douglas fir, the last of which provided a date of 1428, the outside ring being an undetermined distance from the bark (Bannister, Robinson, and Warren 1967, p. 11). Over the beams had been laid a matting of grass and brush as was also probable in Room 788.

At a level of 1.90 m. below the beam sockets a slab-paved floor was reached, but test pits discovered no specific features.

On the exposed areas of the walls were at least 35 layers of plaster, but no evidence of painted decoration was found.

Since the volume excavated was very small, the ceramic specimens were few, and they were not stratigraphically separated. The collection belonged, however, within Ceramic Group A-1, and was characterized by the predominance of post-Sikyatki types.

ROOM 908, SHERD COUNT

Depth	B/W		B/O		Awa. B/Y		Equiv. B/Y		Jed. B/Y		Siky. Poly.		Post-Siky.		Totals
	No.	%	No.	%	No.	%	No.	%	No.	%	No.	%	No.	%	
0–Floor	—	—	—	—	1	1	26	26	19	19	10	10	43	44	99

The date of construction was probably not earlier than the second half of the 15th century, and occupancy must have extended very late in the prehistoric period; abandonment probably occurred, as with Room 788, after the coming of the Franciscans.

TEST 22, ROOM 10

The kiva in Test 22 (fig. 43) was situated about 46 meters northwesterly from the Franciscan convento in a part of the village that had been inhabited up to and perhaps during the time of Spanish occupancy. This is not to say, however, that the kiva itself was necessarily in use after the establishment of the mission, for the padres would doubtless have sought to suppress any pagan observances in the village. Possibly, too, this kiva may have been revived and put to use after the departure of the Franciscans in 1680, as will be considered below.

According to modern Pueblo practice it is customary to accept and tolerate extraneous religions as they come, and to adapt elements of them into the native observances. Many examples could be noted from a survey of the literature, but it is sufficient for present purposes to refer to the discussions by Mrs. Parsons (1939, vol. 1, pp. viii, 542–549, vol. 2, pp. 848–849, 1068–1080, 1101–1103, 1132–1133, 1155). Although the degree of borrowing from other religions seems to be less marked among the Hopi than among other Pueblo peoples today, the Hopi do manifest a complacent attitude toward missionaries without, however, succumbing to their persuasions. Numerous Christian missions have been active in the Hopi villages for many years, Catholic, Mormon, Mennonite, Baptist, and others, all of which appear to have had little effect upon the Hopis' way of life and faith. If this is so today, it is reasonable to assume that it also obtained in the 17th century, when there were at most never more than two or three Spanish priests in the Awatovi mission establishment. It seems almost certain that indigenous ceremonials continued to be observed, if perhaps clandestinely. This hypothesis is not inconsistent with that of the deliberate and ostentatious filling in of certain kivas (such as Room 788) by the Franciscans. The Indians could not have prevented that except by force, which they were probably not prepared to exert. Outward acceptation with quiet deviousness doubtless better served their purpose.

The kiva in Test 22 was the second largest excavated at Awatovi and was exceeded in area only slightly by Test 31, Room 1. It was almost a perfect rectangle measuring 5.70 m. along its right side, 5.90 m. along its left side, 4.95 m. across its rear, and 5.05 m. across its front. It was oriented

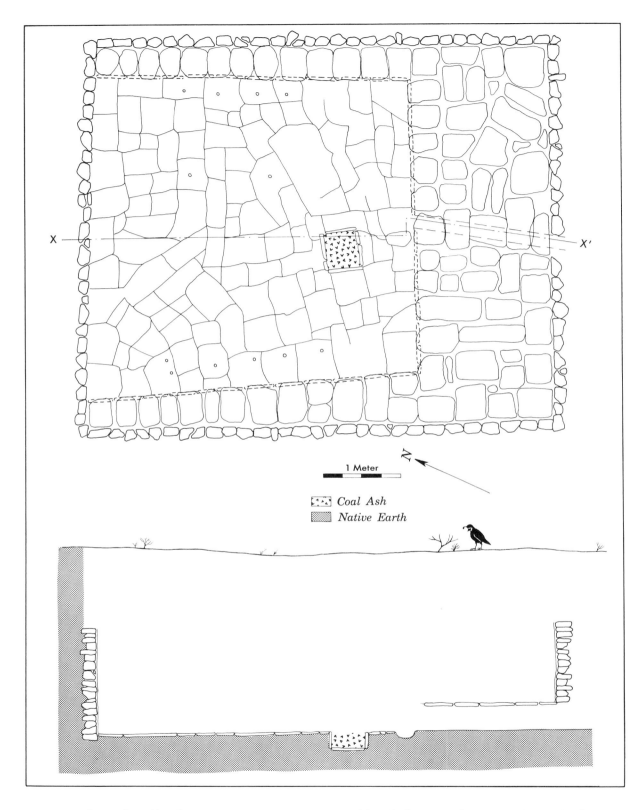

1 Meter

Coal Ash
Native Earth

Fig. 43. Plan and profile of Test 22, Room 10, at Awatovi. Although this was a large room it contained no unusual features.

about N. 27° W., and was surrounded by a block of domestic rooms.

A bench extended across the rear, 1.65 m. broad at its left end, 1.70 m. at its right, and 30 to 33 cm. high. A narrow ventilator tunnel passed beneath the rear bench, not quite perpendicular to either the face of the bench or the rear wall. At the face of the bench the tunnel was 2.60 m. from the left wall and 2.30 m. from the right. Its width of only 12 cm. was unusual, but the details of its construction were not recorded. A vertical shaft extended upward from the outer end of the tunnel beyond the rear wall, but it was not excavated. A small round hole, 9 cm. in diameter, penetrated the rear wall near its center line and 47 cm. above the surface of the bench. Perhaps it entered the ventilator shaft like the hole in Test 14, Room 6 (p. 33), though no plug was found in it.

Benches also existed along right and left sides of the room, each about 30 cm. high, but there was none across the front. That on the right side was 45 cm. broad at its rear end and 40 cm. at its front. That on the left side was 70 cm. broad at its rear end and 40 cm. at its front. All benches were completely paved with neatly fitted slabs of varying shapes and sizes, and all were faced with vertical slabs. No niches or cists were discovered.

The floor was approximately 2.00 m. above caprock and 2.20 m. below the modern surface, but whether any earlier structures existed beneath the floor was not ascertained.

A rectangular slab-lined firepit was located 75 cm. in front of the rear bench, and about 35 cm. to the left of the midline of the room. It measured 38 cm. fore-and-aft by 48 cm. transversely by 20 cm. deep, and was filled with coal ash. An irregularly ovoid basin lay just to the left of the ventilator opening and almost contiguous to the face of the rear bench. Whether it had been a firepit was not certain. No deflector was found. No evidence of a sipapu or footdrum was discovered in the floor.

Rows of small circular holes had been drilled through the floor slabs, a set of seven about 35 cm. from the left bench at intervals of 40 to 60 cm., and a set of four about 25 cm. from the right bench at intervals of 40 to 50 cm. A few others were scattered about, seemingly unrelated to one another.

Walls stood to a height of 1.40 to 1.50 m. above the floor. They were all tied at the corners and not abutted. To their interior surfaces had been applied a coating of adobe mortar, into which had been pressed horizontal bundles of grass supported by vertical sticks or reeds, in the manner

described for Room 788 (pp. 61–62). Some coats of finish plaster remained on the walls but only in small patches, and no evidence of paint was recorded.

Test 22, Room 10, had apparently burned but whether this had caused its abandonment or had occurred later could not be determined.

The kiva was situated in a part of the village immediately northwest of the large plaza that also surrounded Test 31, Room 1, and it was very likely occupied at about the same time as that kiva, perhaps even up to the date of the final destruction and abandonment of Awatovi in 1700–1701. It may indeed have played a role in the tragedy of that destruction, the legendary circumstances of which are summarized herein as part of the discussion of Test 31, Room 1 (pp. 73–74). Both kivas had burned, and displayed evidence of violence.

The nature of the debris that had accumulated was consistent with the hypothesis of violent destruction. To a depth of about 75 cm. below the surface of the mound, the fill consisted of loose windblown sand with relatively small quantities of potsherds or other artifacts. For the next 75 cm. it was hard-packed sand, in which sherds were still not very abundant, although numerous pieces of charred wood were found at depths between 1.00 and 1.75 m. But a varied assemblage of objects occurred in the fill between the depth of 1.50 m. and the floor, which lay at 2.20 m.

At about 1.50 m. were a human mandible and a human ilium. Between 1.60 and 1.70 m. were fragments of a human skull and a partially charred log, 25 cm. in diameter by 2.40 m. long. At 1.72 m. were two restorable jars, both of post-Sikyatki types. Also from this level downward the walls were blackened and burned. At 1.78 m. a human scapula was found, and on top of the rear bench was a pile of charred cornhusks. At 1.95 m. was a restorable post-Sikyatki jar, and at 2.15 m. were three more restorable vessels near the left-rear corner of the room.

From the fill above the 1.75 m. level came a full-grooved object of vesicular basalt in the general shape of an axe or maul, 13 cm. long, with a notch in each end. The function of this artifact is not clear, but Woodbury (1954, pp. 178–179, fig. 39, d) discusses it in the context of similar objects from other proveniences that have been called "weights." In the fill below the 1.75 m. level was found a stone pestle, illustrated in Woodbury (ibid., fig. 18, b).

Four loom-weight blocks lay on the tops of the benches, discolored and cracked by fire. A feature noted in this kiva but not in any other was a series of small holes about 1 cm. deep and 5 to 6 cm. apart, arranged horizontally in groups in the masonry faces of all three benches. The holes were at the same distance above the floor as were holes of similar size in the loom-weight blocks. They may have served to hold one end of a warp bar, the opposite end of which was held by a movable loom-weight block, as discussed by Woodbury (ibid., p. 154).

The skeleton of a dog lay on the floor against the face of the right side bench. Scattered profusely over the floor and the tops of the benches were quantities of charcoal, ashes, charred logs, planks, twigs, and grass, all suggesting burned

remnants of roofing material, although no structural pattern could be made out.

The sherd content of the fill was meagre in comparison with that in most other kivas of comparable size. In the lower levels, associated with the bones and charred wood, the pottery was within Ceramic Group A-2, characterized by a very high percentage of black-on-yellow sherds, with only about 10 percent each of Sikyatki Polychrome and post-Sikyatki types. Above the level of 1.75 m., however, the black-on-yellow fell off considerably, Sikyatki Polychrome remained at about 9 percent, but the post-Sikyatki types accounted for a high 26 percent, indicative of Ceramic Group A-1.

TEST 22, ROOM 10, SHERD COUNT

Depth in cm.	B/W No.	B/W %	B/O No.	B/O %	Awa. B/Y No.	Awa. B/Y %	Equiv. B/Y No.	Equiv. B/Y %	Jed. B/Y No.	Jed. B/Y %	Siky. Poly. No.	Siky. Poly. %	post-Siky. No.	post-Siky. %	Totals
0–175	14	1	12	1	—	—	409	42	184	20	84	9	254	26	957
175–222	4	1	1	—	—	—	188	38	195	40	48	10	47	10	483

Seventeen charcoal samples from various locations within the fill were dated (Bannister, Robinson, and Warren 1967, p. 11), but an undetermined number of the outer rings was missing from each. In most instances it was impossible to estimate the missing number of rings, but in three cases the investigators gave their opinion that the outermost ring was "within a very few years of the cutting date." These three dates were respectively 1422, 1657, and 1696. The less certain dates ranged from 1393 to 1660.

Most of the specimens were of Douglas fir or Ponderosa pine and may reasonably be regarded as remnants of the principal members of the roof structure rather than casual bits from firepits or

similar sources. In view of the uncertainty of the actual cutting dates only two reliable conclusions are possible as to the probable dates of construction and occupancy of the kiva: it was probably built not earlier than 1393 and was perhaps reconstructed as late as 1696. The earlier of these dates appears unacceptable since the geographical location as well as the ceramic content of the fill strongly point to a much later beginning date, but the presence of a beam with a precutting date of 1696 is almost conclusive that the kiva had undergone repair during the interregnum when the padres were absent, and an inference that it was in use at the time of the destruction of the village in 1700–1701 is almost certain.

TEST 31, ROOM 1

The kiva in Test 31 (figs. 44, 45) was the largest excavated at Awatovi, its area exceeding that of Test 22, Room 10, by about 2 square meters. It also was unusual in shape, with length almost exactly twice its width. It was located in the center of what appeared to have been a large plaza, occupying the area between the Spanish church and convento, 24 meters to the south and southwest, and a house block of native dwellings 31

meters to the northwest, which contained the kiva designated Test 22, Room 10.

Room 1 in Test 31 was nearly a rectangle, the rear wall measuring 4.05 m., the right wall 7.95 m., the front wall 4.00 m., and the left wall 7.65 m. The floor lay about 1.35 m. above bedrock, and the kiva was oriented N. 38° E.

Across the rear end was an unusually broad but low bench, 2.80 m. broad and from 23 to 25 cm.

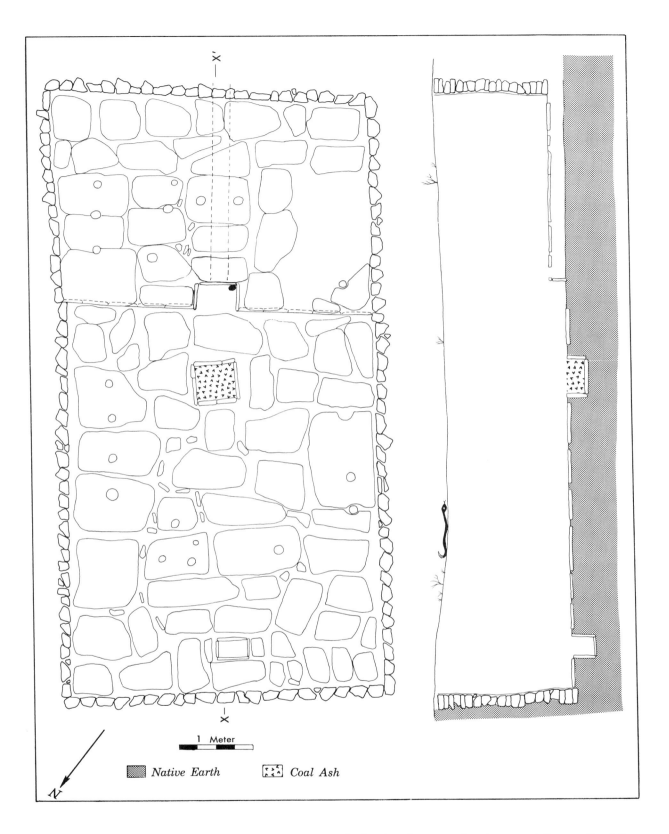

Fig. 44. Plan and profile of Test 31, Room 1, at Awatovi, showing the unusual embrasure at the mouth of the ventilator tunnel, with a wooden post in its rear corner.

1 Meter

▦ *Native Earth*   ⬚ *Coal Ash*

high. The bench was characterized by a unique feature in the form of an embrasure extending from floor level to the upper surface of the bench and exactly in the center of its face. This embrasure was 50 cm. wide and extended backward into the bench about 35 cm. The front of the bench and the side walls of the embrasure were faced with large vertical stone slabs, and the inner wall of the embrasure was closed by another slab (supported by a wooden post) through which a small semicircular aperture, 11 cm. high, led into a ventilator tunnel that extended beneath the bench and through the rear wall of the kiva, where it connected with a square vertical shaft. The ventilator was not fully excavated, but two spherical stone balls were found inside and just behind its mouth. The surface of the bench was entirely paved with neatly fitted slabs; some of the slabs also covered the ventilator tunnel, their ends resting solidly on the fill of the bench so that supporting sticks or lintels were not necessary.

At least nine small circular holes had been drilled through some of the paving slabs on top of the bench. A row of three occurred from 45 to 50 cm. from the right wall, at intervals of 45 cm. A second row of three was placed almost parallel to the first, but from 1.15 to 1.45 m. from the right wall, at intervals of 45 and 95 cm. The other three holes appeared to be haphazardly placed. There were no side or front benches.

The floor of the kiva was completely paved with neatly fitted stone slabs of irregular sizes and shapes. At a point from 65 to 70 cm. in front of the face of the bench, almost exactly in the midline of the kiva, its sides not quite parallel to the walls, was an almost square firepit, measuring 45 cm. fore-and-aft by 50 cm. transversely by 20 cm. in depth. All four sides and the hearth were formed of squared slabs, and the pit was filled with coal ash. No trace of a deflector was found.

Near the front of the kiva and only 45 cm. from the front wall was a rectangular pit measuring 50 cm. transversely by 30 cm. fore-and-aft and 28 cm. in depth. All four sides were faced with rec-

Fig. 45. Test 31, Room 1, from the front, showing rear bench, recessed ventilator opening with perforated deflector slab, pavement, firepit, loom-anchor holes, and loom weights.

tangularly shaped boards, badly rotted, and there was a horizontal stone slab in the bottom. It was not apparent how this pit had been covered, but it probably functioned as a footdrum or a sipapu like analogous features in other kivas. Nothing was found within it.

At least 13 small circular holes appeared in the floor slabs. A row of 4 extended parallel to the right wall, about 50 cm. from it, at intervals of 45 to 50 cm. The forward hole was 2.60 m. from the front wall, the rear hole 1.00 m. from the face of the rear bench. Another row of 4 holes extended parallel to the left wall and from 35 to 40 cm. from it at intervals of 40 to 45 cm. The forward hole was 2.25 m. from the front wall, the rear hole 1.25 m. from the face of the rear bench. The remaining 5 holes did not appear to have been arranged according to a definable pattern.

The walls of the kiva, which stood from 75 cm. to 1.75 m. high, were of the usual flimsy construction of coursed but irregularly laid blocks and slabs; remnants of plaster survived, but without evidence of paint. No niches or other features were noted in the walls.

The fill within the kiva was composed almost entirely of sand, and the quantity of sherds was small. But certain other items of its contents were notable. On the floor near the front were at least six restorable jars of post-Sikyatki types, as well as three pottery objects that resembled what had been elsewhere identified as candlesticks, certainly of Spanish inspiration. Also on the floor were a turquoise bead and five loomblocks, two against the right wall, one near the face of the bench, one near the right-front corner of the kiva, and one on the right portion of the bench. They were all of the usual breadloaf form with small circular sockets in the sides for warp beams and elongated finger notches in the ends. One is illustrated in Woodbury (1954, fig. 33, d).

Just above the floor and against the left wall was a metal arrow point and a bit of copper wire, and a three-quarter-grooved hammerstone was on the bench (ibid., fig. 15, d). On the left half of the bench were several disarticulated human bones that lay on top of an area of burned earth from which a few paving slabs had previously been removed. The bones appeared to have been thrown into the kiva after it had burned. A fractured human skull lay face down near the front wall.

It seems clear that this kiva had burned, for remains of charred beams lay on the bench, and fragments of charred grass and reeds were scattered about on or just above the floor. Further-

more some of the stone and plaster showed discoloration by fire. The evidence of burning is a provocative factor, because it may suggest the identity of this kiva with one described by Dr. J. Walter Fewkes and equated by him with a famous Hopi legend. In brief, the story was that during the winter of 1700–1701, after the people of Awatovi had permitted the Franciscan friars to return and to reestablish their mission, following their expulsion during the rebellion of 1680, some groups of Hopis from villages on the other mesas attacked Awatovi, burned much of it, stifled and burned some of the men in at least one of the kivas, abducted the women, many of whom were tortured and dismembered at a place near Second Mesa, and carried a few women and most of the children into captivity. The documentation of this story is summarized in Montgomery, Smith, and Brew (1949, pp. 20–24). (See also Bourke 1884, pp. 90–91; Bandelier 1890–92, part II, p. 372; Valverde 1732 [1937], pp. 385–387; Stephen 1936, p. 388; Hackett 1937, pp. 385–386; Smith 1970, p. 7; Wilson 1972.)

In 1892 Fewkes spent ten days at Awatovi, and excavated, among other things, part of a kiva which he believed to be the one in which the men had been stifled and burned (Fewkes 1893). Because human bones were uncovered, Fewkes's Hopi workmen were reluctant to continue and he did not complete the excavation. He dug a trench along the southerly wall and a second trench at right angles to the first extending to the center of the kiva. He found stone paving slabs on the floor, and much evidence of fire, as well as a human skull and other human bones. Fewkes was not satisfied that he had found the actual kiva of the legend, but he said (p. 373):

I believe that I have excavated the po-wa'-ko sorcerers' kib-va, and tradition supports this identification. Still I have not proven that to be the case, although the discovery of human bones supports the legend. It seems pretty true that a tragedy took place in this kib-va, for there is no evidence that the bodies were buried there, but whether this chamber is the original po-wa'-ko kib-va or not will always be in doubt.

In 1895 Fewkes again visited Awatovi, and expanded his excavations in and around the same kiva. In his subsequent report (1898b, pp. 612–613) he wrote:

In 1892, while removing the soil from a depression about the middle of the eastern court of Awatobi, about 100 feet north of the northern wall of the mission,

I laid bare a room 28 by 14 feet, in which were found a skull and many other human bones which, from their disposition, had not been buried with care. The discovery of these skeletons accorded with the Hopi traditions that this was one of the rooms in which the men of Awatobi were gathered on the fatal night, and the inclosure where many died. I was deterred from further excavation at that place by the horror of my workmen at the desecration of the chamber. In 1895, however, I determined to continue my earlier excavations and to trace the course of the walls of adjacent rooms. The results obtained in this work led to a new phase of the question, which sheds more light on the character of the rooms in the middle of the eastern court of Awatobi. Instead of a single room at this point, there are three rectangular chambers side by side, all of about the same size (plate CVIII). In the center of the floor of the middle room, 6 feet below the surface, I came upon a cist or stone shrine. As the workmen approached the floor they encountered a stone slab, horizontally placed in the pavement of the room. This slab was removed, and below it was another flat stone which was perforated by a rectangular hole just large enough to admit the hand and forearm. This second slab was found to cover a stone box, the sides of which were formed of stone slabs about 2 1/2 feet square. On the inner faces of the upright slabs rain-cloud symbols were painted. These symbols were of terrace form, in different colors outlined with black lines. One of the stones bore a yellow figure, another a red, and a third white. The color of the fourth was not determinable, but evidently, from its position relatively to the others, was once green. This arrangement corresponds with the present ceremonial assignment of colors to the cardinal points, or at least the north and south, as at the present time, were yellow and red, respectively, and presumably the white and green were on the east and west sides of the cist. The colors are still fairly bright and may be seen in the restoration of this shrine now in the National Museum.

There was no stone floor to this shrine, but within it were found fragments of prayer-plumes or pahos painted green, but so decayed that, when exposed to sunlight, some of them fell into dust. There were likewise fragments of green carbonate of copper and kaolin, a yellow ocher, and considerable vegetal matter mixed with the sand. All these facts tend to the belief that this crypt was an ancient shrine in the floor of a chamber which may have been a kiva.

When the Peabody Museum excavated Test 31, Room 1, in 1938, abundant evidence of its destruction by fire was noted, in the form of quantities of charcoal, ashes, charred roof beams, stones and plaster burned to shades of pink and orange. Furthermore, parts of a human skull and

other human bones were found. The room was about in the position in which Fewkes had dug, as can be seen by a comparison of plate 1 in his 1893 report or plate 107 in his 1898 report (on which the kiva is indicated by the letter P) with figure 2 herein, and except for the length of the front wall his dimensions corresponded fairly closely with ours. Fewkes measured the rear (or as he called it the "south") side at 14 ft., whereas our measurement was 13 ft., 4 in. (4.05 m.). He estimated the right (east) side at 28 ft., 6 in. (our measurement being 7.95 m. or 25 ft., 3 in.); the left (west) side at 24 ft., 6 in. (our measurement being 7.65 m. or 25 ft., 2 in.), and the front (north) side at 18 ft. (our measurement being 4.00 m. or 13 ft., 1 in.). The dimensions of the front wall as just given do not agree very closely but since Fewkes actually exposed only the south wall, all his other calculations were only estimates made from surface indications.

Thus while we cannot be sure, there is a reasonable basis for identifying Test 31, Room 1, with Fewkes's kiva, and thus possibly with the po-wa'-ko kiva of legend.

The legend itself may have been further substantiated by dramatic evidence provided through a discovery in 1964 by Mr. Rex Gentry of a mass human burial about 15 miles southwest of Awatovi and 10 miles south of Second Mesa. Subsequent excavation by Dr. Alan P. Olson disclosed the dismembered and mutilated remains of about 30 individuals buried beneath a rounded hummock. Although Olson believed it to be a secondary burial without evidence of violence, examination of the bones by Dr. Christy G. Turner and Nancy Tucker Morris led them to the conclusions that the mass burial was primary, that evidence of great violence and deliberate butchery was abundant, that individuals of both sexes and of ages from one year to more than 45 years were represented, and that the age of the bones, as determined by radiocarbon dating, was about 370 ± 95 years. While the evidence is purely circumstantial, it could be consistent with a hypothesis that the burial site was the place of a massacre corresponding to that reported in the legend of Awatovi. (For full details see Olson 1966; Turner and Tucker 1968; and Turner and Morris 1970.)

As already stated, the ceramic content of the fill was comparatively meagre, with a heavy predominance of post-Sikyatki types, only moderate quantities of black-on-yellows, and a small component of Sikyatki Polychrome. Thus it fell within Ceramic Group A-1, the latest pottery complex at Awatovi. Furthermore, the ratios were only slightly different from the lowest to the highest levels.

TEST 31, ROOM 1, SHERD COUNT

Depth in cm.	B/W		B/O		Awa. B/Y		Equiv. B/Y		Jed. B/Y		Siky. Poly.		post. Siky.		Totals
	No.	%	No.	%	No.	%	No.	%	No.	%	No.	%	No.	%	
0–75	8	1	—	—	—	—	211	29	178	24	76	10	258	36	731
75–125	—	—	2	1	2	1	66	24	70	26	22	8	108	40	270
125–175	6	1	4	1	—	—	113	21	110	21	39	7	261	49	533

Sixteen datable specimens of charcoal were recovered, nearly all from the floor or just above it, and apparently representing members of the roof structure. Most were of Douglas fir or Ponderosa pine, with a few of pinyon. There was not a single cutting or near-cutting date, and it was impossible to determine on any specimen the position of the outermost surviving ring relative to the actual bark (Bannister, Robinson, and Warren 1967, p. 12). Nevertheless, some useful inferences can be drawn from the data.

The dates can be grouped as follows: one at 1354, four between 1392 and 1433, three between 1459 and 1476, four between 1546 and 1567, and four between 1599 and 1628. Despite the inherent uncertainties, and disregarding the single date of 1354, it appears that the room was probably not built before about 1400, and that it had undergone repairs as late as 1630 or perhaps considerably later. It is quite plausible to infer that it could have been in use after 1680 and up to the final destruction of the village in 1700–1701, although it might have suffered a period of abandonment between 1630 and 1680, when the friars would have attempted to suppress any pagan observances.

TEST 57, ROOM 1

The kiva in Test 57 was situated in the northerly part of the village, about 60 meters west of Test 22, Room 10, in what had probably been a large plaza lying between the house blocks used during the later years of the occupation. The kiva itself was hurriedly excavated toward the end of the final season as a test of the area, but none of the surrounding structures was investigated. As usual, it was rectangular, and although its exact dimensions were not recorded, it measured about 3.00 m. wide by about 3.75 m. long. It was oriented about N. 15° E.

A broad bench extended across the rear, paved with large stone slabs; and a horizontal ventilator tunnel, the exact position and dimensions of which were not recorded, lay very near the midline of the bench. No investigation was made of the vertical shaft. The face and surface of the bench had been largely destroyed, and it was thus impossible to determine whether it had once been paved or whether there had been cists within it. No benches existed along the other sides of the room.

The floor was paved with stone slabs, irregularly shaped but neatly fitted; about 80 cm. in front of the rear bench was a small firepit about 28 cm. square filled with coal ash and underlaid with clean sand. A deflector had once stood about halfway between the bench and the firepit, but no remnant of it survived. No evidence of a sipapu or footdrum was found. A row of three small circular holes existed parallel to the left wall and a little closer to the front wall than to the face of the bench.

Walls were of the usual unstable type characteristic of the late period at Awatovi, and stood to a maximum height of about 1.35 m. No evidence of niches, plaster, or other wall features had survived.

The kiva had been filled with the usual debris of sand, refuse, sherds, and stray artifacts. The ceramic complex of the fill fell within Ceramic Group A-2, a late but not the very latest period of Pueblo IV. It was strongly dominated by Jeddito Black-on-yellow, with moderate components of

Sikyatki Polychrome, and of various post-Sikyatki types. It is notable that Sikyatki Polychrome decreased by almost one-half between the bottom and top strata, while the post-Sikyatki types correspondingly more than doubled. No datable wood specimens were recovered.

TEST 57, ROOM 1, SHERD COUNT

Depth in cm.	B/W		B/O		Awa. B/Y		Equiv. B/Y		Jed. B/Y		Siky. Poly.		post-Siky.		Totals
	No.	%	No.	%	No.	%	No.	%	No.	%	No.	%	No.	%	
0–50	3	—	1	—	—	—	391	33	410	35	131	11	235	20	1171
50–100	—	—	2	—	7	—	792	37	758	34	424	19	211	10	2194
100–135	6	—	—	—	10	—	579	35	609	37	323	20	133	8	1660

In addition to the sherds, several turquoise and bone beads, bone awls, hammerstones, two pottery pipes, one projectile point, several polishing pebbles, some fragments of painted wood, a discoidal stone chopper, and a fragment of turquoise mosaic containing at least 13 small bits of turquoise (Woodbury 1954, figs. 27, v, 32, h), were recovered, but none of these items was chronologically helpful. It must be concluded, on the basis of the sherd complex, that the kiva had probably been abandoned during the latter part of Pueblo IV, perhaps in the late 16th century.

I V

Excavations of Kivas at Kawaika-a

Oh, to be wafted away
From this black Aceldama of sorrow,
Where the dust of an earthy to-day
Is the earth of a dusty to-morrow!

W. S. Gilbert, *Patience*, Act I

Along the southeasterly rim of Antelope Mesa, northeasterly from Awatovi, lie the ruins of several large pueblos that were built and occupied approximately contemporaneously with Awatovi. None was quite so large as Awatovi and most appear to have been abandoned prior to the coming of the Spaniards, but one of them may have been visited by Don Pedro de Tovar in 1540.

In July of that year, after having stormed the town of Hawikuh near modern Zuni, Coronado sent a small group of men under Tovar to explore the area toward the northwest. Some members of this party proceeded as far as the Grand Canyon of the Colorado River, and thus became the first Europeans to see that natural wonder. En route, however, they came upon a pueblo occupied by Indians who were at first somewhat less than hospitable. The Spaniards promptly made a show of force, and the Indians then submitted and allowed the strangers to enter their village.

The identity of this town has always been in doubt, and has been thought by some to have been Awatovi. Other commentators, however, have believed that it was actually another village somewhat to the east of Awatovi, the most likely site being what is called Kawaika-a by the modern Hopis. Although its orthography is various, the most common form in the literature being Kawaiokuh, Kawaika-a is today a mound of rubble covering the remains of a large pueblo of more than 20 acres, about 4 miles northeast of Awatovi. It lies on the mesa top just at the edge of the escarpment, in a position closely analogous to that of Awatovi, looking out toward the southeast across the Jeddito Valley.

For our present purposes it is not important to solve the vexed question of whether or not Kawai-

ka-a was ever visited by Tovar or any other Spaniard, but a summary of the authorities bearing on that problem can be found in Montgomery, Smith, and Brew (1949, pp. 3–7).

During the final season of the Awatovi Expedition, in the late summer of 1939, evidence of painted plaster was noticed on the walls of several rooms at Kawaika-a. In order to investigate these mural decorations a crash program was instituted, and 15 kivas in varying states of preservation were excavated. These kivas were situated in two clusters on the southwest and southeast edges of the village. All had been built close to the edge of the mesa and there were no other structures between them and the escarpment. Their locations are shown in figure 3. The excavation along the southwesterly edge was designated Test 4 (fig. 46) and that along the southeasterly edge Test 5 (fig. 57). General views of Tests 4 and 5 are shown in Smith (1952a, fig. 30, *a, b*). Tests 1, 2, and 3 were made in other parts of the site, but did not expose kivas and are therefore not relevant to the present discussion.

The mural decorations discovered at Kawaika-a have been fully reported in Smith (1952a), and we shall not deal further with that feature. In the discussion to follow, each kiva will be described in terms of its architectural details, the nature of its fill, and its probable date, in the same framework that has been applied to the kivas at Awatovi.

Because the major purpose of the excavations at Kawaika-a was the discovery of kiva mural decorations, and also because time and labor were limited, complete examination of all architectural details was not always ideally fulfilled. Although the recorded data are in some cases inadequate for fully detailed descriptions, the following dis-

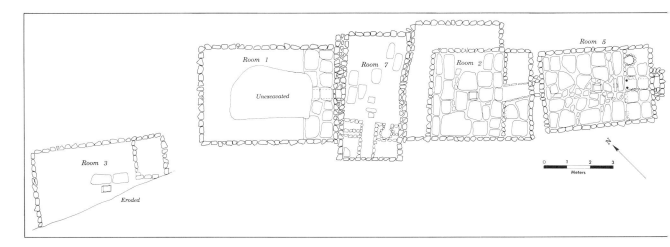

Fig. 46. Plan of all rooms excavated in Test 4 at Kawaika-a. The left half of Room 3, which was very near the escarpment of the mesa, had been destroyed by erosion. Room 2 was rebuilt several times, as explained on page 79.

cussion is presented as completely as the records permit. It is relevant to note that Dr. Walter Hough excavated at least one painted kiva at Kawaika-a in 1901 (Hough 1903, p. 340, pl. 89), but we were unable to identify it among those that we investigated.

TEST 4, ROOM 1

Room 1 in Test 4 was located near the edge of the mesa in the extreme southwesterly part of the site. It was one of a cluster of at least five kivas that were contiguous or almost so in this area. It was almost a perfect rectangle, measuring about 5.70 m. on right and left sides and 4.10 m. on front and rear. Orientation was about N. 38° W., and the long dimension lay almost parallel to the escarpment of the mesa.

Across the rear end was a bench 1.37 m. broad at its right end, 1.42 m. at its left end, and 38 cm. high. Its surface was neatly paved with fitted stone slabs, and a ventilator tunnel extended beneath it at about the midline. The tunnel was, however, not investigated.

Since the main purpose of the excavation was to study mural decorations, the kiva was not fully excavated, but a trench was dug along each wall, leaving a large mass of fill in the center of the room. Thus, most of the floor and the face of the bench remained obscured. It was clear, however, that no benches had existed along the right, left, and front walls. The exposed area of the floor was not paved, but was covered with a thin stratum of clean sand, beneath which was a firm layer of coal ash mixed with adobe. Of course, slabs may originally have been used and subsequently scavenged for use elsewhere. The areas normally occupied by firepit, deflector, and sipapu were not uncovered.

The walls were of poorly laid masonry exactly like that of the later periods at Awatovi and stood to a maximum height of only about one meter. All had once been coated with numerous layers of plaster, an undetermined number of which had been painted. The surviving remnants were so fragmentary, however, that no effort was made to record the designs.

Room 1 as excavated may have represented a modification of its original form. The right wall abutted the rear wall, which continued beyond and behind it. Plaster on the rear wall also continued behind this abutment, suggesting the existence of an earlier right wall behind the later one. But lack of time prevented further investigation.

Due to the limited nature of the excavation, only a few sherds were recovered, and these were not segregated as to depth. The ceramic complex showed a predominance of black-on-yellow, with a moderate quantity of Sikyatki Polychrome and only a small component of post-Sikyatki types. It

suggested Ceramic Group A-2, with a chronologically median placement in Classical Pueblo IV.

TEST 4, ROOM 1, SHERD COUNT

Depth in cm.	B/W		B/O		Awa. B/Y		Equiv. B/Y		Jed. B/Y		Siky. Poly.		post-Siky.		Totals
	No.	%	No.	%	No.	%	No.	%	No.	%	No.	%	No.	%	
0–100	3	1	2	1	5	2	83	27	143	47	39	13	25	8	300

Four charcoal specimens recovered from the fill gave dates recorded by Hall between 1321 and 1452 but in each case the outer ring was an undeterminable distance from the bark. It can be said, however, that the kiva was probably occupied at least as late as the end of the second quarter of the 15th century, which is consistent with the rather meagre ceramic evidence.

TEST 4, ROOM 2

Room 2 in Test 4 had had at least two, perhaps three, phases of occupation and had undergone considerable modification. Although the precise nature and sequence of the changes were not clear we may hypothesize a tentative history by reference to the lettered points indicated on the plan in figure 47.

The wall between Room 2 and Room 7 in this cluster was double-faced, suggesting that the two kivas may have been constructed simultaneously. A vertical break occurred in this wall at point G, which was directly in line with a prolongation of the wall D–J, and a wall may once have extended from D to G, creating a room within the points E–D–J–G–A–H–F–E. This room would have measured 4.84 m. along its right side, 5.52 m. along its left side, 3.96 m. across the front, and 4.04 m. across the rear. Later, perhaps, the kiva was enlarged by the removal of the postulated wall from G to D, and the incorporation of the area enclosed by the wall G–B–C–D. The kiva in this phase would have measured 4.84 m. along its right side, 5.52 m. along its left side, 5.20 m. across the front, and 5.50 m. across the rear, thus being the only kiva wider than it was long. Finally it may have been reduced in size by the building of new walls from D to J and from J to H. This hypothesis is substantiated by the fact that these walls abutted the earlier walls at both points D and H.

In the previously published report on mural paintings (Smith 1952a) only the final phase of this kiva (E–J–H–F) was called Room 2. The extended portion of its earlier phase embraced within the area A–G–B–C–D–J–H–A was called Room 4. It appears preferable, however, on more mature consideration, to regard the entire structure as a single kiva with successive architectural phases, all of which are referred to herein as parts of Room 2.

Plaster layers, which will be more fully discussed later, bear on the problem. No single layer of plaster extended across the break in the wall at G, and the decorative paintings on the area A–G were unrelated to those on the area G–B. Painted designs were continuous, however, from G to B to C to D, and were very different in style from those between A and G. Furthermore, the plaster layers were continuous from C to E, around the corner D and behind the abutting wall J–D.

Since the final phase of the kiva was within the area E–J–H–F, we shall describe it as an entity. In this phase it was generally rectangular but approached a square more nearly than did most other kivas at either Kawaika-a or Awatovi. It measured 4.20 m. along its right side, 4.52 along its left side, 4.04 m. across its rear, and 3.90 across its front. It was oriented about N. 38° W.

Across the rear was a bench 1.02 m. broad at its right end, 1.22 m. broad at its left, and about 40 cm. high. Its surface had originally been paved with large stone slabs, but these had all been removed from the right half of the area. The face of the bench was composed of poorly laid masonry, which had partly collapsed (fig. 48, a).

A ventilator tunnel extended diagonally beneath the bench; its opening was offset about 22 cm. to the right of the midline of the kiva, and the point

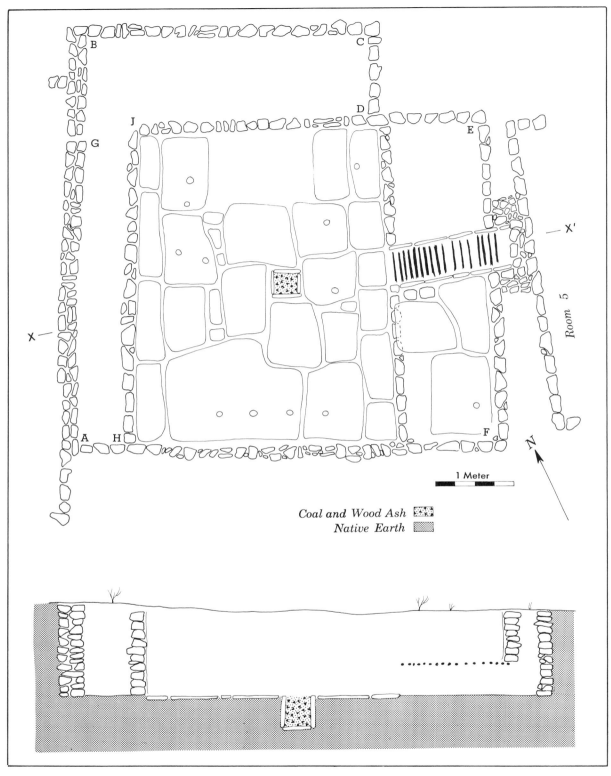

Fig. 47. Plan and profile of Test 4, Room 2, at Kawaika-a, showing the diagonal ventilator tunnel with roof beams *in situ*, firepit containing mixed wood and coal ash, and ventilator shaft between the walls of Rooms 2 and 5. The superimposed letters indicate the rebuilding sequence, as discussed on page 79.

at which it penetrated the rear wall was about 80 cm. to the right of the midline, so that it formed an angle with the face of the bench of about 73°. The opening of the tunnel had collapsed so that its exact size and manner of construction was not determinable, but the tunnel itself was 37 cm. wide at the front and 48 cm. wide at the rear. Its walls were lined with vertical stone slabs, across which were laid 17 wooden sticks, from 3 cm. to 7 cm. in diameter, either contiguous to one another or with intervals of only 2 cm. to 3 cm. (fig. 48, b). They lay parallel to the face of the bench, not perpendicular to the sides of the tunnel. Over the sticks lay large paving slabs.

A vertical shaft was located in the narrow space between the rear wall of Room 2 and the front wall of Room 5. Within it were found a small ladle and a rectangular bowl. No benches existed along the other walls of the room.

The floor was paved with large stone slabs, most of them nearly rectangular and neatly fitted. An almost square firepit lay 1.15 m. in front of the face of the bench. It was not directly in front of the mouth of the ventilator tunnel, but lay almost exactly on the midline of the kiva. Its sides were respectively 24, 26, 26, and 28 cm. long and it was 40 cm. deep. All sides and bottom were lined with stone slabs, and the contents contained both wood and coal ash. No evidence of a deflector was found.

At least 13 small circular holes existed in the floor slabs, but most seemed haphazardly placed, as if the slabs containing them had been used previously in other places. Near the right wall, however, parallel to it and from 40 to 44 cm. from it, was a row of four such holes at intervals of 39 to 43 cm., the rearmost being 93 cm. from the face of the rear bench. No evidence of a sipapu or footdrum was found.

The walls varied somewhat in character. The older front wall, which was also the right wall of Room 7, was double-faced and fairly well built, but all other walls were single-faced, laid in the usual careless manner characteristic of most of the later masonry, with blocks of variable sizes and shapes and only approximate coursing. Almost exactly in the middle of the earlier wall B–C was a large vertical post that had been set into a prepared embrasure so that its outer edge was flush with the face of the masonry. The area around the post was packed with adobe, and plaster layers applied to the wall had originally extended across it, obscuring it. At the time of excavation, however, some plaster had collapsed, exposing the

decayed remnants of the post (Smith 1952a, fig. 30, a).

Although all surviving walls showed remnants of plaster, many areas were too fragmentary to show significant elements of painted decoration. This was especially true of the final phase of the room, within the area E–F–H–J–E, where the only surviving bits of plaster were around the right-rear corner E. There had been about ten coats of plaster there, two or three of them painted, but it was not feasible to preserve them or to record their decorative details.

On the walls of the earlier phase of the kiva, however, 25 or more layers survived in the area A–G, and about 18 layers in the area G–B–C–D, of which 8 in each area had been painted. As already stated, there was a complete break in these layers at the point G, and the designs on opposite sides of this break bore no apparent relation to one another. In the area A–G only 3 of the 8 painted layers displayed remnants sufficiently large to be recorded in detail (ibid., fig. 39, b, c, d). Of the 8, 1 was assigned to Layout Group I, while the others were tentatively assigned to Layout Group III. It thus appears that most of these murals were executed at a fairly early date, comparable to those of Test 19, Room 3, Test 14, Room 3, and Kiva C at Awatovi, but somewhat earlier than those in any other kivas excavated at Kawaika-a. They were also earlier than the paintings on other walls in Room 2, which is consistent with the hypothesis already expressed that an early wall, later demolished, had once extended along the line G–D and had been integral with the wall A–G.

More interesting and much more nearly complete were the painted designs on walls G–B–C–D. There were eight paintings on each segment of those walls, and although some could not be positively linked on all three walls, several were physically continuous along the entire area. Some were classified with Layout Group I, but most belonged to Layout Group II, indicating a middle chronological position within Pueblo IV. Those that were recoverable are illustrated in Smith (ibid., figs. 50, d, 51, e, 52, b, 55, a, 56, a, 57, c, 60, a, b, 76, a, 89, b, 91, a, d; plate D).

The fill in the later phase of the kiva, E–F–H–J–E, was excavated separately from that in the probably earlier area that lay behind the wall H–J–D. The maximum depth in each was about 1.50 m. In the presentation of the ceramic complexes these two volumes will be referred to as early and late phases, respectively.

There was not much difference in the relative

a

b

Fig. 48. *a*. Test 4, Room 2, from the front, showing rear bench, cover supports over ventilator tunnel, pavement, and firepit.

b. Detail of cover supports over ventilator tunnel in Test 4, Room 2, with covering slabs removed.

TEST 4, ROOM 2, SHERD COUNT

Depth in cm.	B/W		B/O		Awa. B/Y		Equiv. B/Y		Jed. B/Y		Siky. Poly.		post-Siky.		Totals
	No.	%	No.	%	No.	%	No.	%	No.	%	No.	%	No.	%	
							Early Phase								
0–100	4	1	—	—	—	—	97	37	103	40	40	15	15	6	259
100–150	7	2	8	2	1	—	122	30	141	35	96	24	26	7	401
							Late Phase								
0–50	2	—	3	2	—	—	46	25	88	48	18	10	26	14	183
50–100	4	1	7	2	3	—	148	33	155	35	94	21	33	8	444
100–150	14	4	8	2	3	1	138	37	103	28	61	17	41	11	368

quantities of various pottery types as between the two phases, and both fell between Ceramic Groups A-2 and A-3, with a predominance of black-on-yellows, rather unusually large components of Sikyatki Polychrome, and moderate quantities of post-Sikyatki types. The slightly larger showing of Sikyatki Polychrome and the smaller showing of post-Sikyatki types in the early phase as opposed to the late phase, however, does support the inference of a slight chronological precedence of the former.

Only one piece of datable charcoal was recovered; it came from the fill of the early phase and its outer ring was dated by Hall at 1356, which was not very significant since the distance below the bark was indeterminable.

All factors considered, the entire room seems to have been occupied during middle and late Pueblo IV, but was probably abandoned before the latest span of that period, and before the coming of the Spaniards, if indeed the latter ever actually visited this village.

TEST 4, ROOM 3

Room 3 in Test 4 was located very close to Room 1 but nearer to the escarpment of the mesa. Its right-rear corner was about 1.25 m. west of the left-front corner of Room 1 and the corresponding walls of the two kivas were nearly parallel to one another. Room 3 was probably almost rectangular, although the erosion of its entire left side and about half of its rear made exact measurement impossible. It was 5.60 m. long on its right side and at least 4.30 m. wide across its front. Its orientation was about N. 45° W.

A bench had existed across the rear but only part of its right half remained evident, and its left half had completely disappeared. Single courses of stones marked the position of the face of the bench and the right side of the ventilator tunnel. These masonry remnants were respectively 1.20 m. from the rear wall and 1.85 m. from the right wall. It was impossible to determine whether the bench had once been paved or whether it had contained cists. The size and character of the ventilator were also indeterminable. No benches existed along any of the other walls.

There had apparently been two occupations of this kiva. At a depth of 90 cm. below the surviving top of the right wall was a stratum of clean sand about 5 cm. thick. Upon it lay two large

sandstone paving slabs, marking the floor level, and through it was sunk a rectangular firepit measuring about 25 by 35 cm. and located 1.00 m. in front of the face of the bench. This firepit was lined on all sides by vertical slabs and a slab formed its bottom. It was filled with wood ash.

Below the stratum of sand was a layer of coal ash, 8 cm. thick, and below that a second stratum of clean sand about 3 cm. thick. Several coats of plaster on the front wall reached downward to this point and curved outward just above the top of the lower sand layer, as if there had once been an earlier floor at that level. Below the sand was a stratum of hard earth mixed with some coal ash extending to bedrock.

The surviving masonry of the walls was of the usual poor quality that characterized the later period of construction. About 20 layers of plaster extended over almost the entire right wall, 4 or 5 layers bearing paint, but they were so fragmentary and fragile that no significant details were recovered.

Because the modern surface of the mound sloped away from a maximum height of about 1.00 m. at the right-rear corner of the kiva to bedrock at the left and front, the contents of the fill were meagre. It was excavated in two levels, the ceramic complex of both heavily dominated by Jeddito Black-on-yellow with very small components of Sikyatki Polychrome and post-Sikyatki types, and with unusually large proportions of black-on-whites and black-on-oranges, characteristic of Ceramic Groups A-3 or B-4.

No datable wood specimens were recovered.

Except for the somewhat inexplicably large proportions of black-on-white and black-on-orange, the pottery collections would fall within the Classical period of Pueblo IV, or somewhere about the late 15th century.

TEST 4, ROOM 3, SHERD COUNT

Depth in cm.	B/W		B/O		Awa. B/Y		Equiv. B/Y		Jed. B/Y		Siky. Poly.		post-Siky.		Totals
	No.	%	No.	%	No.	%	No.	%	No.	%	No.	%	No.	%	
0–50	17	7	17	7	5	2	69	29	99	42	9	4	20	9	236
50–100	36	6	25	4	8	1	332	54	126	21	60	10	23	4	610

TEST 4, ROOM 5

Room 5 was at the southeasterly extremity of the cluster of kivas in Test 4 (fig. 49). It was adjacent to Room 2, but the walls of the two kivas were not actually contiguous, and a few centimeters of fill lay between them. Room 5 was almost exactly rectangular, measuring 3.33 m. across the rear, 3.40 m. across the front, 4.75 m. along the right side, and 4.50 m. along the left. Its orientation was about N. 44° W.

A bench extended across the rear, 1.10 m. broad and 45 cm. high. Its face was of fairly well-laid, coursed masonry, and its surface was paved with neatly fitted stone slabs, most of them nearly rectangular. A ventilator tunnel, 46 cm. wide and 33 cm. high, extended through the bench, at right angles to its face and exactly centered. Its sides were of coursed masonry, over which had been laid 15 wooden sticks from 4 to 7 cm. in diameter and placed almost tangentially to one another (figs. 50, 51). Over the sticks lay a matrix of clay and small pebbles about 6 cm. to 8 cm. thick, and above that the paving slabs of the bench surface. The floor of the tunnel was of sand.

The tunnel penetrated the rear wall, which was double, and between the two faces of this wall rose a vertical shaft fully framed by coursed masonry, and of unusual proportions, measuring 55 by 25 cm., its longer dimension being parallel to the direction of the wall within which it was built.

The mouth of the tunnel was unusual, having been constructed for the reception of a door slab. All around the orifice was a molded collar of clay that extended backward about 8 cm. from the face of the bench, where it turned inward to form a jamb. Just behind the jamb on each side and providing support for it was a vertical wooden post about 4 or 5 cm. in diameter, and upon these posts

lay a wooden lintel. A carefully shaped stone slab, which exactly fitted the opening and was obviously the door, lay within the mouth of the tunnel.

Through the face of the bench on its right side was an opening 25 cm. wide, 15 cm. high, 35 cm. from the right wall, and 9 cm. above the floor. It led through the wall into a roughly semicircular cist 35 cm. in diameter and about 40 cm. high (figs. 51, 52). The circumference of the cist was lined with masonry of small stones and within it was set a globular yellow utility jar about 35 cm. deep, its orifice 24 cm. in diameter. The orifice was directed outward and upward at an angle of about 45° to the horizontal and lay just behind the back of the stones that formed the facing wall of the bench. Small stones and chunks of adobe were packed tightly all about the jar, and a wooden lintel was set into the masonry to form the upper limit of the opening. Resting on this lintel and extending directly backward to the rounded masonry lining of the cist were 12 small sticks that formed a roof. Above them was packed a fill of clay and small stones which supported the paving slabs of the bench top. The jar contained nothing.

The bench had originally been narrower, for a plastered masonry face existed 22 cm. behind the outer face. This earlier face had been partly destroyed when the cist was constructed in association with the later extension. There was no surviving evidence that a cist had existed in the early phase of the bench. No benches existed along the side or front walls.

The floor was fully paved with stone slabs of irregular shapes and varying sizes fairly neatly fitted. A deflector stood 40 cm. in front of the mouth of the ventilator tunnel. It was larger and

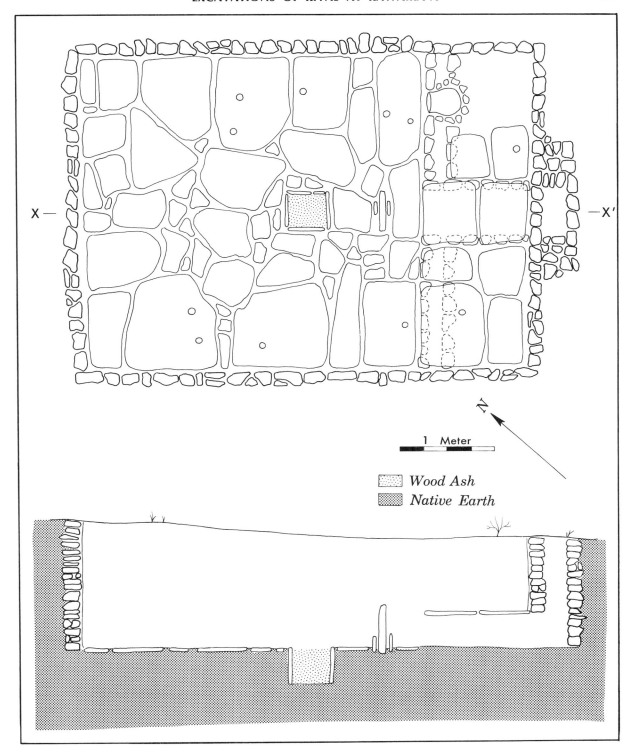

Fig. 49. Plan and profile of Test 4, Room 5, at Kawaika-a, showing the earlier front face of the rear bench, and the emplacement of a large utility jar beneath the right-hand side of the bench.

a

b

Fig. 50. *a.* Test 4, Room 5, from the front, showing rear bench with utility jar emplaced beneath it at the left, deflector, pavement, and firepit.

b. Detail of cover supports for ventilator tunnel in Test 4, Room 5, with covering slabs removed.

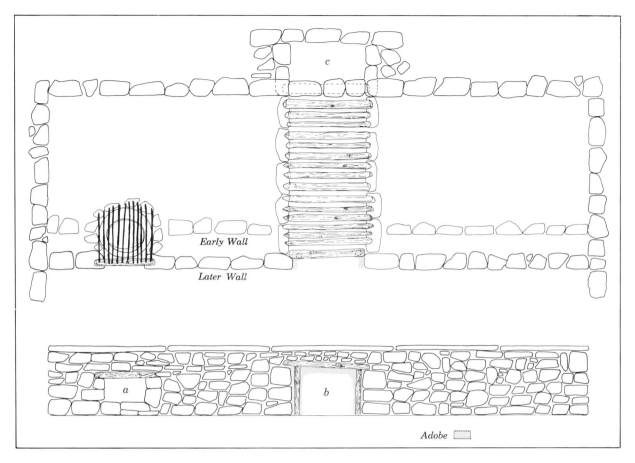

Fig. 51. Plan and front elevation of rear bench in Test 4, Room 5, at Kawaika-a. A globular utility jar was embedded in a cist beneath the surface, with access through the opening a. The cist was roofed with a series of small sticks. The mouth of the ventilator tunnel (b) was surrounded by a collar of adobe, reinforced by two upright wooden posts. The slabs covering the tunnel were supported by wooden sticks, and the vertical shaft (c) rose inside the heavy rear wall. In this drawing the surface slabs have been omitted in order to show the underlying structure.

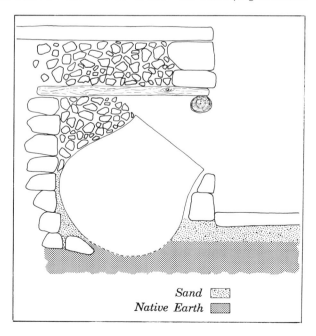

Fig. 52. Profile of a cist containing a large utility vessel beneath the rear bench of Test 4, Room 5, at Kawaika-a.

more substantially constructed than usual, being composed of a roughly rectangular vertical slab 44 cm. high above the floor, 46 cm. long, and 2.5 cm. thick. It was set into a slot in the floor and was supported by the insertion of a small triangular slab on either side.

A firepit about 35 cm. square and 40 cm. deep was located on the midline of the kiva, 55 cm. in front of the deflector and 98 cm. from the face of the bench. Its bottom was earthen, and stone slabs extended upward on each side for a distance of 30 cm. from the bottom, above which the sides were unlined.

Nine small circular holes were present in the floor slabs and two in the surface of the bench, but their irregular placement suggested that the slabs in which they occurred had been taken from another kiva and reused. No evidence was found of a sipapu or footdrum.

The walls were fairly substantial, but formed of irregular blocks laid in very approximate courses. Fragments of plaster remained on the rear and front walls, and over almost the whole area of the right wall. The plaster in the latter area was penetrated by copious roots and was so badly cracked that although a good many painted layers apparently had existed, parts of only two designs were recoverable. These are illustrated in Smith (1952a, figs. 54, c, 70, b); they were classified as belonging to Layout Groups II (2) and I (2), respectively. Two others, whose details were undefined, probably also belonged to Layout Group II. This suggests an occupation somewhat earlier than middle or Classical Pueblo IV.

The fill contained only moderate quantities of pottery, heavily dominated by Jeddito Black-on-yellow, with smaller quantities of Sikyatki Polychrome and very small components of post-Sikyatki types, as in Ceramic Groups A-2 or A-3.

Four specimens of wood from the fill yielded dates. For three of them, dated respectively 1233, 1378, and 1433, it was impossible to determine the distance from the bark of the outermost surviving ring. The fourth was dated 1430 with a subjective judgment that the outer ring was actually close to the bark (Bannister, Robinson, and Warren 1967, p. 17). The last specimen was dated by Hall at 1440 ± 10. It appears, thus, that the kiva was probably occupied until the second quarter of the 15th century, a date that is corroborated by the hypothetical dates of the mural paintings and the ceramic evidence.

Two small test pits were sunk into adjoining rooms, one just west of Room 1, the other just north of Room 5. Neither was further excavated, but a good many charcoal specimens were recovered from the fill of the pits. They were dated by Hall between 1311+x and 1367+x. These dates were as much as a century earlier than many of those from other excavated rooms, but since the position of the outer rings was indeterminate in each case, their actual cutting dates could have been very much later. Collectively, however, they do suggest a time not earlier than the late 14th century, or about early Pueblo IV, for the construction of this room, an inference consistent with the evidence provided by the ceramic complex and the mural paintings.

TEST 4, ROOM 5, SHERD COUNT

Depth in cm.	B/W		B/O		Awa. B/Y		Equiv. B/Y		Jed. B/Y		Siky. Poly.		post-Siky.		Totals
	No.	%	No.	%	No.	%	No.	%	No.	%	No.	%	No.	%	
0–100	7	2	6	2	5	2	61	22	152	54	35	13	14	5	280
100–135	11	2	11	2	7	1	189	31	220	36	130	21	38	6	606

TEST 4, ROOM 7

Room 7 in Test 4 was a kiva of unusual shape, relatively long and narrow, crowded between Room 1 on its left side and Room 2 on its right (figs. 46, 53). Although the inference is not certain, it appeared that Room 7 had been built later than either of its adjoining rooms, not only be-

cause of its unusual shape, apparently dictated by the space available, but also because its walls appeared to have been constructed independently of the others, although contiguous to them.

Room 7 was rectangular but its right wall bowed inward somewhat; whether this was because of

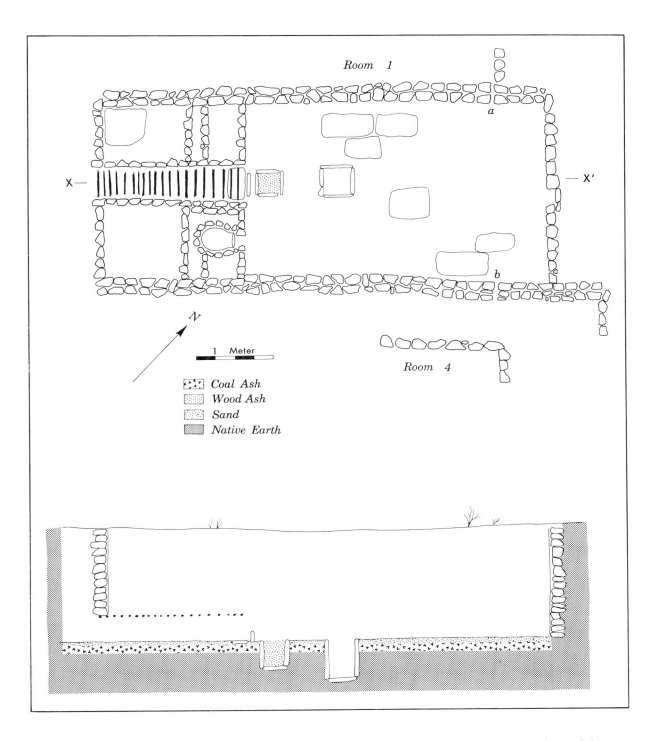

Fig. 53. Plan and longitudinal profile of Test 4, Room 7, at Kawaika-a, showing three successive faces of the rear bench and the points (a, b) from which the side walls had been extended forward in the remodeling.

original malconstruction or because of subsequent slumping was not certain. It measured 5.50 m. along its right side, 5.60 m. along its left, 2.35 m. across its front, and 2.26 m. across its rear. It was oriented N. 47° E., or almost exactly at right angles to Rooms 1 and 2.

Across the rear was a bench, 1.77 m. broad at its right end, 1.83 m. at its left, and 33 cm. high.

Fig. 54. Test 4, Room 7, from the front, showing rear bench with niche leading into cist containing utility jar at the left. A low deflector and two firepits appear in the floor.

A horizontal ventilator tunnel extended beneath the bench, nearly parallel to the long dimension of the kiva but about 25 cm. off-center toward the left. The tunnel was about 47 cm. wide at its mouth but about 40 cm. wide where it penetrated the rear wall. Its side walls were of masonry and it had been roofed with about 15 to 20 small sticks from 4 to 7 cm. in diameter, all of which had almost completely decomposed. The vertical shaft outside the rear wall was not excavated. The floor of the ventilator tunnel was not paved but a stone sill existed just inside the mouth, which was partly obstructed by a vertical slab, 7 cm. high and 23 cm. long, set into the floor and luted on both sides with adobe. It had probably functioned as a deflector (figs. 54, 55).

The surface of the bench had probably once been paved with stone slabs, but only one slab remained *in situ*. The face of the bench was of plastered masonry, which had partly collapsed.

The bench had been twice rebuilt as shown in the plan in figure 55. In its original form it had been 1.09 m. broad at its right end and 1.17 m.

at its left, with a masonry face. Later it had been extended forward 17 to 19 cm. with a new face, also of masonry. The earliest face remained intact, without surviving evidence of cists set into it, but the right-hand part of the second face had been partly destroyed when a large cist associated with the third face had been built, as will be explained below.

The third and final face, also of masonry, was 49 cm. in front of the second. There was no evidence of plaster on the original face, but fragments of plaster survived on the second, and blended continuously with the plaster on those parts of the left and right walls of the kiva that had been exposed before the building of the final extension.

Approximately in the center of that part of the third face to the right of the ventilator tunnel was a rectangular opening 9 cm. wide by 12 cm. high, its sill 7 cm. above the floor (fig. 56). This opening extended back 10 cm. and led into the mouth of a large yellow utility jar that had been imbedded in a cist below the surface of the bench. The

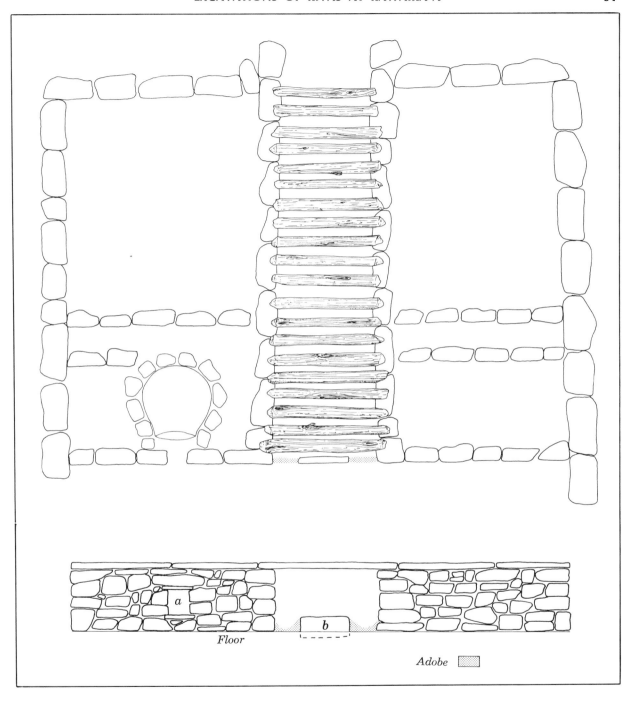

Fig. 55. Plan and front elevation of the rear bench in Test 4, Room 7, at Kawaika-a, showing the positions of three successive front walls, the second of which was partly demolished for the placement of a large utility jar in connection with the latest phase of the structure. The aperture (a) gave access to the jar. The vertical stone slab (b) partially blocked the ventilator tunnel entrance and was set firmly in an adobe collar.

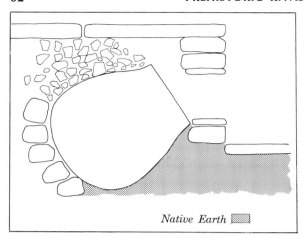

Native Earth

Fig. 56. Profile of a cist containing a large utility jar beneath the rear bench of Test 4, Room 7, at Kawaika-a.

orifice of the jar was inclined upward and outward at an angle of about 30° to the horizontal. The jar itself measured about 35 cm. in both depth and maximum diameter.

The sides of the cist containing the jar were fully lined with masonry and it was covered with a circular stone slab, apparently cut to fit. It extended backward beyond the line of the second face of the bench, which had been partly destroyed by its insertion. The space beneath and behind the jar was stuffed with wads or pads of grass serving as a cushion. At the time of excavation the jar contained nothing.

The floor of the kiva had once been paved with stone slabs, but only a few remained in position. Beneath the slabs was a layer of clean sand about 2 cm. thick, and below that a layer of coal ash.

Two firepits existed. One lay about 1.00 m. in front of the latest face of the bench exactly in the midline of the kiva. It was about 30 cm. square by 53 cm. deep, lined on all sides with sandstone slabs and filled with wood ash and charcoal. The other firepit lay directly in front of the ventilator opening, contiguous to the small deflector. It was about 25 cm. square by 36 cm. deep, and its sides were formed of crudely laid small-stone masonry. It too was filled with wood ash and charcoal. Apparently the second firepit had been in

use during an earlier period of occupation, because it had been covered by floor slabs, and was invisible until these were lifted.

No evidence was found of a sipapu or footdrum.

The walls of the kiva were of the usual late-style masonry and stood to a maximum height of about 1.50 m. at the time of excavation. The right-side wall had bowed inward but had not collapsed.

Both side walls were discontinuous at a point 60 cm. from the front wall, as if the kiva had originally been shorter by this amount and had later been enlarged by the removal of an original front wall and the extension forward of the side walls by the building of stub prolongations, which were then tied into a new front wall. In this context it is interesting to note that the supposed position of an earlier front wall was in alignment with the existing right wall of Room 1 and the original right wall of Room 2. The newer stub wall at the right side of Room 7 extended beyond its intersection with the newer front wall and seemed to be integral with the adjoining wall of Room 2. Clearly there had been renovations of Rooms 1, 7, and 2, all of them related in some way to one another, but the precise circumstances and sequence of events were not determined.

Fragments of plaster existed on the left, right, and front walls, but only on the right wall were significant painted designs recoverable. Three fairly elaborate remnants were found there, all classified within Layout Group I (2). Two are illustrated in Smith (1952a, figs. 86, a, 88, c).

A niche had been let into the front wall, 58 cm. above the floor, and almost exactly in the center from right to left. It was trapezoidal in shape, 14 cm. high by 12 cm. wide across the top and 17.5 cm. across the bottom. The entire interior had been coated with several layers of plaster and a small hammerstone lay within it.

The fill of Room 7 was excavated in two levels and the quantity of sherds was comparatively small, dominated by Jeddito Black-on-yellow, with smaller components of Sikyatki Polychrome and very few of post-Sikyatki types, characteristic of Ceramic Group A-3. No datable wood specimens were recovered.

TEST 4, ROOM 7, SHERD COUNT

Depth in cm.	B/W		B/O		Awa. B/Y		Equiv. B/Y		Jed. B/Y		Siky. Poly.		post-Siky.		Totals
	No.	%	No.	%	No.	%	No.	%	No.	%	No.	%	No.	%	
0–100	4	2	7	3	1	—	68	30	94	41	33	14	20	9	227
100–150	3	2	4	2	3	2	67	36	80	43	21	11	5	3	183

The ceramic evidence is consistent with the assignment of the wall decorations to Layout Group I (2) as already stated. The period of occupancy was thus probably around middle Pueblo IV.

TEST 5, GENERAL

At least seven adjacent kivas that bordered the southeasterly escarpment of the mesa formed a cluster that was called Test 5 (fig. 57). All were oriented generally toward the northwest, that is, approximately at right angles to the edge of the mesa, and all except Room 4 had been completely eroded across their rear or downslope ends. Surviving front walls stood at varying heights between 1.00 and 1.80 m., with surviving side walls sloping downward at angles of 30° to 45° to floor level, which was usually at or just above the caprock or surface of the mesa. In only one case had the rear bench, presumably once always present, survived, and in consequence the details of this feature and the longer dimension of the room were usually not determinable.

TEST 5, ROOM 1

Room 1 in Test 5 was at the southwestern extremity of the cluster of kivas in this area. It measured 3.90 m. across the front and its side walls extended backward a distance of about 3.50 m. before disappearing. Its orientation was N. 30° W.

No benches existed along either the front or side walls.

The floor had originally been paved with large stone slabs laid on a stratum of coal ash, but only a few slabs remained in position. An almost square firepit, measuring about 25 by 30 cm. and 25 cm. deep lay 2.90 m. from the front wall. It was slab-lined on all sides. The area in which a deflector might have stood had been removed by erosion. No evidence of a sipapu or footdrum was found.

What was left of the walls was very unstable, and parts of the left wall collapsed of their own weight during excavation. About 20 layers of plaster remained on the left wall, and parts of 4 painted designs were recovered. They are illustrated in Smith (1952a, figs. 67, a, b, 87, c) and belonged to Layout Group I, having thus been executed relatively late in Pueblo IV. Remnants of plaster on the front and right walls were too fragile for investigation.

The fill was composed of the usual debris with large numbers of building stones that had fallen from the walls and from the slope above. The pottery complex was heavily dominated by Jeddito Black-on-yellow, with moderate quantities of Sikyatki Polychrome and post-Sikyatki types, characteristic of Ceramic Group A-2.

No datable charcoal was recovered, but the ceramic complex indicated an occupation at some time during middle Pueblo IV.

TEST 5, ROOM 1, SHERD COUNT

Depth in cm.	B/W		B/O		Awa. B/Y		Equiv. B/Y		Jed. B/Y		Siky. Poly.		post-Siky.		Totals
	No.	%	No.	%	No.	%	No.	%	No.	%	No.	%	No.	%	
0–100	3	1	—	—	5	2	123	39	142	45	19	6	20	6	312
100–150	—	—	—	—	2	1	81	36	93	46	25	12	9	4	210

TEST 5, ROOM 2

Room 2 in Test 5 (fig. 58) adjoined Room 1 immediately northeast of the latter. The masonry wall that separated them was integrally constructed, evenly faced on both surfaces, and 55 cm. thick. The front wall of Room 2 was, however, not a prolongation of that of Room 1 but lay a few centimeters behind the extended line of the latter. The room measured 3.90 cm. across its front, and the side walls extended back 3.95 cm. to the partly eroded masonry face of a rear bench, all the remainder of which had been destroyed. Orientation of the kiva was N. 32° W.

The breadth and height of the rear bench were not determinable but the mouth of a ventilator

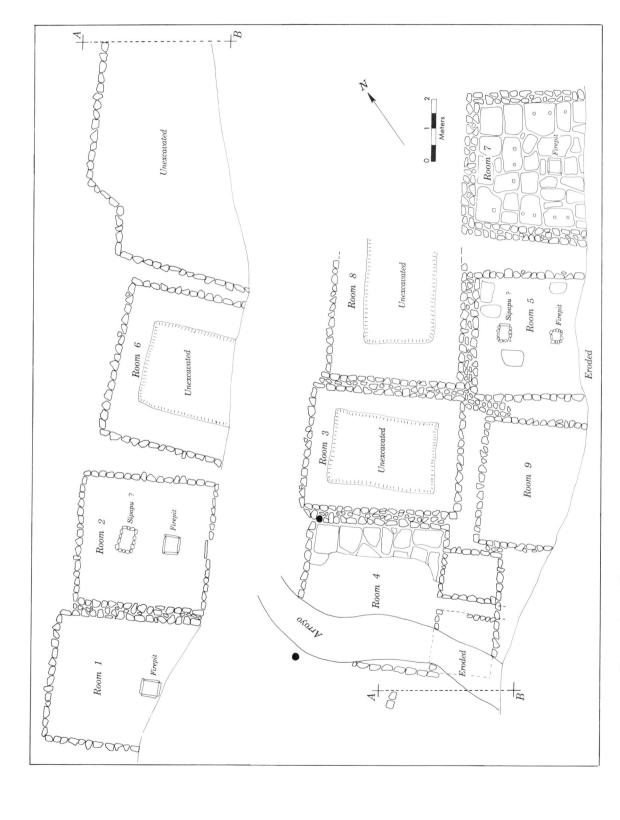

Fig. 57. Plan of all rooms excavated in Test 5 at Kawaika-a. The upper half of the drawing adjoins the left end of the lower half along the line A-B. The rear portions of most of the rooms had been destroyed by erosion and part of the left-hand area of Room 4 had been obliterated by a small water channel. Since the examination of these rooms was carried out with very limited time, at the end of the final season of 1939, some areas were left unexcavated.

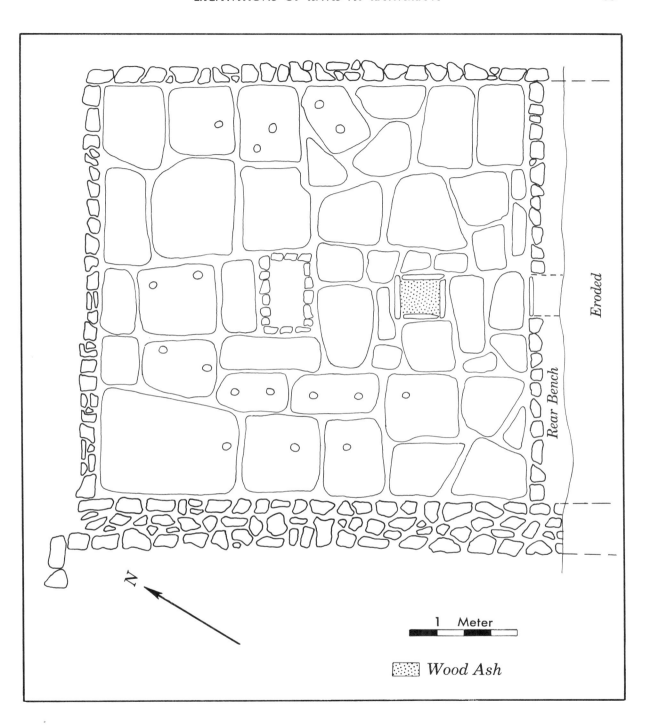

Fig. 58. Plan of the surviving portion of Test 5, Room 2, at Kawaika-a. The rear bench had been almost entirely destroyed by erosion, although the lower course of its masonry face remained in position.

tunnel was very nearly at the midline, with a rectangular slab fitted into it as a door. No benches existed along the front or side walls.

The floor was entirely paved with stone slabs, through which at least 16 small circular holes had been drilled. Some of these were haphazardly placed, but two rows of 3 and 5, respectively, were arranged in straight lines parallel to the left wall, respectively 50 cm. and 1.00 m. from it, and about equidistant from the front wall and the face of the rear bench.

A rectangular firepit was located about 80 cm. in front of the mouth of the ventilator tunnel, slab-lined and filled with wood ashes. Its exact dimensions were not recorded.

Another rectangular pit with masonry sides and sand bottom lay about 80 cm. in front of the firepit. It may have been a sipapu or footdrum, but no evidence of a covering board or slab survived.

The exact dimensions of this rectangular pit were not recorded.

The front wall had almost completely collapsed but the forward ends of the right and left walls stood to heights of about 1.80 and 1.40 m., respectively. Plaster existed on both side walls, but only on the left wall was it sufficiently intact to warrant investigation. There were about ten layers, of which seven yielded decipherable painted designs. These have been illustrated in Smith (1952a, figs. 58, *b*, 66, *c*, *d*, 67, *d*, 74, *c*, 75, *b*, 88, *a*), and all belonged to Layout Group I, indicating a date during middle or late Pueblo IV.

The fill contained much fallen building stone and a copious quantity of sherds, heavily dominated by Jeddito Black-on-yellow, with relatively small components of Sikyatki Polychrome and post-Sikyatki types, characteristic of Ceramic Group A-2.

TEST 5, ROOM 2, SHERD COUNT

Depth in cm.	B/W		B/O		Awa. B/Y		Equiv. B/Y		Jed. B/Y		Siky. Poly.		post-Siky.		Totals
	No.	%	No.	%	No.	%	No.	%	No.	%	No.	%	No.	%	
0–100	—	—	—	—	—	—	83	27	146	48	46	15	29	10	304
100–180	2	—	—	—	4	1	150	32	232	49	44	10	34	7	466

A single large piece of charcoal, which may have come from a beam, was recovered from the fill. The outermost surviving ring was complete and probably close to the original bark. It was dated at 1416–17 by Hall and at 1415 by the Laboratory of Tree-Ring Research (Bannister, Robinson, and Warren 1967, p. 17). This may represent a fairly close indication of the actual date of construction and occupation.

Among the artifacts were two paint-grinding slabs lying on the floor.

The ceramic evidence places the kiva within Classical Pueblo IV, consistent with the probable date indicated by the mural paintings.

TEST 5, ROOM 3

Room 3 was in the upper rank of kivas in Test 5. It was tested by a trench along the rear wall and another in the right-front corner, where about 20 layers of plaster were evident, some of them painted, but all too fragmentary for analysis. Limited time precluded further excavation. The walls all stood to a height of at least 2.30 m. above the floor, and the kiva measured about 4.60 m. along its left side, 4.30 m. along its right, 3.80 m. across its front, and 3.60 across its rear. It was oriented about N. 32° W.

The pottery from the small excavated area was representative of Ceramic Group A-2. The kiva was probably occupied during middle Pueblo IV.

TEST 5, ROOM 3, SHERD COUNT

Depth	B/W		B/O		Awa. B/Y		Equiv. B/Y		Jed. B/Y		Siky. Poly.		post-Siky.		Totals
	No.	%	No.	%	No.	%	No.	%	No.	%	No.	%	No.	%	
0–floor	3	1	—	—	—	—	78	39	69	35	39	20	11	5	200

TEST 5, ROOM 4

Room 4 in Test 5 (fig. 59) lay directly southwest of Room 3 and west of Room 9. Most of its right wall was integral with the left wall of Room 3, but there was a jog or pier toward the rear, made

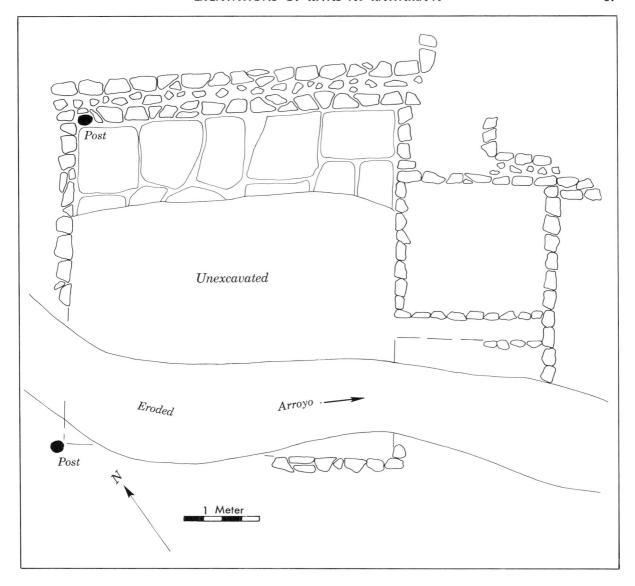

Fig. 59. Plan of the surviving portion of Test 5, Room 4, at Kawaika-a. As indicated also in figure 57 a small arroyo had destroyed much of the left half of the room, and the upper part of the rear bench had also been eroded. Two wooden posts were set into the masonry at the front corners of the room.

necessary to permit the right-rear corner to fit around the already constructed left-front corner of Room 9. Room 4, therefore, must have been built subsequent to the construction of Room 9 and while the latter was still in use.

Although much of the left-hand area of the kiva had been completely destroyed by the action of a small water channel that led from the top of the mound to the escarpment, its original shape and size could be pretty closely determined, because

an upright wooden post that probably marked the position of the left-front corner still stood, and a section of the left wall also survived.

The kiva was generally rectangular, measuring 5.80 m. along its right side, 6.10 m. along its left, 4.20 m. across its front, 4.50 m. across the face of the rear bench, and 3.75 m. across the rear of the bench. The difference between the two dimensions of the bench was caused by the pier, already mentioned, at its right end. This pier extended completely across the bench from back to front, and 75 cm. outward from the right wall. Orientation of the kiva was about N. 30° W.

The rear bench was 1.80 m. broad but its height was undeterminable because the entire upper surface had been eroded. The face had been formed of masonry of which part of the lowest course remained in position. A ventilator tunnel had existed beneath the bench, but it was not quite parallel to the sides of the room. Its center line was about 2.20 m. from the right wall at the face of the bench and about 2.50 m. at the back. The tunnel was thus very nearly on the midline of the kiva at its open or forward end but somewhat to the left of the midline at the rear wall. No constructional features of the tunnel remained. No benches existed along the other three sides of the room.

The floor had probably been fully paved with slabs, but the central and left portions were badly eroded, so that evidence for a firepit and deflector was lacking.

Walls survived only along the right side, about two-thirds of the rear, one-third of the front, and a small fragment of the left. They stood to a height of almost 1.50 m. at the right-front corner, but sloped away almost to floor level at the rear and left sides. The masonry was of poor quality and the right wall was coated with an unrecorded number of layers of plaster, of which eleven had been painted.

Apparently the kiva had burned, at least in part, for the remaining masonry and plaster along the front wall and the front portion of the right wall showed evidence of discoloration from heat and smoke. Set into the masonry of the right wall just at its junction with the front wall was an upright wooden post about 10 cm. in diameter. Its upper portion had been charred but the lower part was not burned. At a point 4.20 m. to the left of this corner post was a similar post about 10 cm. in diameter, also partly charred. Although the masonry in this area had mostly collapsed, this post appeared to have been set into it exactly at the left-front corner, the location of which could thus be determined.

Of the painted layers of plaster, ten were sufficiently intact to provide recoverable details. Nine were classified as belonging to Layout Group I, and one (the second from the earliest) to Layout Group II. They are illustrated in Smith (1952a, figs. 56, *b*, 66, *a*, *b*, 68, *b*, 69, *e*, 70, *c*, 72, *a*, 77, *b*, 84, *b*, 86, *b*).

The ceramic contents of the fill were similar to those in the other kivas at Kawaika-a, heavily dominated by Jeddito Black-on-yellow, with moderate amounts of Sikyatki Polychrome and small components of post-Sikyatki types. These ratios placed the collection within Ceramic Group A-2 characteristic of Classic Pueblo IV.

No dates were derived from the two posts or from wood specimens in the fill.

TEST 5, ROOM 4, SHERD COUNT

Depth in cm.	B/W		B/O		Awa. B/Y		Equiv. B/Y		Jed. B/Y		Siky. Poly.		post- Siky.		Totals
	No.	%	No.	%	No.	%	No.	%	No.	%	No.	%	No.	%	
0–100	3	—	—	—	—	—	347	40	366	43	94	11	40	5	850
100–150	1	—	—	—	2	—	106	38	129	46	35	13	8	3	281

TEST 5, ROOM 5

Room 5 was another in the row of kivas in Test 5 (fig. 60), situated between Rooms 9 and 7 and directly east of Room 3. It seems to have been constructed at the same time as Room 3 because the masonry of its left-front corner was tied into that of the right-rear corner of Room 3. It was not, however, structurally related to Room 9 or 7, as was evident from the fact that its left and right walls, while close to and approximately parallel to the adjacent walls of those kivas, were separated from them by narrow columns of rubble fill from 20 to 60 cm. thick.

Not more than two-thirds of the original area of Room 5 remained intact, and the rear part, presumably once including a bench and ventilator tunnel, had been entirely eroded away. The kiva was 3.70 m. wide across the front and its surviving left and right walls extended backward about 3.30 and 2.90 m., respectively, before disappearing. Its orientation was about N. 36° W. No benches had existed along either side walls or front wall.

The floor had apparently once been paved with slabs, but only three or four remained in position, the others probably having been scav-

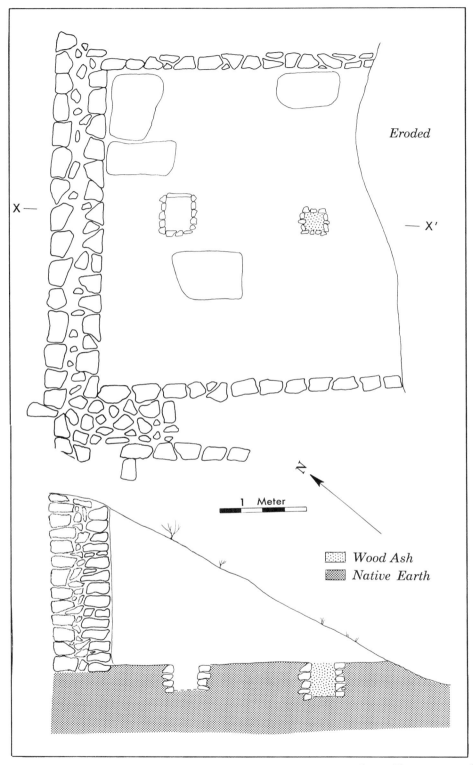

Fig. 60. Plan and profile of the surviving portion of Test 5, Room 5, at Kawaika-a. The rear area, including the bench, had been destroyed by erosion.

enged for use elsewhere. An almost square fire-pit was situated 1.50 m. from the right wall, 1.60 m. from the left wall, and 2.40 m. from the front wall. Its sides were constructed of masonry and it had a slab hearth. It measured 25 by 26 cm. in plan, 40 cm. in depth, and was filled with wood ash. The area in which a deflector might once have stood had been obliterated.

About midway between the firepit and the front wall was a similar pit, measuring 30 cm. front-to-back by 40 cm. transversely, and 45 cm. deep. Three of its sides were formed of masonry and one of a vertical slab. Its bottom was clean sand without evidence of fire, and it contained only loose fill. Perhaps this feature had been a sipapu or footdrum.

Small remnants of plaster, perhaps 20 layers thick, appeared on the left, right, and front walls, but all were too badly broken to warrant detailed investigation.

Only a small quantity of sherds was recovered from the fill, the complex heavily dominated by black-on-yellow with minor quantities of Sikyatki Polychrome and only one post-Sikyatki sherd, corresponding with Ceramic Group A-2 or A-3, characteristic of middle Pueblo IV.

No datable wood or charcoal specimens were recovered.

TEST 5, ROOM 5, SHERD COUNT

Depth in cm.	B/W		B/O		Awa. B/Y		Equiv. B/Y		Jed. B/Y		Siky. Poly.		post-Siky.		Totals
	No.	%	No.	%	No.	%	No.	%	No.	%	No.	%	No.	%	
0–185	—	—	1	2	—	—	31	52	20	34	6	10	1	2	59

TEST 5, ROOM 6

Room 6 in Test 5 was located along the southeast slope near the escarpment and like nearly all the others was badly eroded, so that approximately its entire rear half had disappeared. It lay just northeast of Room 2 and its left wall was integral with the right wall of Room 2 toward the rear. Toward the front, however, the two walls diverged, so that a rubble-filled space of about 80 cm. separated them at their respective front corners. Each wall was finished only on the face exposed to the interior of its kiva, the other face being left rough. Both side walls of Room 6 were at right angles to the front wall.

The front wall was 4.20 m. long and stood about 1.00 m. high at the time of excavation. The surviving remnants of the side walls extended backward about 4.00 and 3.60 m., respectively, sloping downward to bedrock at points behind which erosion had entirely removed them. No benches existed along either front or side walls. The area in which a rear bench and ventilator might have been had completely disappeared.

The kiva was not fully excavated and no floor features were recorded. Its orientation was approximately N. 25° W.

An area of painted plaster approximately 1.00 m. high extended along the front wall from the left-front corner to a point somewhat to the right of the midline of the wall. Remnants of three designs had survived, the first and third belonging to Layout Group I and the second to Layout Group III. They are illustrated in Smith (1952a, figures 62, c, 47, a, 62, a; pl. G).

Comparatively few sherds were recovered from the fill, much of which had been washed over the escarpment of the mesa, and which probably also contained some debris brought down from the higher slope above. The collection, however, was dominated by Jeddito Black-on-yellow, with a fairly large component of Sikyatki Polychrome and a small amount of post-Sikyatki types, characteristic of Ceramic Groups A-2 or A-3 indicative of a period in middle Pueblo IV, which is consistent with the surviving mural designs.

No datable wood or charcoal specimens were recovered.

TEST 5, ROOM 6, SHERD COUNT

Depth in cm.	B/W		B/O		Awa. B/Y		Equiv. B/Y		Jed. B/Y		Siky. Poly.		post-Siky.		Totals
	No.	%	No.	%	No.	%	No.	%	No.	%	No.	%	No.	%	
0–100	—	—	—	—	—	—	33	43	57	25	29	22	13	10	132

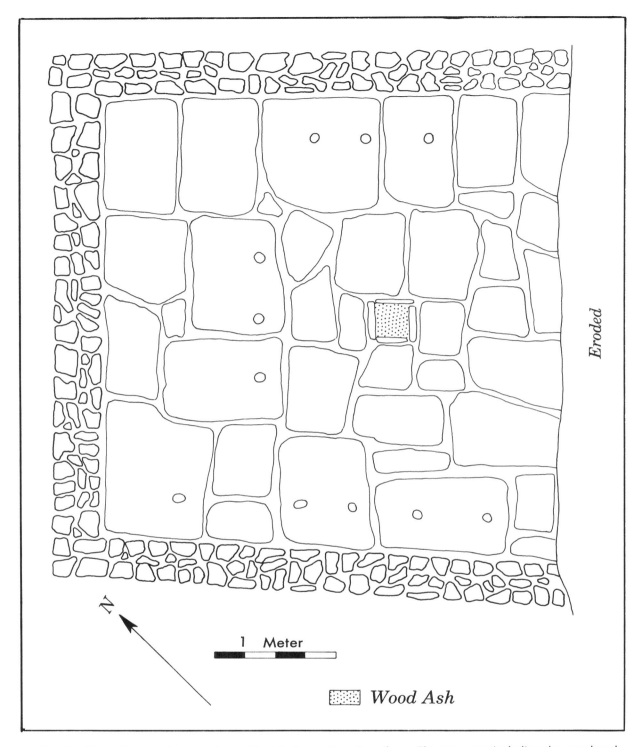

Fig. 61. Plan of the surviving portion of Test 5, Room 7, at Kawaika-a. The rear part, including the rear bench, had been destroyed by erosion.

TEST 5, ROOM 7

Room 7 in Test 5 (fig. 61) was at the right (or northeast) end of the rank of kivas located along the southeast slope of the village, just above the escarpment of the mesa. It was adjacent to Room 5 on its left side, but was not actually contiguous to it, since the walls of the two rooms had been independently constructed and were separated horizontally by from 40 to 70 cm. of fill.

Like almost all other kivas in this part of the site, Room 7 had lost approximately the entire rear half of its area including any bench and ventilator that might have been there. The front wall was about 3.70 m. long and stood about 1.50 m. high at the time of excavation, while the side walls, which were not quite at right angles to the front wall, diverged slightly toward the rear, sloping downward to bedrock at a horizontal distance of about 3.70 m. from the front, at which point they were about 4.00 m. apart. No benches existed on the front or side walls. Orientation of this kiva was approximately N. 45° W.

The floor was completely paved over its surviving area with slabs of varying sizes, mostly rectangular, laid with their edges parallel to the walls of the room and fairly carefully fitted. A rectangular firepit measuring 27 by 29 cm. was situated on the midline of the kiva, 2.25 m. from the front walls. It was slab-lined, 42 cm. deep, and filled entirely with wood ash. No trace of a deflector was found, but it may have been removed by erosion.

Eleven small circular holes were arranged in three rows in the floor slabs. Five holes extended in a straight line about 30 cm. from the left wall and parallel to it; the length of the row was 2.60 m. and intervals between adjacent holes varied from 25 cm. to 1.00 m. A row of three holes ran parallel to the right wall and about 30 cm. from it; and another row of three holes ran parallel to the front wall and about 1.30 m. from it. Each row was 1.20 m. long, and the individual holes were almost evenly spaced, at intervals of about 55 cm.

No niches or other features were found in the walls, but small bits of plaster, some of them painted, and from 18 to 20 layers thick, survived on each wall. The designs were too fragmentary to warrant recording.

The fill was excavated in two strata, in which the ceramic complexes were closely similar. Both were dominated by Jeddito Black-on-yellow, with small components of Sikyatki Polychrome and minor quantities of post-Sikyatki types, characteristic of Ceramic Group A-2, and indicating a position in middle Pueblo IV, or slightly later. No datable wood or charcoal was recovered.

TEST 5, ROOM 7, SHERD COUNT

Depth in cm.	B/W		B/O		Awa. B/Y		Equiv. B/Y		Jed. B/Y		Siky. Poly.		post-Siky.		Totals
	No.	%	No.	%	No.	%	No.	%	No.	%	No.	%	No.	%	
0–100	2	—	—	—	—	—	110	41	118	44	30	11	6	4	266
100–150	—	—	—	—	—	—	51	34	64	43	18	12	15	11	148

V

Summary Notes on the Physical Features of Kivas at Awatovi and Kawaika-a

The prototype of the scientist is not the liberator releasing the slaves, or the good Samaritan lifting up the fallen, but a dog sniffing tremendously at an infinite series of rat holes.

H. L. Mencken

CHRONOLOGY

All kivas excavated at Awatovi and Kawaika-a had probably been constructed and occupied during the period of Pueblo IV, which is to say approximately between the years from about 1300 to 1630. Most of them, indeed, probably represented the middle and late portions of that range, and only one (Test 14, Room 10, at Awatovi) seemed to have been built and abandoned during the earlier years. Although the Franciscan friars must have done what they could to prevent the use of kivas during the period of their ascendancy, it is quite possible that some surreptitious native religious observances continued notwithstanding. Almost certainly kiva ceremonies flourished during the Hopi risorgimento of 1680–1699, and in the light of the evidence and the legend of the final holocaust, some kivas must have been in use even after the return of the Spaniards and up to the very end in about 1700.

These chronological hypotheses are based on a consideration of several factors, none in itself conclusive, but all taken together providing a reasonably convincing mass of evidence. The specific data have been set forth above in the descriptions of particular kivas, and will be only briefly discussed here.

No kiva excavated at the two major villages contained, either in the debris that filled it or *in situ* upon its floor, any significant quantity of black-on-white pottery or of the polychromes and gray utility types that normally were associated with black-on-white in the Western Anasazi area. If we take that ceramic complex as one of the diagnostics for Pueblo III, it is clear that no ex-

cavated kiva at Awatovi or Kawaika-a belonged to that period. Only Test 14, Room 10, at Awatovi, which had been almost destroyed by the construction of a later kiva within and above it, contained debris characterized by substantial quantities of Jeddito Black-on-orange pottery, a type that has usually been regarded as marking the period of transition between Pueblo III and Pueblo IV, from the late 13th to the late 14th century (Smith 1971, pp. 353, 602, fig. 12). It was during the latter part of the former period and the early part of Pueblo IV that Jeddito Black-on-orange became the dominant painted ceramic type and black-on-white examples practically disappeared. The presence in Test 14, Room 10, of only 9 percent black-on-white to 33 percent black-on-orange and more than 50 percent black-on-yellow strongly suggests that the kiva was occupied and abandoned during the very latest years of Jeddito Black-on-orange, when the black-on-yellows were supplanting it and becoming statistically dominant, perhaps in the early 15th century.

All other excavated kivas were characterized by a predominance of black-on-yellow pottery on the floor and in the fill, though the mix varied from complexes containing fairly heavy components of Awatovi Black-on-yellow with little Sikyatki Polychrome and no post-Sikyatki types (Rooms 218 and 229 at Awatovi) to complexes with 50 to 80 percent of post-Sikyatki types (Rooms 529, 788, and 908 at Awatovi). The latest of these kivas were almost certainly in use at the time of the establishment of the mission, as indicated in the case of Rooms 788 and 908 by the placement of the sanctuary and sacristy of the church directly above them, with their roof structures left intact, and their beams providing dates indicative of construction in the late 16th century (Montgomery, Smith, and Brew 1949, pp. 65–66, fig. 10).

These conclusions do not mean, of course, that there had been no kivas at Awatovi or Kawaika-a earlier than Pueblo IV. During the excavation of the Western Mound at Awatovi many domestic rooms were found containing ceramic complexes composed almost wholly of black-on-white types and their associated orange polychromes and gray utility vessels. The site had evidently been occupied at least during the latter part of Pueblo III, before 1300. We failed to discover a kiva in those horizons, but it is hardly imaginable that they did not exist. With further excavation they would almost certainly be found, but from our present data nothing can be said about them.

PLACEMENT

The kivas at Awatovi and Kawaika-a were apparently subterranean or partly so. In analogy to modern Hopi kivas, their roofs may have been level with the surface of the ground or perhaps slightly above it. The only two roofs that remained intact (Rooms 788 and 908 at Awatovi) both lay beneath the sanctuary and sacristy of the Franciscan Church where all trace of the original surface had disappeared, and in almost all other cases the walls had partially collapsed, making a determination of their upper limits impossible.

In some cases, individual kivas appear to have been isolated in open plaza areas between blocks of domestic rooms, although this was never perfectly certain, inasmuch as the immediately surrounding areas were not fully excavated. Furthermore, even when adjacent domestic rooms existed, it was not clear whether they had been in use contemporaneously with the kiva or whether the kiva had been intruded among them after their abandonment and filling.

In many instances, perhaps in most, several kivas were built in clusters, each one adjacent to one or more of the others, and probably contemporaneously occupied. Examples at Awatovi were Rooms 2–6 in Test 14; Kivas A, C, D, and E; Rooms 218 and 229; Rooms 788 and 908; and perhaps others. At Kawaika-a two clusters were formed by the five kivas in Test 4 and the seven or more in Test 5, respectively.

A striking feature of at least three kiva clusters, namely Test 14 at Awatovi and Tests 4 and 5 at Kawaika-a, was their location very close to the escarpment of the mesa and along the very edge of

the village. In these situations the rear or "ventilator" ends of the kivas were usually nearest to the escarpment, and their floors lay on or just above the level of bed rock. Although the forward parts of these kivas might have been rendered pseudo-subterranean by the piling of earth or the building of other structures around them, their rear portions must have been almost wholly above ground, because there was simply not sufficient depth for their concealment. Most kivas thus situated, especially in Test 5 at Kawaika-a, had suffered erosion to such an extent that much of their rear portions had disappeared entirely.

The same practice may be observed today in Hopi mesa-top villages, where some kivas close to the escarpment have rear walls entirely above ground, as described by Dorsey and Voth (1902, pp. 170–171):

The two kivas or underground chambers occupied by the Snake and Antelope Fraternities for their secret mysteries were, respectively, those of the Wowochim (Adult's) and Ahl (Horn) Societies; henceforth in this paper they will be called the Snake and Antelope kivas. Both lie outside the limits of the village on the southeast side, occupying a position just as the mesa begins to slope down toward the first terrace. . . . As a consequence of their position the outer walls and a portion of the end walls of both kivas are almost entirely exposed, being built up from the sloping side of the hill. The lower portion of both outer walls is now, however, partially covered by refuse, as this side of the village is a favorite dumping ground for the refuse of the streets. The exposed walls are roughly built, the lower half being of a double course of undressed stones with the remainder of the wall of a single course. At no place in any of the exposed walls is there evidence of careful masonry or plaster. The two kivas are separated from each other by an interval of a few feet, this being occupied by one of the trails. The fact that the orientation of Hopi kivas is largely a matter of convenience is well illustrated by the position of these two — that of the Snake kiva having its long diameter to the southeast, while that of the Antelope kiva is west of south. There is a still greater discrepancy in the orientation of these two kivas, as the Snake kiva faces southeast, while the Antelope kiva faces the southwest. Inasmuch, however, as the Hopi south is rather southeast, it would be proper to say that the Snake kiva faces nearly east and that the Antelope kiva faces nearly west: these and their related terms will consequently be used in any reference which may be made to direction when speaking of either kiva.

SHAPE AND SIZE

All kivas at Awatovi and Kawaika-a were essentially rectangular in shape, though all varied to some degree from the ideal, and in very few cases were corners exactly square or opposite walls of exactly equal length. These variations seemed quite fortuitous, and were the result of the generally slovenly character of the architectural craftsmanship. They will generally be disregarded in the discussion, and overall dimensions will usually be stated as the mean of corresponding extremes.

Lengths varied from about 3.25 to about 7.80 m. with nearly all fairly evenly distributed between 4.00 and 7.00 m. The ratio of width to length varied from 42 to 90 percent with almost all lying between 57 and 80 percent. Areas varied from 8 to 33 sq. m., with most lying between 11 and 29 sq. m. The data for these factors are shown graphically in figures 62 to 65, from which several inferences may be drawn. Both areas and width-length ratios varied fairly widely and did not seem to conform to any discernible chronological or local pattern, although the three earliest kivas (Test 14, Room 10, and Rooms 218 and 229 at Awatovi) were smaller than the later ones. An exception to this rule, however, was provided by Test 57, Room 1, at Awatovi, which was actually smaller than Test 14, Room 10, although its position in the extreme northeastern part of the village and the abundance of post-Sikyatki sherds in its fill marked it as chronologically late.

The data also indicate a slight, but probably not significant tendency for the small kivas to be more nearly square than the larger ones, although none was precisely square. Only one, the second phase of Test 4, Room 2, at Kawaika-a, may have been slightly wider than long, but since its recorded dimensions are hypothetically inferred they may be in some degree inexact.

Several kivas, though basically rectangular, were complicated in plan by the existence in them of corner pilasters or piers of masonry, or by an outward extension on one side to form a bay or alcove. Pilasters varied in size and position but were always in either the right-rear corner (Room 229, Test 14, Room 2, at Awatovi; Test 4, Room 2, intermediate phase, and Test 5, Room 4, at Kawaika-a) or the left-rear corner (Kiva A and Rooms 218 and 529 at Awatovi). Test 14, Room 3, at Awatovi, in its early phase, appeared to have had a pier in the left-front corner, but this was in fact an offset in the front wall made necessary in order to avoid encroachment on the adjacent Room 2, which was already in existence and use.

Bays or alcoves were rare and occurred at most in three kivas (Test 14, Rooms 4 and 10, at Awatovi; Test 4, Room 2, intermediate phase, at Ka-

Kiva No.	Median Length in m.	Median Width in m.	Area in sq. m.	Width: Length Ratio
Awatovi				
A	6.60	4.00	26.40	60%
C	4.72	2.62	13.78	55%
E	4.55	3.80	17.29	83%
218	3.26	2.59	8.44	79%
229	3.22	2.65	8.63	82%
529	* 7.08	4.17	29.52	58%
529	** 5.45	4.17	22.73	76%
788	4.70	3.48	16.36	74%
T 14, R 2	5.78	4.11	23.75	71%
T 14, R 3	* 4.96	3.94	19.54	79%
T 14, R 3	** 4.40	3.94	17.33	87%
T 14, R 4	6.34	4.02	25.49	63%
T 14, R 5	5.97	4.66	27.82	78%
T 14, R 6	* 6.86	4.85	33.27	70%
T 14, R 6	** 6.86	4.20	28.81	61%
T 14, R 10	* 4.31	2.63	11.33	61%
T 14, R 10	** 4.47	2.95	13.19	66%
T 19, R 3	5.97	4.47	27.58	75%
T 22, R 10	5.80	5.00	29.00	86%
T 31, R 1	7.80	4.02	31.36	51%
T 57, R 1	3.75	3.00	11.25	80%
Kawaika-a				
T 4, R 1	5.70	4.10	23.37	72%
T 4, R 2	* 5.25	3.97	20.84	75%
T 4, R 2	** 5.16	5.35	27.60	103%[x]
T 4, R 2	** 4.36	3.97	17.31	90%
T 4, R 3	5.60	4.30	24.08	76%
T 4, R 5	4.62	3.36	15.52	73%
T 4, R 7	* 4.96	2.30	11.38	48%
T 4, R 7	** 5.55	2.30	12.76	41%
T 5, R 3	4.45	3.70	16.46	83%
T 5, R 4	5.95	4.35	25.88	73%

* Early occupation.   ** Intermediate occupation.

** Late occupation.   [x] Width exceeds length.

Fig. 62. Chart showing dimensions, areas, and proportions of all kivas excavated at Awatovi and Kawaika-a.

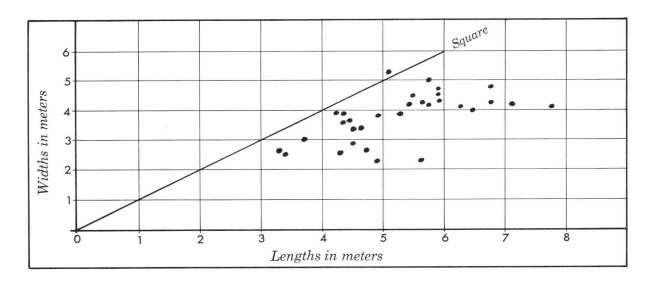

Fig. 63. Scatter diagram showing distribution of all excavated kivas at Awatovi and Kawaika-a in terms of the ratios of widths to lengths. Each dot represents one kiva. Nearness to the diagonal indicates relative approach to square. One kiva (Test 4, Room 2, at Kawaika-a) was slightly wider than long.

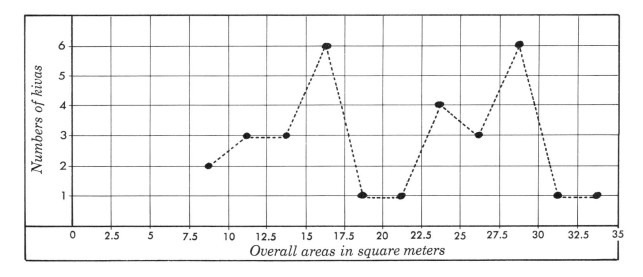

Fig. 64. Numbers of kivas excavated at Awatovi and Kawaika-a distributed according to overall areas, including benches.

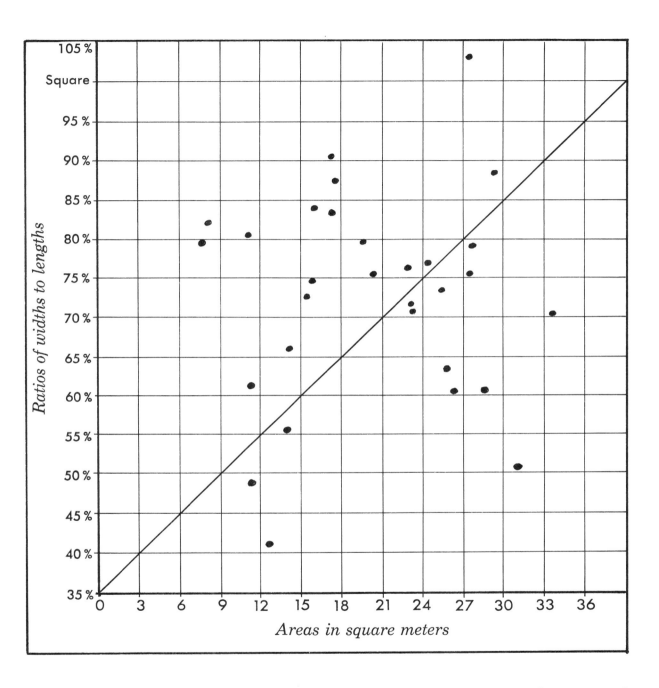

Fig. 65. Scatter diagram showing areas in relation to width-length ratios of all kivas excavated at Awatovi and Kawaika-a. Each dot represents one kiva. There is a slight, but perhaps not significant, tendency for smaller kivas to be more nearly square than larger kivas.

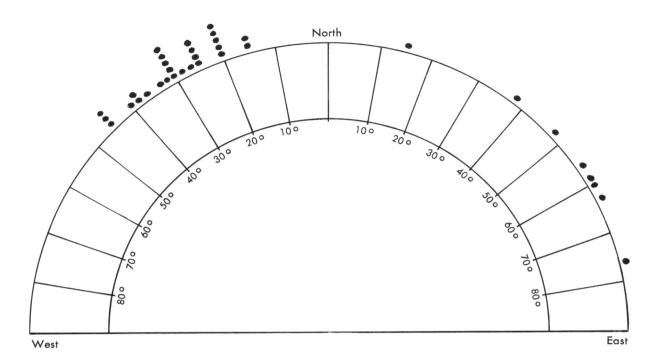

Fig. 66. Chart showing orientations with relation to true north of all excavated kivas at Awatovi and Kawaika-a. Each dot represents one kiva with orientation in the position indicated. There is no discernible pattern in terms of chronology or position in the two sites. The early orientation of Test 14, Room 10 (S. 55° W.), is not shown on this chart.

waika-a). But even these were not clear, because of the uncertain nature of architectural revisions that had been made in the kivas during occupancy.

ORIENTATION

Regarding as the rear that end of the room with broad bench and ventilator, the orientation from rear toward front varied widely with relation to true north. Ten kivas were scattered between N. 15° W. and N. 75° E., but 25 were concentrated between N. 20° W. and N. 45° W., as shown on figure 66. It can thus be said that there was a strong tendency for orientations to be grouped closely around north–northwest, with a few scattered throughout the entire northeast quadrant, and only one in any other direction: the early phase of Test 14, Room 10, at Awatovi, which faced S. 55° W. No correlation was discernible, however, between orientation and any other variable, and convenience and the exigencies of location were probably influential factors. It should be emphasized, however, without refer-

ence to specific comparative data, that an approximately northerly orientation was the rule in most prehistoric Anasazi kivas. The same feature at Awatovi and Kawaika-a thus conformed to the general cultural pattern.

WALLS

The excavations at Awatovi clearly indicated that there had been at least three major building periods during the development of that village, each of them characterized by a distinct style of masonry construction.*

All examples of the early style occurred in the lower strata of the Western Mound, where the walls were pretty uniformly constructed with a

* A thorough and careful analysis of the several masonry techniques used at Awatovi, illustrated by drawings and photographs of typical examples, was prepared by Dr. Thomas N. Campbell, who was a member of the field staff in 1937. I am greatly indebted to Dr. Campbell for permission to use his unpublished manuscript, from which I have compiled the following brief summation.

relatively high degree of care and technical skill. Their major components were large blocks of the laminated sandstone that formed the upper strata of Antelope Mesa itself, from which they had evidently been quarried. These blocks had been more or less carefully shaped or at least selected, their upper, nether, and outer faces fairly smooth and approximately at right angles to one another. Sizes and proportions varied, but the outer faces usually approached squares or not greatly elongated rectangles. The blocks were laid approximately in courses and fairly neatly fitted, though stone-to-stone contact was rare. Intersecting walls were usually aligned fairly closely but almost never exactly at right angles to each other. They were always double-faced and from about 40 to 48 cm. thick. Within the core, the edges of the blocks were not carefully finished and those of the two surfaces tended to interlock, the interstices being filled with rubble.

Numerous thin sandstone spalls were used between the blocks, both as stop spalls to aid in the retention of the mud mortar and as true-bearing spalls to stabilize the blocks themselves. Occasionally a potsherd was used as a spall. Wall intersections were sometimes bonded but frequently they were not.

In some instances walls of this type varied somewhat on their opposite faces. Exterior faces were often more carefully laid and composed of larger and more precisely shaped blocks than were interior faces, perhaps because the exteriors were exposed to weathering while interiors were normally thickly coated with varying numbers of coats of plaster, thus requiring less nicety in the surface finish of the stone work.

The fill in most rooms that were built in this style was characterized by a predominance of black-on-white or black-on-orange pottery types, indicating construction and occupation during late Pueblo III or early Pueblo IV. Characteristic examples of such early walls are shown in figure 67, a, b, although none of the excavated kivas belonged to this period.

Walls of the intermediate style were found in the upper part of the Western Mound and in rooms lying easterly from it toward the area of the mission buildings. They differed notably from those just described, being formed largely of unshaped slabs of greatly varying thickness and length, laid without much effort at coursing and in abundant mortar. These stones usually extended completely through the wall, so that both faces were uneven and there was no rubble core. Spalls were few and served normally a true-bearing func-

tion. Walls of this style were comparatively thin, from 20 to 30 cm., and were generally insubstantial.

The ceramic fill in most rooms with such walls was characterized by a predominance of Awatovi Black-on-yellow or of Jeddito Black-on-yellow and Sikyatki Polychrome. These rooms were apparently built and occupied, therefore, during early Pueblo IV, although precise dating is difficult. Examples are illustrated in figure 67, c, d.

It should be noted that in most rooms in the Western Mound there was a sharp differentiation between the lower and earlier double-faced, block-built walls and the upper and later single-faced slab walls. The latter in most cases were built directly upon the uppermost courses of the former, usually along almost exactly the same alignments, as if there might have been a temporary abandonment of that part of the village, followed by the filling of the older rooms and the subsequent construction of newer ones of a different style of masonry during a second period of occupation.

Although there was no sharply defined change in the ceramic content of the fill in the two strata they did seem to coincide approximately with the transition from black-on-orange to black-on-yellow pottery. Whether the combination of these changes was indicative of an incursion of alien people or marked merely a local evolutionary development is an important and difficult question. It has been discussed elsewhere (Smith 1971, pp. 599, 611–612) and will not be further considered here. Inasmuch as we have no kivas from the older horizon, no comparison between them and the later ones is possible.

Examples of kivas representative of the secondary masonry style at Awatovi were Rooms 218, 229, all rooms in Test 14 (except Room 10), Room 3 in Test 19, Kivas A, C, D, E, and perhaps others.

In the eastern part of the village, surrounding and beneath the Franciscan Mission area, still a third masonry style had developed. This was not markedly different from the intermediate style just described, and could be regarded as simply an evolutionary modification of it. The walls were still about 20 to 30 cm. thick, built of unshaped slabs of sandstone, laid in abundant mortar, quite without any semblance of coursing. Normally the stones extended entirely through the wall, and the faces were very uneven. There were many spalls of varying shapes and sizes, mostly serving to stop the mortar rather than as bearings for the major stones. These walls were inferior even to their earlier counterparts; the stones rarely rested even-

a   *b*

Fig. 67. *a.* Part of the surface of a wall of Room 327 in the Western Mound at Awatovi. The large blocks were probably not shaped, but had been selected for their relative regularity. The wall was 45 to 48 cm. thick and faced on both surfaces with rubble core. Spalls were small, thin, and irregularly shaped; one (at upper left) was a potsherd. Some were true-bearing, others were stop spalls. Part of the mortar has been removed for purposes of illustration. This type of wall construction is characteristic of the earliest or "black-on-white" period, at Awatovi, from which no kivas were excavated.

b. Part of the surface of a wall of Room 321 in the Western Mound. The blocks were selected but not shaped, and they varied in size and shape to a greater degree than did those in *a.* Spalls were fewer and larger than in that example. This style represents the time of transition between the "black-on-white" and "black-on-orange" periods, from which no kivas were excavated.

c. Part of the surface of a wall of Room 240 in the Western Mound. Notable is the irregularity and comparative thinness of the stones, and the almost complete absence of spalls. Coursing was very uneven and the wall was relatively insubstantial. It was only about 28 cm. thick and was not double faced. This style represents the early part of the "black on yellow" period, of which kivas 218, 229, and 240 were characteristic.

d. Part of the surface of a wall in Room 264 of the Western Mound. A few long thin slabs were used, but for the most part the stones were small, irregularly shaped blocks. Spalls were almost completely absent. The wall may represent two periods of construction, with fairly even coursing toward the top, above an area of very haphazard placement of larger but more irregular stones. A greater proportion of mortar was used here than in the earlier walls. This style represents the early or middle part of the "black-on-yellow" period.

c   *d*

ly on one another, and were supported mainly by the mortar. Examples are illustrated in figures 67, e, f, 68, a, b.

The fill in rooms with walls of this late masonry style was characterized by late Jeddito Black-on-yellow, some Sikyatki Polychrome, and comparatively large components on post-Sikyatki types. They must have been built late in Pueblo IV and some were occupied up to the establishment of the mission or afterward (e.g., Rooms 788, 908, and Test 22, Room 10).

Despite the appearance of taxonomic clarity induced by the three-fold classification adumbrated above, there were in fact few sharp distinctions between the styles, especially between the intermediate and late, which blended into each other through many gradations and deviations. Many walls could have been classified equally well with either the intermediate or late style, and despite the greater contrast between the early and intermediate styles, there were examples that partook

of the characteristics of both. The styles as described are, like all typological entities, idealized abstractions, but nevertheless there was evident throughout the period of occupation of the village a continuing trend from heavy, double-faced, fairly well-constructed masonry to a thin, single-faced, insubstantial, and inferior product.

In a few instances adobe bricks had been employed, usually in secondary walls built inside and against already existent stone walls, as in Room 229 at Awatovi (fig. 5). The use of adobe bricks in Pueblo architecture was fairly widespread though not common in pre-Spanish times, and has been reviewed by Smith (1952a, p. 9).

The walls of all periods were coated with plaster layers of varying thickness composed of the same gray to gray-brown mud that was used for mortar. It had not been refined or sifted and contained bits of rubbish in the form of bones, twigs, grass, sherds, charcoal, ashes, and gravel. In many cases this layer of mortar plaster was reinforced by the

e   f

e. Part of the surface of a wall of Test 22, Room 10, just north of the Franciscan mission. The masonry was composed of fairly large unselected blocks haphazardly laid, with little mortar, almost in the manner of a New England dry wall. A few true-bearing spalls were used, with a good many stones of intermediate size that were apparently shoved into interstices where necessary to provide added support. The entire structure was crude and insubstantial, and was one of the very latest rooms to be occupied at Awatovi.

f. Part of the surface of a wall of Kiva E at Awatovi. Individual stones were completely irregular in size and shape, and were laid with minimal attempt at coursing. In contrast to the wall shown in e, spalls were fairly frequent here and mortar was more copious. The structure was extremely insubstantial, however, and some stones had cracked from internal stress. This style represents a late, but not the latest, pre-Spanish building period.

embedding in it of a network of vertical and horizontal reeds, withes, or bundles of grass (figs. 68, f, 69, b). In other cases, sheets of twilled matting were embedded as binding and supporting agents (figs. 68, e, 69, a).

Evidently the builders had attempted to eliminate the uneven surfaces of the bare masonry by applications of plaster of varying thickness to produce a relatively even surface. Usually, however, this purpose was inadequately achieved, and the surfaces remained markedly undulating rather than plane.

Over the base coating of mortar were then applied thin coats of finish plaster composed of a reddish-brown sandy clay that must have been carefully prepared, for it was usually homogenous in character and free of extraneous matter (fig. 68, c, d). These finish coats appeared to have been renewed from time to time, and in at least one instance (in Room 218 at Awatovi) more than a hundred superimposed coats had survived, their total thickness being about 11 cm. (fig. 70; Smith 1952a, pp. 13–21, fig. 34, c). On these finish coats were painted the colorful mural designs that distinguished most kivas at Awatovi and Kawaika-a, as fully discussed by Smith (1952a).

The preceding descriptions of walls have been based on notes and photographs from kivas as well as domestic rooms at Awatovi, for there were no differences in the masonry of the two kinds of chambers at any given period of time.

The excavations at Kawaika-a were hurried and the field notes often incomplete, but it may be said generally that the walls of excavated kivas there conformed essentially to the features of the second and third styles as characterized above.

NICHES AND DOORWAYS

Small niches of varying sizes, shapes, and positions existed in the walls of some kivas, but not in all, and their placements conformed to no discernible pattern. They had probably been originally used as repositories for fetishes, sacred objects, or food, but nothing remained in any of them at the time of excavation.

Only nine niches were recorded in seven kivas, but inasmuch as many walls had collapsed wholly or in part prior to excavation, many more may once have existed. All niches were in front walls at various heights and at various horizontal positions, three about at the center, three to the right of center, three to the left of center. One kiva (Room 229 at Awatovi) had three niches, others only one each. Most were rectangular, but one was circular, one triangular, and one trapezoidal. Dimensions varied from about 12 to 35 cm. wide, about 9 to 20 cm. high, and about 10 to 32 cm. deep. Most were simply apertures in the masonry formed by the omission of a single stone; a few had slab sills; and almost all were fully lined with smoothed coats of plaster. These wall niches are differentiated from the much larger cists often contained under rear benches, as discussed below.

In two kivas (Test 14, Room 6, and Test 22, Room 10, at Awatovi) there occurred an unusual

Fig. 68. a. Part of the surface of a wall in Room 410 in the mission area of Awatovi. The masonry here, despite its appearance of utter incompetence, was in fact more substantial than some others. Although the stones varied enormously in size and shape they were firmly embedded in mortar and had been placed with some degree of care for the transmission of weight, so that the entire structure was less flimsy than its appearance would suggest. It was built close to the end of Awatovi's occupancy, during the Spanish period.

b. Part of the surface of a wall in Room 514 in the mission area of Awatovi. This example was about contemporary with that shown in a, and superficially appears of much better construction. The general character and method were similar, however, but with a more careful arrangement of larger and smaller stones in an effort at coursing. Most of the small stones acted as bearing spalls, but some were used to stop the copious mortar.

c. Part of the plastered surface of a wall in Room 242 in the Western Mound at Awatovi. The masonry beneath the plaster coating was characteristic of the middle part of the "black-on-yellow" period, but the appearance after plastering was nearly the same on all walls, regardless of underlying masonry technique.

d. Part of the plastered surface of a wall in Room 218, the earliest kiva excavated in the Western Mound. The surface has been heavily weathered and exhibits something of the materials frequently included with the mud of the matrix: bits of bone, small pebbles, potsherds, charcoal.

e. Impression in wall mortar of Room 788, under the second church at Awatovi, of twilled matting that had been inserted to provide support for the surfacing plaster.

f. Part of a wall in Room 788, showing remnants of horizontal bundles of grass and vertical reeds used as reinforcements in the rough mortar underlying the finish plaster.

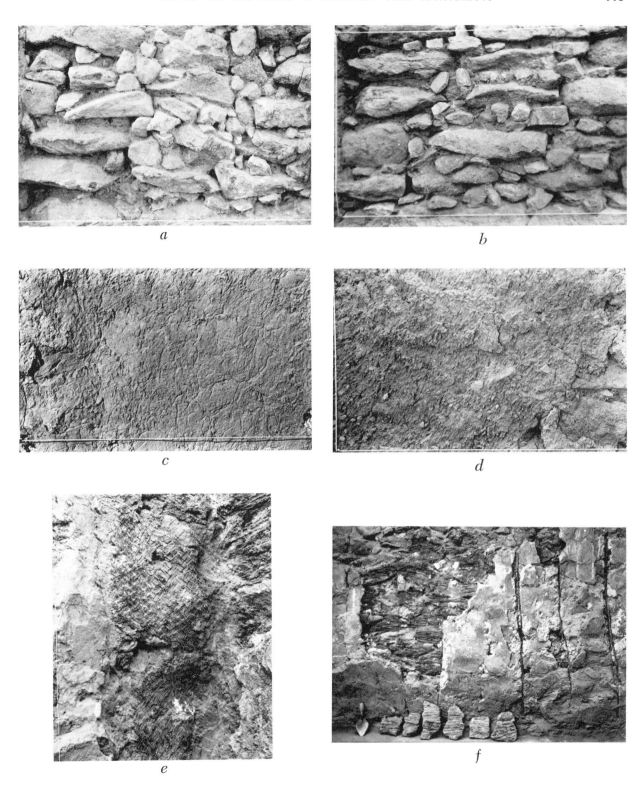

a

b

c

d

e

f

feature, consisting of a small circular hole that penetrated the rear wall at its center line and entered the exterior vertical ventilator shaft. In one case (and probably originally in both) an adobe plug was fitted snugly into the hole.

Only two passageways were found through kiva walls. Both existed through the common wall that formed the front of Room 218 and the left side of Room 229 at Awatovi. They were large enough to permit the passage of a human being, and their sills were at or near floor level. Both had been sealed during occupation of the two kivas, one with masonry, the other with a fitted stone slab.

BENCHES

Probably every kiva was once equipped with a broad raised bench across its rear portion, beneath which ran a horizontal ventilator tunnel. Certainly such a bench did exist in every excavated kiva whose rear area had not been destroyed by erosion.

These benches were generally rectangular and flat on top, the face of each being approximately parallel to the rear wall and extending fully across the kiva from left to right. Some qualification of these generalizations should be made, however, inasmuch as few benches, like the kivas themselves, were in fact very precise in their geometry, so that parallelism and rectangularity are expressions of ideals that were hardly ever fully achieved in practice. In most cases such deviations were not great, but in a few they were marked. In several instances, also, the rear bench was abbreviated at one end or the other by the existence of a masonry pier or pilaster built into the corner of the room. The purpose of such piers was not usually apparent. Rarely a bench was broader at

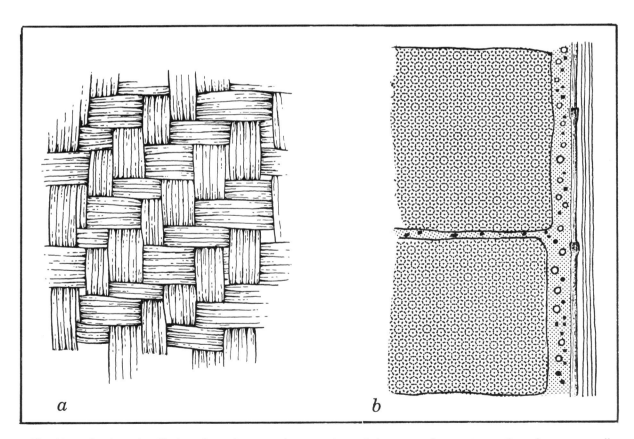

Fig. 69. *a.* Section of twilled reed matting sometimes used as reinforcement for mortar coating of masonry walls.

b. Schematic profile of kiva wall, showing, from left to right: masonry blocks, coarse mortar reinforced by embedded horizontal reeds and grass, vertical reeds pressed into the mortar, and successive layers of finish plaster.

Fig. 70. Cross section of a block of wall plaster from Room 218 in the Western Mound at Awatovi. Each lamination represents a single coat of plaster, of which there were approximately 100, 26 of them painted. The total thickness was about 11 cm., or an average thickness of about 1.1 mm. per coat.

one end than at the other (e.g., Kiva A at Awatovi).

Figure 71 is a scatter diagram showing the distribution of average breadths and heights of those rear benches that were intact when excavated. Nearly all cluster between 1.00 and 1.85 m. in breadth and between 30 and 50 cm. in height. No significant relation between height and breadth was apparent, nor was there any significant relation between bench and kiva dimensions, except in the case of Test 31, Room 1, at Awatovi. This was by far the largest kiva excavated, and its rear bench, measuring 2.80 m. broad by 24 cm. high was much broader and also lower than any other. No consistent chronological change in bench dimensions was noted.

Surfaces of rear benches were probably almost always paved with large smooth sandstone slabs,

and evidence of such paving survived in at least 22 instances, from earliest to latest. In 12 other cases the surface of the bench had been destroyed, and in a few the paving slabs may have been scavenged after abandonment of the kiva. The faces of 18 rear benches were built of coursed masonry, 2 were of vertical slabs, 2 were of masonry and slabs in combination, and the character of others was indeterminate.

Cavate recesses or cists had been inset into the rear benches in several instances. These varied in shape and size, but each one usually consisted of a square or rectangular aperture through the stone face of the bench. This aperture gave access to a large cavity or cist in most of which had been emplaced a globular utility jar, its mouth inclined upward and forward and often containing food or objects of ceremonial significance. In each of four kivas there were two such cists, each approximately in the center of that portion of the face of the bench between the mouth of the ventilator tunnel and one of the side walls. These were all relatively early (Room 229, Test 14, Rooms 2, 5, and 6, at Awatovi). In each of five other kivas only one cist was present, three in the left half of the bench, two in the right half. These were mostly chronologically later (Rooms 529 and 788 at Awatovi; and Test 4, Rooms 5 and 7, at Kawaika-a), but one (in Test 14, Room 4, at Awatovi) was intermediate in date. In 10 kivas there were definitely no cists, and in 13 this feature was indeterminate, because of erosion of the critical area.

Benches along front and side walls existed in some kivas but not in most. At Awatovi only seven kivas had front benches and only eight had side benches. In six instances front and side benches existed together; one kiva had a front bench but no side benches (Test 14, Room 4, at Awatovi); two kivas had side benches but no front bench (Room 218, on the left side only, and Test 22, Room 10, on both sides, both at Awatovi). There were no front or side benches at Kawaika-a, which seems to suggest some possible difference between the ceremonial organizations of the two villages, unless there is a chronological explanation, as implied in the next paragraph.

In breadth these benches varied between extremes of 45 and 72 cm., most of them clustering between 50 and 60 cm. In height they varied between extremes of 30 and 50 cm., most of them between 36 and 45 cm. No consistent relationship was noted between breadths and heights. There seemed to be a tendency for such benches to occur with greater frequency in those kivas that

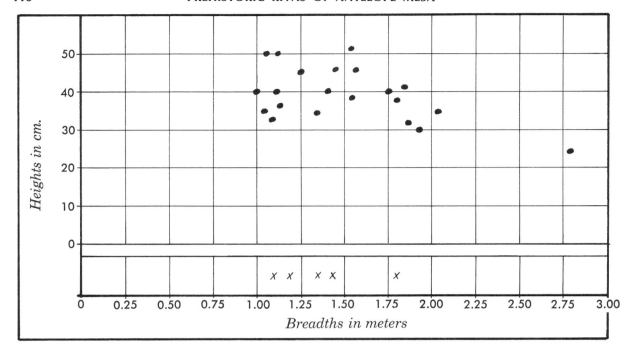

Fig. 71. Scatter diagram showing heights and breadths of all rear benches recorded in kivas at Awatovi and Kawaika-a. Each dot represents one bench.

Five benches were partially eroded. Their heights were undeterminable, but their breadths are indicated at the bottom of the chart by X's. Eight other benches were completely eroded or were not excavated and are not recorded.

Nearly all recorded benches fell within a fairly tight cluster, the only markedly erratic example being the one in Test 31, Room 1, at Awatovi.

occupied a median chronological position. For example, at Awatovi all kivas in Test 14 (except the very early one, Room 10) had them, whereas they occurred in only two very late kivas (Room 529, and Test 22, Room 10), and in only one early kiva (Room 218, along the left side only). Moreover no occurrence was found at Kawaika-a, where all excavated kivas were relatively late.

In five instances the surfaces of front and side benches were slab-covered, and it is probably reasonable to assume that slabs originally existed elsewhere, having been scavenged after abandonment. Faces were of masonry in five instances and of vertical slabs in three, the latter occurring relatively late in time (Room 529, Test 19, Room 3, and Test 22, Room 10, all at Awatovi).

VENTILATORS

Every kiva excavated at Awatovi and Kawaika-a which had not suffered erosion in the critical area was equipped with a ventilator system, consisting of a tunnel beneath the rear bench and a shaft rising to the surface just beyond the rear wall. Tunnels were always rectangular in section, always at floor level, and except in a few cases extended along or nearly along the midline of the room, perpendicular to the face of the rear bench. There were only two exceptions in which the tunnel lay at a sharp angle (Test 14, Room 10, at Awatovi, and Test 4, Room 2, at Kawaika-a).

Twenty tunnels survived in whole or in part. In width they varied between extremes of 25 and 60 cm., and in height between 25 and 50 cm. None was exactly square, and only three were wider than high. Most measured from 35 to 45 cm. high by 25 to 37 cm. wide.

Sides were usually of coursed masonry, with vertical slabs used about half as frequently. Floors were sometimes paved with slabs, but much more frequently simply with earth. The nature of the roof construction was frequently indeterminable due to the fact of erosion or collapse, but in those that survived a series of small poles or sticks had usually been laid transversely and resting on the side walls to support a superstructure. Such sticks were recorded in ten instances, twice with a twilled matting of reeds lying upon them. Above the sticks or matting were usually laid horizontal stone slabs, either at or slightly below the surface of the bench. In three instances sticks were absent and the slabs lay directly on the side walls. It is probable that sticks had also been used in other cases but had decayed before excavation.

The inner apertures or "mouths" of ventilator tunnels usually opened into their kivas at floor level and without obstruction, but some had been partially closed. Three, all at Awatovi (Kiva A, Room 788, and Test 31, Room 1), held vertical slabs, snugly fitted around their edges, each with a small semicircular notch 10 to 12 cm. in diameter at the center of its lower edge. One (Test 4, Room 7, at Kawaika-a) contained an unnotched slab extending from floor level halfway to the top of the tunnel; another (Test 14, Room 5, at Awatovi) was reduced by the placement of a stone block within one side and two adobe bricks within the other; another (Test 4, Room 5, at Kawaika-a) had a neatly molded adobe frame and jamb into which a fitted slab could be inserted at will; and still another (Kiva E at Awatovi) was partly closed by masonry. In only two of these seven kivas was a conventional deflector set into the floor between the opening of the tunnel and the firepit.

There seemed to be no chronological significance in any of the details of tunnel construction, except that the two cases of twilled matting over sticks occurred in Rooms 529 and 788, two of the very latest kivas to be occupied at Awatovi.

All ventilator systems must have terminated in a vertical shaft outside or within the rear wall of the kiva, but in most cases this feature had been destroyed or was not carefully investigated. In only five cases were details recorded. Four of these shafts were rectangular and three of them were contained actually within the masonry of the rear wall of the kiva itself; two of the latter were pierced by a circular hole through the inner face of the wall, which was stopped by a removable adobe plug (Test 14, Room 6, and Test 22, Room 10, both at Awatovi). The other rectangular shaft (Kiva A at Awatovi) was independently constructed of masonry outside the wall of the kiva, as was a circular shaft (Kiva D at Awatovi).

PAVEMENTS

Slab paving was recorded on the floors of 31 kivas and had probably once existed in all. Slabs were not recorded in Room 528, at Awatovi, or in Test 4, Room 1, at Kawaika-a, but those kivas were only partially excavated, and slabs might have been present in the unexposed areas. Room 10 in Test 14 at Awatovi, the earliest kiva excavated, had only a sand floor, but since it had been remodeled and then largely destroyed by the construction of Room 4 above it, any original slabs might have been removed. Floor slabs were usually laid upon clean sand but sometimes on a bed of coal ash. Seven instances of the latter were recorded, but there may have been others, since the underpinning of the slab floors was not always investigated. Coal ash as used in this way occurred in chronologically late kivas (Kiva A and Rooms 528 and 788, at Awatovi, and Test 4, Rooms 1, 3, and 7, and Test 5, Room 1, at Kawaika-a).

FIREPITS

All kivas had firepits. They were almost always on or near the midline of the room and closer to the mouth of the ventilator than to the front wall. They were almost always rectangular or nearly square, their sides almost always parallel to the walls of the room, and usually lined with vertical stone slabs, which never rose above the level of the floor. None was surrounded by a coping. Three (Room 229 at Awatovi, Test 4, Room 7, and Test 5, Room 5, at Kawaika-a) had masonry sides. Bottoms were sometimes sealed with a horizontal slab. Data are shown in figure 72.

Longitudinally the firepits were usually situated between 80 cm. and 1.20 m. in front of the mouth of the ventilator tunnel. Five lay between 50 and 75 cm., two about 2.00 m., and three less than 20 cm., from the tunnel. No chronological pattern was apparent in their positions (fig. 73).

The horizontal dimensions of most firepits varied between 20 and 40 cm., and only four exceeded those measurements. One firepit was a rhombus, 28 by 28 cm., and two (in the successive stages of Test 14, Room 10, at Awatovi, which was the earliest kiva excavated) were basin-shaped, 35 and 45 cm. in diameter, respectively. In depth most firepits were between 25 and 45 cm. Only two were deeper and five shallower (fig. 74).

The contents of most firepits consisted of wood ash, although ten contained coal ash. Coal was distributed chronologically from the earliest kiva (Test 14, Room 10, at Awatovi) to some of the latest (for example, Test 22, Room 10, Test 31, Room 1, and Test 57, Room 1, all at Awatovi).

In four kivas two firepits occurred and in one kiva, four, but it was not always clear whether

| | Distance in m. from | | Dimensions | | Interior | | | Proportion of distance from front to rear | Remarks |
	front	rear	Plan (Long / Trans)	Depth	Sides	Hearth	Fuel		
Awatovi									
A	3.70	0.10	50-60	?	Earth	Earth	Coal	8%	
A	2.75	1.20	35-40	40	Slabs	Slabs	Wood	32%	
C	2.40	0.85	30-35	30	?	?	?	29%	
E	2.40	1.15	24-23	18	Slabs	Slabs	?	34%	
218	2.30	1.00	39-40	?	Slabs	?	?	34%	
229	1.53	0.95	27-26	37	Masonry	?	Wood	41%	
529	2.62	0.90	34-34	42	Slabs	Slabs	Wood	39%	
788	2.55	1.00	28-28	44	Slabs	Slabs	Wood	30%	Rhomboidal
T 14, R 2	2.95	1.00	28-33	?	Slabs	?	Wood	28%	Left of Center
T 14, R 3	2.45	1.05	30 28 / 32 31	35	Slabs	Earth	?	33%	
T 14, R 3	1.40	2.16	38 41 - 26	43	Slabs	Sand	Wood	62%	Covered by Slabs
T 14, R 4	3.15	0.50	22-37	36	Slabs	Sand	Wood	16%	Diagonal
T 14, R 4	2.45	1.05	41 41 / 39 38	?	Slabs	Slabs	Wood	31%	
T 14, R 4	0.50	3.00	37 30 / 27 30	48	Slabs	Earth	Coal	84%	Right of Center Covered by Slabs
T 14, R 4	3.40	0.16	30-32	20	Slabs	Slabs	Wood	9%	Covered by Slabs
T 14, R 5	2.60	1.00	26 26 / 28 28	36	Slabs	Sand	Coal	29%	Right of Center Covered by Slabs
T 14, R 6	4.15	0.60	30-25	35	Slabs	Slabs	Wood	15%	
T 14, R 6	3.65	1.14	25 30 / 28 33	21	Slabs	Slabs	Coal	32%	
T 14, R 10	1.87	1.00	35 diam.	9	Clay	Clay	Coal	36%	Basin-shape
T 14, R 10	1.07	1.70	45 diam.	15	Clay	Clay		59%	Basin-shape
T 19, R 3	2.30	1.05	31-33	35	Slabs	Slabs	Coal	34%	
T 22, R 10	3.00	0.75	38-48	20	Slabs	?	Coal	23%	Left of Center
T 31, R 1	3.85	0.70	45-50	20	Slabs	Slabs	Coal	19%	
T 57, R 1	1.80	0.80	28-28	?	Slabs	?	Coal	33%	
Kawaika-a									
T 4, R 2	1.85	1.15	26 24 / 28 26	40	Slabs	Slabs	Wood and Coal	43%	
T 4, R 3	3.05	1.00	35-25	?	Slabs	Slabs	Wood	27%	
T 4, R 5	2.70	0.55	35-35	40	Slabs	Earth	?	21%	
T 4, R 7	2.30	1.00	30-30	53	Slabs	Earth	Wood	33%	
T 4, R 7	3.25	0.10	25-25	36	Masonry	Earth	Wood	8%	Covered by Slabs
T 5, R 1	2.90	?	25-30	25	Slabs	Earth	?	?	Bench eroded
T 5, R 2	2.85	0.80	?	?	Slabs	?	Wood	21%	
T 5, R 5	2.40	?	25-26	40	Masonry	Slabs	Wood	?	Bench eroded
T 5, R 7	2.25	?	27-29	42	Slabs	?	Wood	?	Bench eroded

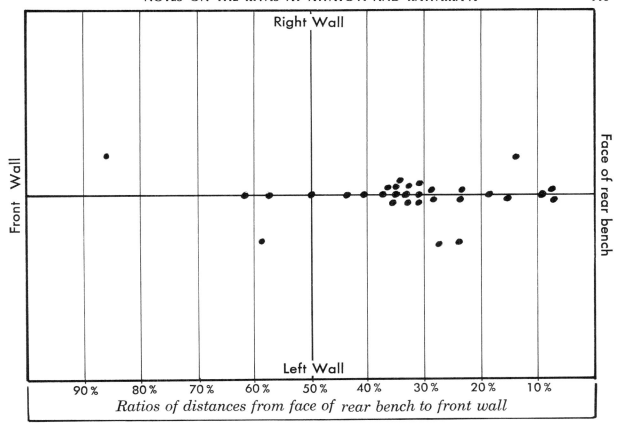

Fig. 73. Scatter diagram showing positions of all firepits in excavated kivas at Awatovi and Kawaika-a, in terms of their proportional distances from the face of the rear bench to the front wall of the kiva. Each dot represents a firepit.

they had been in use simultaneously or successively. In three cases (Test 14, Rooms 3 and 6, at Awatovi, and Test 4, Room 7, at Kawaika-a) successive use was indicated by the fact that one firepit in each kiva had been abandoned and covered over by paving slabs, while the other remained open. In Kiva A at Awatovi two firepits remained open, one containing wood ash, the other coal ash. In Test 14, Room 4, at Awatovi, two firepits

had been abandoned and covered, but two others remained open. One of the abandoned firepits contained both coal ash and charcoal, the only instance in which both fuels appeared to have been mixed.

The almost complete separation of wood and coal as fuels was striking, and suggests that they may have had different ceremonial significance. We know that wood smoke can have special

Fig. 72. This chart shows dimensions, positions, and other characteristics of firepits in floors of all kivas excavated at Awatovi and Kawaika-a.

Positions are expressed in meters from the front wall of the kiva and from the face of the rear bench. Almost all firepits were located along the longitudinal center line of the kiva, except those designated as right or left of center.

Dimensions are expressed in centimeters; those firepits with plans of two dimensions were rectangles; those with three or four dimensions were quadrilaterals with unequal edges.

An interrogation point indicates uncertainty or incomplete field record.

The notation "Covered by Slabs" indicates that the firepit referred to had been abandoned and obscured by floor-paving slabs during the continued occupation of the kiva.

In several instances the distance from the rear bench was indeterminable, because the bench had been obliterated by erosion prior to excavation.

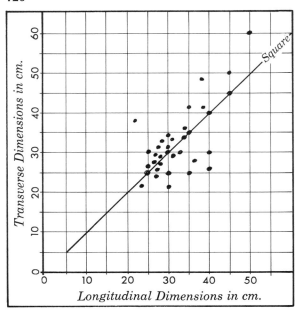

Fig. 74. Scatter diagram showing distribution, according to sizes and shapes, of all recorded firepits in excavated kivas at Awatovi and Kawaika-a. Those in the upper left are greater in transverse dimension, those in lower right are greater in longitudinal dimension, and those along the diagonal are square. Each dot represents one firepit.

prophylactic powers in modern Hopi usage. For example, the Hopi hunter on his return from the chase fumigates himself in juniper smoke, and exorcism of possible disease can be effected in the same way under some circumstances (Parsons 1939, vol. 1, pp. 466–467).

Early in our excavations we were surprised and interested to find that most of our Hopi workmen did not seem to be dismayed by the uncovering of human skeletons. Because of Fewkes's experiences at Awatovi thirty years before (pp. 73–74), we had had qualms in advance about this kind of confrontation. In explanation of the seeming lack of concern, however, we subsequently found that the men who had been working on or near the skeletons would make a small fire of juniper wood when they returned to camp and would jump through the smoke to ward off evil effects. It is interesting to record that the only man who would under no circumstances go near a skeleton was a nominal Christian.

DEFLECTORS

Although in a good many kivas no deflector was found, probably having been removed or broken

after abandonment of the kiva, such devices must normally have existed between the firepit and the tunnel mouth. Those that were recorded at Awatovi and Kawaika-a were almost always formed of a single vertical slab of stone. Sizes of the slabs varied considerably, as did their relative positions, though they tended to be closer to the firepit than to the mouth of the tunnel.

A few variations occurred, however. One deflector was constructed of two vertical slabs placed snugly face-to-face (Test 14, Room 4, at Awatovi). In lieu of a conventional deflector a movable slab had been inserted directly into the tunnel mouth in five kivas (Kiva A, Room 788, and Test 31, Room 1, at Awatovi, and Test 4, Rooms 5 and 7, at Kawaika-a); and in Kiva E and Test 14, Room 5, at Awatovi, the tunnel mouth had been partly closed by masonry.

SIPAPUS AND FOOTDRUMS

One of the most important features in Hopi ceremonies and those of most other Pueblo peoples is the sipapu, usually represented by a small hole in the central plaza of a village or in the floor of a kiva. Every Hopi village must have one, and there is one in most, though not in all, Hopi kivas. The sipapu provides a ritual connection with the netherworld, and is the place of emergence through which the people once came up to the surface of the earth. The kachinas also come and return through it. It is thus the most sacrosanct of all places in the village. Sometimes it serves as an altar in which are placed sacred things, such as prayer feathers or kick balls. (Mindeleff, 1891, pp. 117, 122, 135; Stephen, 1936, part 1, pp. 10, 137, part 2, 928, 1076, 1295; Parsons, 1939, vol. 1, pp. 309, 311, 383.)

A subfloor feature that certainly fulfilled the function of a sipapu occurred in many kivas at Awatovi and Kawaika-a about halfway between the firepit and the front wall of the kiva. This was usually in the form of an elongated pit, sunk into the floor, the longer dimension transverse to that of the kiva, with a recessed sill or ledge surrounding the pit, on which a plank or slab could be fitted so that its upper edge would be flush with the surface of the floor. Such things are common in modern Hopi kivas, though they do not occur in all, and the planks are fitted with a small circular hole that can be plugged when not in use on ceremonial occasions. During ceremonies celebrants may stamp on the plank, which thus acts as a resonator or footdrum (Mindeleff 1891, pp.

121–122, 123, 126, 130–131, figs. 22, 27, 30; Stephen 1936, part 1, pp. 10, 34, 536, 708, 720, figs. 6, 31, 70, 302, 313, 321, 385, and under sipapu in the index; Parsons 1939, vol. 1, pp. 309–310, 382–383, vol. 2, pp. 768, 981).

Of course at Awatovi and Kawaika-a the planks had decayed and disappeared, but there seems no doubt that they had once been present. Ten such pits existed in the kivas at Awatovi and two at Kawaika-a, usually slab-lined. At least five contained moderately sized utility jars, each set in a bed of adobe, sand, small stones, or coal ash. Such pits occurred in kivas of middle to late date, but not in earlier ones. At least 17 kivas were without them, while the situation in others was indeterminate.

The positions of sipapus of this kind varied between 90 cm. and 1.90 m. from the front wall of the kiva, although one (Test 31, Room 1, at Awatovi) was only 45 cm. from the front wall. In length they varied from 25 to 50 cm. (although one was 70 cm. long) and in width from 22 to 50 cm. Depths varied from 24 to 40 cm. Proportions varied from exactly twice as long as wide to almost square. Three were circular, each about 22 cm. in diameter.

Kivas without devices of this kind may have had sipapus in the form of a small circular hole, 5 to 8 cm. in diameter, drilled through a floor slab, like those that have often been reported in prehistoric Anasazi kivas. Similar small holes also occur in modern Hopi kivas, usually closed with a wooden plug when not in use (Mindeleff 1891, pp. 126, 130–131, fig. 25). Such holes could have been obliterated where floor slabs had been removed, or might have been indistinguishable from similar holes that had been used for other purposes. There were, however, some kivas in which a sipapu had apparently never existed.

Professor Brew, the Director of the Expedition, was interested in the reason for the absence of sipapus in some kivas. In his previous excavations of Pueblo I pithouses and Pueblo II and III kivas on Alkali Ridge in southeastern Utah, many of those structures had also apparently lacked a sipapu (Brew 1946, p. 211), although this feature had been thought to be standard in San Juan kivas. Questions addressed to some of our Hopi friends elicited a simple but reasonable answer, namely that a sipapu must be present only in a kiva that is used for ceremonies in which a sipapu is necessary. There is further observation of the fact that not all modern Hopi kivas have sipapus (Stephen 1936, part 2, p. 1076), and a review of reported data from the Western Anasazi area indicates that the sipapu was not a universal feature in prehistoric kivas of that time (Smith 1952b, pp. 154–165).

Mindeleff (1891, pp. 130–131) in discussing Hopi kivas states that they are of two kinds, "marked by the distinction that only certain ones contain a sipapuh, and in these the more important ceremonies are held. . . . It is also said that a stone sipapuh was formerly used instead of the cottonwood plank now commonly seen. The use of stone for this purpose, however, is nearly obsolete, though the second kiva at Shipaulovi . . . contains an example of this ancient form." (See also Stephen 1936, part 2, p. 1076.)

LOOM-ANCHOR HOLES

Small circular holes, 5 to 8 cm. in diameter, were numerous and appeared in the floors of almost every kiva in which paving slabs survived. Normally they were arranged in straight rows of three, four, or five holes, each running parallel to the side walls of the kiva and half a meter or so from the wall. Very often, however, they occurred haphazardly without evident pattern, probably because the paving slabs in which they were drilled had been reused after earlier removal from original positions elsewhere. It is quite possible that some of these holes may have served as sipapus but were not recognized as such, but most of them had probably served as sockets for loom-anchoring devices. Sometimes similar holes occurred in paving slabs on the surfaces of benches.

In modern Hopi kivas, vertical weaving looms are frequently set up near the side walls. In order to fix such looms firmly in place the upper horizontal beam of the loom is attached to roof beams of the kiva by means of a series of loops or ties. The lower beam is held by inserting its ends into sockets in the kiva walls or drilled into the ends of heavy squared blocks of stone that rest upon the floor, thus acting as weights to hold down the loom beam gravitationally. But in addition there are attached to the lower beam loops of rope, leather, or other flexible material that are in turn fixed to anchors inserted into small holes in the floor.

In describing modern Hopi kivas, Mindeleff (1891, p. 132) says: "In most of the existing kivas there are planks in which stout loops are secured, fixed in the floor close to the wall, for attaching the lower beam of a primitive vertical loom. . . . The planks or logs to which is attached the lower part of the loom . . . are often partly buried in the ground and under the edges of adjacent paving stones in such a manner as to be held in place very securely. . . . The holes pierced in the upper surfaces of these logs are very neatly executed. . . . Strips of buckskin or bits of rope are passed through these U-shaped cavities and then over the lower pole of the loom." Mindeleff's figures 22, 24, 25, 27, and 31 illustrate the placement of such planks and the manner in which the U-shaped sockets are carved into them.

Although no such planks were found in any of the Jeddito kivas, the rows of circular holes in the floor slabs doubtless served the same purpose. Exactly similar rows of holes have been found in ancient San Juan kivas, some of them with anchors emplaced within them.

Kidder and Guernsey (1919, pp. 50–51, 60, 70, 73, figs. 22, 26, pl. 21, a) discuss and illustrate the manner in which such holes and anchors were used in kivas of the Kayenta area. In a kiva at Olla House, a Pueblo II or III cave ruin in Comb Ridge, 7 or 8 miles below Kayenta, one floor hole contained "a loop of braided yucca anchored in the adobe floor by means of a cross-stick and so placed that the top of the loop was just below the floor level (fig. 22). The underside of the top of the loop shows such wear as would have been caused by the play of a string or rope running through it. It is possible that [two other holes] once contained loops, and formed part of a series of loopholes such as were later found in other kivas."

In a kiva at "Cliff-house B," a ruin near Marsh Pass (ibid., p. 60, fig. 24, pl. 21, a), seven holes were arranged in two straight rows, one on each side of the kiva, this time in an adobe floor. "All but one contained loops resembling that found in the kiva of Olla House. These loops are made of bent twigs, except in a single case, where a double yucca string is employed. As all were left in position, the method of anchoring could not be observed, but it was, perhaps, by means of a cross-piece, as in Olla House (fig. 22). . . . There can be little doubt that these series of loop holders served as attachments."

Near Nakaito a slightly different arrangement was found, this time cut into the sandstone ledge that formed the kiva floor (ibid., p. 70, fig. 26). Here there occurred a "row of five small holes in perfect alignment and exactly 15 inches apart. Their shape is difficult to describe, but as the illustration (fig. 26) shows, they doubtless served as sockets for wooden crosspieces, which like the loops observed in the floors of several kivas, held the lower bar of a loom." The socket was circular with its lower edges expanded outward to receive and retain a horizontal stick set into it, closely

similar to those later found by Neil Judd at Betatakin. In still another case Kidder and Guernsey (ibid., p. 73) found two rows of five holes each, "containing yucca loops," parallel to the side walls of a kiva.

When Judd excavated Betatakin, a large Pueblo III ruin in Tsegi Canyon, he also found in the floors of several rooms identified as kivas, rows of small circular holes that he carefully described (Judd 1930, pp. 24, 28, 31, 34, fig. 3). The holes as illustrated in his figure 3 were circular with two vertical grooves extending downward at opposite points of the circumference to intersect undercut notches so that a horizontal stick longer than the diameter of the hole could be lowered through the grooves and then revolved slightly into the undercuts, after which it could not be pulled out.

Judd described a form of anchor (p. 62, fig. 18) made of "an oak branch, knotted and tied with yucca, and buried so that the loop lay just below the floor level." These objects were looped over the anchor sticks and their upper ends presumably were tied to the lower beam of a loom. Rows of circular holes also occurred in a kiva at Kiet Siel (Vivian and Reiter 1965, p. 99). In a kiva at Hawikuh, Hodge reported rows of holes through the slabbed floor, exactly similar to those at Awatovi (Hodge 1939).

There can be little doubt that the rows of circular holes in kiva floors in the Jeddito area were analogous to those of the Marsh Pass-Kayenta kivas, and we have therefore identified them as loom-anchor holes. It is noteworthy that they could function even in adobe floors (Kidder and Guernsey 1919, p. 60, pl. 21, a), similar to that in the Pueblo III D-shaped kiva at Jeddito Site 4 (p. 129 below).

At Pecos Dr. Kidder found many rows of such holes in the earthen floors of at least six kivas, which he identified as receptacles for "loom-loop holders," and described as follows (1958, p. 179):

The great majority of these were round, 3–3 3/4 inches deep. They were packed solidly with very hard white wood ash, evidently stuffed in wet, and pounded down. The ash plug in each example that was sufficiently well preserved for examination showed two 1/2-inch round holes in its upper surface, as did those in Kiva 5. These holes were casts of a twig, probably a pliable willow switch, that had been tied on itself into a long narrow loop and set in the excavation in the kiva floor, where it was held firmly in place when the ash paste solidified. . . . The top of the loop protruded about 1 inch.

and again (ibid., pp. 159–162):

The holders were set in holes about 4 inches in diameter by 8 to 10 inches deep dug into the floor with a sharp-pointed stick which left vertical marks in the clay sides. Then a flexible withe, probably willow, 1/4 to 1/2 inch in diameter was bent on itself to form a long, narrow loop, its two ends apparently always tied together. This was held by hand in the empty hole with its top about 1 inch above the level of the kiva floor, the knot near, but usually not on, the bottom of the hole. Then white wood ash, worked into a thick paste with water or possibly some plant juice, was packed tightly in and tamped down. It preserved perfect casts of the holes and the withe loops. [Some holes] had been filled with clean clay of lighter color than the floors instead of with ash.

There is no doubt that each row of loops served for attachment of the lower bar of a loom, the length of which was evidently about 5 feet.

(See also ibid., pp. 159, 162, 172, 179, 184, 194, 198, 203, 252–257; figs. 42, 43, g, 44, d, 46, 49, 50, c, d, e, 52, a, 54, e, 56, 65, e.)

Kidder also reviewed other reported instances of such devices in the Southwest, noting that they were absent from Mesa Verde and Chaco kivas, and had apparently occurred only in the Kayenta and Hopi areas, whence he rather reluctantly concluded they must have been introduced to the upper Rio Grande Valley and Pecos (ibid., pp. 252–257).

INCISED FLOOR DESIGNS

In two kivas designs had been incised into slabs on the floor or on the rear bench, each consisting of a hollow square outlined by a single row of shallow, basin-shaped, circular pits a few centimeters in diameter, gouged into but not through the slabs (Kiva A and Room 529 at Awatovi). In the latter case each individual pit was embellished by a lightly incised line extending radially outward from it, suggestive of a tadpole.

LADDER SOCKETS

In each of three kivas (Rooms 229, 529, Test 14, Room 2, all at Awatovi) a small pit filled with sand was situated between the mouth of the ventilator tunnel and the firepit, probably to receive the pole of a ladder reaching upward to a hatchway in the roof.

ROOFS

Roofs had completely disappeared from nearly all kivas excavated, but in two cases they had remained sufficiently intact to provide data for reconstruction. The two kivas referred to were Rooms 788 and 908 at Awatovi, both of which had been deliberately filled with clean sand, leaving their roofs undisturbed. This had probably been done by the Franciscan friars to make possible the construction of the sanctuary and sacristy of the mission church above them, as has been discussed elsewhere (Montgomery, Smith, and Brew 1949, pp. 64–67, 77, 85, 134–137, 265–272). Only Room 788 was completely excavated, but testing in Room 908 indicated that its roof had been similar. Although these kivas were chronologically among the very latest in the village, it seems reasonable to infer that other kivas had been covered in a similar manner.

As discussed above on pages 62–63 and illustrated in figures 40 and 41, the roof in Room 788 was supported on two main transverse beams with five or six smaller beams laid at right-angles across them, leaving a rectangular open hatchway in the center. The hatchway was surrounded by a low parapet of stone blocks and adobe. The side areas of the roof were spanned by small poles or savinos, over which was laid brush, grass, or perhaps twilled yucca matting, finally sealed with a coating of adobe. The entire structure resembled that of modern Hopi kivas. Beams varied from 1.90 to 2.30 m. above the floor. Presumably a ladder provided access from hatchway to floor but none was discovered.

On the whole, as is evident from the foregoing summary, the kivas of Pueblo IV age at Awatovi and Kawaika-a conformed closely to an accepted architectural and functional pattern. It is equally striking that their style has changed so little during the three subsequent centuries and that their modern successors in the Hopi villages of today resemble them so closely. Evidently the basic pattern of Hopi ceremonial life was well established during early Pueblo IV times and has changed little since.

This pattern, however, while not an entirely new thing in the 14th century, did represent the attainment of a relatively well-stabilized ceremonial and cultural scheme, following several earlier centuries of fluidity and change. From Basket Maker II through Pueblo III there were striking and fairly rapid chronological alterations in the architecture and lifeways of the Anasazi. Insofar as these changes are evident from surviving kivas they will be discussed elsewhere herein, with particular reference to kivas excavated at earlier sites on Antelope Mesa (pp. 126–155).

BUILDING A KIVA

An explicit and detailed description of the building of a Hopi kiva in the 1880s, which must very closely exemplify the procedures followed at

Awatovi and Kawaika-a, is provided by Mindeleff (1891, pp. 119–122):

The men have already quarried or collected a sufficient quantity of stone, and a wall is built in tolerably regular courses along each side of the excavation. The stones used are roughly dressed by fracture; they are irregular in shape, and of a size convenient for one man to handle. They are laid with only a very little mud mortar, and carried up, if the ground be level, to within 18 inches of the surface. If the kiva is built on the edge of the cliff, as at Walpi, the outside wall connects the sides of the gap, conforming to the line of the cliff. If the surface is sloping, the level of the roof is obtained by building up one side of the kiva above the ground to the requisite height as illustrated in Fig. 21. One end of the "Goat" kiva at Walpi is 5 feet above ground, the other end being level with the sloping surface. When the ledge on the precipitous face of the mesa is uneven it is filled in with rough masonry to obtain a level for the floor, and thus the outside wall of the Walpi kivas is more than 12 feet high, although in the interior the measurement from floor to ceiling is much less.

Both cottonwood and pine are used for the roof timbers; they are roughly dressed, and some of them show that an attempt has been made to hew them with four sides, but none are square. . . .

In continuation of the kiva building process, the tops of the walls are brought to an approximate level. The main roof timbers are then laid parallel with the end walls, at irregular distances, but less than 3 feet apart, except near the middle, where a space of about 7 feet is left between two beams, as there the hatchway is to be built. The ends of the timbers rest upon the side walls, and as they are placed in position a small feather, to which a bit of cotton string is tied (nakwakwoci) is also placed under each. Stout poles, from which the bark has been stripped, are laid at right angles upon the timbers, with slight spaces between them. Near the center of the kiva two short timbers are laid across the two main beams about 5 feet apart; this is done to preserve a space of 5 by 7 feet for the hatchway, which is made with walls of stone laid in mud plaster, resting upon the two central beams and upon the two side pieces. This wall or combing is carried up so as to be at least 18 inches above the level of the finished roof. Across the poles, covering the rest of the roof, willows and straight twigs of any kind are laid close together, and over these is placed a layer of dry grass arranged in regular rows. Mud is then carefully spread over the grass to a depth of about 3 inches, and after it has nearly dried it is again gone over so as to fill up all the cracks. A layer of dry earth is then spread over all and firmly trodden down, to render the roof water-tight and bring its surface level with the surrounding ground, following the same method and order of construction that prevails in dwelling-house buildings.

Short timbers are placed across the top of the hatchway wall, one end of which is raised higher than the other, so as to form a slope, and upon these timbers stone slabs are closely laid for a cover. (See Pl. LXXXVII.) An open space, usually about 2 by 4 1/2 feet, is preserved, and this is the only outlet in the structure, serving at once as doorway, window, and chimney.

The roof being finished, a floor of stone flags is laid; but this is never in a continuous level, for at one end it is raised as a platform some 10 or 12 inches high, extending for about a third of the length of the kiva and terminating in an abrupt step just before coming under the hatchway, as illustrated in the ground plan of the mungkiva of Shupaulovi (Fig. 22, and also in Figs. 25 and 27). On the edge of the platform rests the foot of a long ladder, which leans against the higher side of the hatchway, and its tapering ends project 10 or 12 feet in the air. Upon this platform the women and other visitors sit when admitted to witness any of the ceremonies observed in the kiva. The main floor in a few of the kivas is composed of roughly hewn planks, but this is a comparatively recent innovation, and is not generally deemed desirable, as the movement of the dancers on the wooden floor shakes the fetiches out of position.

On the lower or main floor a shallow pit of varying dimensions, but usually about a foot square, is made for a fireplace, and is located immediately under the opening in the hatchway. The intention in raising the hatchway above the level of the roof and in elevating the ceiling in the middle is to prevent the fire from igniting them. The ordinary fuel used in the kiva is greasewood, and there are always several bundles of the shrub in its green state suspended on pegs driven in the wall of the hatchway directly over the fire. This shrub, when green, smolders and emits a dense, pungent smoke, but when perfectly dry, burns with a bright, sparkling flame.

Across the end of the kiva on the main floor a ledge of masonry is built, usually about 2 feet high and 1 foot wide, which serves as a shelf for the display of fetiches and other paraphernalia during stated observances (see Fig. 22). A small, niche-like aperture is made in the middle of this ledge, and is called the katchin kihu (katchina house). During a festival certain masks are placed in it when not in use by the dancers. Some of the kivas have low ledges built along one or both sides for use as seats, and some have none, but all except two or three have the ledge at the end containing the katchina house.

In the main floor of the kiva there is a cavity about a foot deep and 8 or 10 inches across, which is usually covered with a short, thick slab of cottonwood, whose upper surface is level with the floor. Through the middle of this short plank and immediately over the cavity a hole of 2 or 2 1/2 inches in diameter is bored. This hole is tapered, and is accurately fitted with a movable wooden plug, the top of which is flush with the surface of the plank. The plank and cavity usually occupy a position in the main floor near the end of the kiva. This feature is the sipapuh, the place of the gods, and the most sacred portion of the ceremonial chamber. Around this spot the fetiches are set during a festival; it typifies also the first world of the Tusayan genesis and the opening through which the people first emerged. It is frequently so spoken of at the present time.

Other little apertures or niches are constructed in the side walls; they usually open over the main floor of the kiva near the edge of the dais that forms the second level, that upon which the foot of the ladder rests. These are [not] now dedicated to any special purpose, but are used as receptacles for small tools and other ordinary articles. In early days, however, these niches were used exclusively as receptacles for the sacred pipes and tobacco and other smaller paraphernalia.

Dorsey and Voth (1902, p. 171) add some enlightening remarks upon Hopi kivas of the 1890s:

The exterior of the roof of both kivas is approximately the same, each having a hatchway near the center about eight feet square and about sixteen inches at its highest part, sloping gently to a height of eight inches at the opposite side. The hatches are of thin slabs of sandstone, the interspaces being filled with plaster. The limits of both kivas are indicated by means of stones — a single course [for] the Antelope kiva and an irregular course for the Snake kiva, varying from two to four stones in height. There are many points of difference in the interiors of the two kivas. The main floor of the Snake kiva where rites are performed consists of thirteen hewn planks fourteen inches wide. At the south end this is surmounted by a banquette of stone a foot and a half high. Opposite this and in the center of the kiva is a sunken fire hearth, rectangular in

shape and surrounded by a single course of flat stones. At the north end is a raised platform, the spectators' position of the kiva. This is of large, irregularly squared, rough hewn stones. Here the non-active members sit and lounge or work during ceremonial days, and here the members eat on those days when fasting is not prescribed. The walls of the kiva are coated with reddish yellow clay, which in the northeast corner had become detached and exposed the blackened courses of stone which were much evener and more regular than those exposed on the outside. About half way on the east, south and west walls are, respectively, one, two and three deep rectangular recesses about ten inches in width. These serve as receptacles for various small objects, such as moccasins, paints, cotton, feather boxes, etc.

Both the main floor and the platform of the Antelope kiva is [sic] of stone. The banquette extends along the entire northern end, and on the west side for a distance of three feet. It is about sixteen inches in height and is plastered. This kiva has a single recess in the west, north and east walls. There is no mural decoration in either kiva, but in the Antelope kiva each of the seven rafters have [sic] on the under surface four sets of four broad parallel white lines; the rafter on the north end has an additional set of lines.

It is a most ingenious paradox that relative stability and maturity seem finally to have come in the 14th century and to have persisted in the face of the tremendous impact of four centuries of European pressures, which should logically have produced shattering transformations instead of institutionalized conservatism. Ozymandias has fallen on his face, but the Hopi kachinas still stand erect in their ancestral kivas.

VI

Kivas at Other Sites in the Jeddito Area

They use statistics as a drunkard uses a lamppost, for support rather than for illumination.

Andrew Lang

One objective of the Jeddito expedition was to investigate and expound the complete story of Anasazi occupation of the area from its beginnings to modern times. In pursuit of this aim a survey was conducted on Antelope Mesa and the immediately surrounding areas, from which more than 300 sites were recorded, varying from small "sherd areas" to large masonry villages such as Chakpahu, Kokopnyama, and Awatovi itself. These sites represented a range in cultural development from Basket Maker III to Pueblo IV, with Awatovi the lone example of Pueblo V.

In chronological terms the sequence extended from the late 6th century to the end of the 17th — a span of more than a thousand years. A series of representative sites were selected for special study in order to provide a framework for the story, but time and resources limited our investigations to a comparatively small number of them, all chosen on the basis of their surface characteristics as exemplars of the major horizons in the sequence. Some of the selected sites were more or less fully excavated while others were only tested. Altogether seventeen were investigated in considerable extent.

It is not the purpose of this report to discuss all aspects of the investigations but merely to consider those structures within the several sites that were identified as kivas. In addition to the numerous kivas already described from Awatovi and Ka-waika-a, ceremonial chambers were found in only six of the other sites studied (fig. 1). The earliest of the excavated sites, Jeddito 264 (Daifuku 1961), was occupied during the periods of Basket Maker III and Pueblo I, and contained pithouses characteristic of those times, but nothing that could be distinguished as a kiva.

Those sites in which kivas were identified had been occupied at various times during the span from Pueblo II through Pueblo IV. These kivas and certain kiva-like rooms will be individually described and discussed herein.

THE KIVA AT SITE 4

A small Pueblo II–III site designated Jeddito 4 was situated near the southeastern escarpment of Antelope Mesa, a short distance downstream from the Jeddito Trading Post and about 100 meters northeast from Site 4A. It consisted of a single row of at least ten masonry surface rooms arranged in a northeast–southwest orientation, with three or four small outlying masonry structures that may have been either dwelling units or storage rooms. Its excavation was supervised by the late Dr. Charles A. Amsden, and the following description is adapted from his field notes.

Approximately in front of the third room from the northeasterly end of the main row and about 9 m. southeasterly from it was a subterranean kiva, the floor of which was just over 1.50 m. below the modern surface. This kiva was markedly D-shaped, one of several examples of this unusual form discovered in the Jeddito region (figs. 75, 76). The rear boundary of the floor area, which was defined by the face of a rear bench, was straight and measured 3.60 m. across. The front and sides were defined by a continuously curved wall which splayed slightly outward from the two rear corners, in arcs of relatively long radius, to opposite points approximately 2.25 m. from the rear boundary where they were 3.90 m. apart. Thence these side walls converged toward the front along arcs of somewhat shorter radius until they merged at a point 4.00 m. from the rear boundary of the

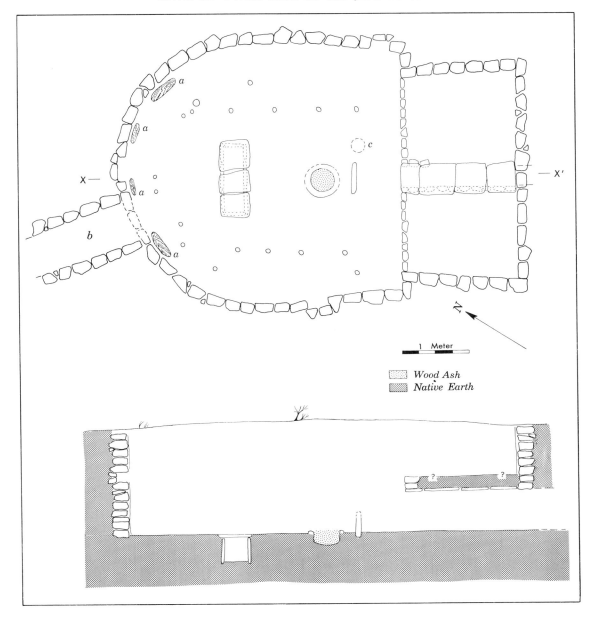

Fig. 75. Plan and profile of the kiva at Site 4. Four wooden battenlike objects (a) lay on the floor near the front wall, and a gray corrugated jar had been set into a cavity beneath the floor (c). A subterranean passageway (b) led from the kiva to a point below one of the rooms of the associated pueblo, to which a vertical shaft gave access through the floor of the room.

floor area. The rear boundary coincided along most of its length with the face of a bench, although the bench itself measured only 2.90 m. along its face. This was 70 cm. less than the full length of the rear boundary of the floor area, which thus extended about 35 cm. beyond the bench at each end. The bench thus occupied what

might be called an alcove or recess. It extended rearward to a breadth of 1.70 m., but its ends diverged slightly so that its rear wall was 3.15 m long.

The floor of the kiva was approximately 1.50 m. below the modern ground surface and the surface of the bench was between 85 cm. and 1.00 m.

Fig. 76. Rear portion of the D-shaped kiva at Site 4, showing bench with ventilator tunnel, deflector, and clay-lined, basin-shaped firepit with raised coping. Adjacent to the deflector was a pit containing a broken utility jar. Note characteristic Pueblo II masonry of the walls, and the loom-anchor holes set into the hard clay floor.

above the floor. The kiva was oriented about N. 38° W.

The face of the rear bench was constructed of well-laid masonry of about seven courses of sandstone blocks similar to those used in the main walls of the room. No paving slabs were found on the surface of the bench except a row that formed the roof for a ventilator tunnel. The tunnel lay almost exactly along the midline of the bench and perpendicular to its face. Its side walls were of masonry and its cover, as stated, was formed of stone slabs laid horizontally across the tunnel and supported by the side walls. These covering slabs were slightly lower than the topmost course of the masonry in the face of the bench, and had probably not constituted a part of the original surface, which must have been at a higher level and may have been formed of earth or other slabs. The tunnel was rather narrow, being only 30 cm. wide by about 65 cm. high. No investigation was made

of the vertical ventilator shaft outside the rear wall.

The floor of the kiva itself was of hard, light-colored, mud plaster about 2 cm. thick laid over a bed of clean sand. A firepit was located 1.00 m. in front of the face of the bench, 1.60 m. from the left wall, and 1.90 m. from the right. It was almost circular, 40 cm. in diameter by 20 cm. in depth, with vertical sides and a slightly concave bottom, and was completely lined with clay. It was surrounded by a convex coping 7 cm. high and about 12 cm. wide at floor level. The firepit contained only wood ashes. A stone slab serving as a deflector was set upright in the floor between the mouth of the ventilator and the firepit and 20 cm. from the latter. Its exact dimensions were not recorded.

About 45 cm. forward from the firepit a rectangular box was sunk through the floor. It was 1.10 m. long by 30 cm. wide by 45 cm. deep, its longer dimension transverse to the midline of the room. This box was lined with upright stone slabs and had an earth bottom. It was covered with stone slabs inset into the kiva floor so that their upper surfaces were flush with it. It probably represented a sipapu and may have served as a resonator or footdrum, as in many kivas at Awatovi and Kawaika-a as well as in modern Hopi kivas.

About 15 cm. to the right of the deflector a gray corrugated jar had been set into a cavity in the floor about 30 cm. deep. It appeared to have been already broken at the time of its emplacement, and had probably once served as the lining for a storage cist.

At least 18 small, neatly made, circular holes, varying between 5 cm. and 8 cm. in diameter, penetrated the earthen floor. Two rows of five each, which must have been used as receptacles for loom anchors (pp. 121–123), extended parallel to the midline of the kiva and from 65 to 80 cm. from left and right walls, respectively. Intervals between holes varied from 25 to 70 cm., and each row was about 2.20 m. long. The other eight holes were haphazardly distributed and are shown in figure 75.

The purpose of these latter holes was not clear. Similar haphazard distribution has been referred to above in descriptions of Pueblo IV kivas, where they occurred in large stone paving slabs. The hypothesis has been proposed that they had originally been drilled as loom-anchor holes in slabs located elsewhere, and that their irregular arrangement resulted from the removal of the slabs from their original positions, and their later installation in other kivas where their earlier and more orderly arrangements were lost. This hypothesis can hardly apply, however, to holes in an earth floor without separable segments that can be moved about independently like paving slabs. Another explanation must, therefore, be sought. Some of the holes might have served as postholes; others possibly as receptacles for prayer sticks (pahos) or standards such as are often used in modern Hopi ceremonials, although there has been found no convincing evidence of the latter usage.

The roof of the kiva had burned, probably at or just after the time of abandonment because its charred remnants lay directly upon the floor. Although the exact form of the original roof structure could not be ascertained, the surviving fragments provided clues that suggested its arrangement. Two main beams had extended across the kiva, and since there was no evidence of supporting pilasters or posts, they must have rested directly upon the walls. Judged from the position of the remnants lying on the floor, one beam had apparently been placed just above the face of the bench, and the other about midway between it and the extreme front of the kiva. These beams appeared to have been from 20 to 25 cm. in diameter, and of course must have been at least 4.50 to 5.00 m. long.

Two similar beams about 1.00 m. apart may have spanned the area between the two main beams at right angles to them. On these secondary beams was probably erected the frame for a hatchway. In a rough radial pattern over the main and secondary beams were laid numerous smaller poles perhaps about 6 to 7 cm. thick, extending outward from the beams to the masonry walls. Upon these poles was a mat of coarse grass, sometimes in double layers at right angles, and from 2 to 3 cm. thick. This mat was chinked here and there in its low spots with bundles of juniper bark, evidently to provide an even surface. The whole fabric was then covered with a layer of clay 4 to 10 cm. thick. A hypothetical reconstruction of the roof is shown in figure 77, although it is admittedly imprecise in detail.

The walls of the entire structure were of unusually good masonry of evenly coursed sandstone blocks, most of them approximately rectangular though some were trapezoidal or trapeziform. The blocks were not artificially dressed but had been selected and laid so that naturally straight edges formed the exposed surface of the wall, while the unexposed edges remained irregular. The blocks varied in size around an average 30 cm. long by 20 cm. thick by 20 cm. broad. They were laid in a bedding of adobe mortar from 2 to 10 cm. thick and without spalls. The surfaces of the walls had been plastered with a brownish silty material to a thickness of about 1 cm., but no evidence of painted decoration was found.

Three niches had been let into the walls, all of nearly the same dimensions. They were formed simply by the removal of one component block in the masonry although sometimes vertical slabs had been set to form the sides and to support the top. One was almost exactly at the center of the frontal curve of the room, 80 cm. above the floor and 23 cm. high. Another was in the right wall almost at its rear corner, 92 cm. above the floor and 20 cm. high. The third was in the left wall, about 1.00 m. from the rear corner, 91 cm. above the floor and 20 cm. high. The depth of the niches was not recorded. All were empty.

An opening through the front wall, about 50 cm. to the left of the foremost point in the curve, led

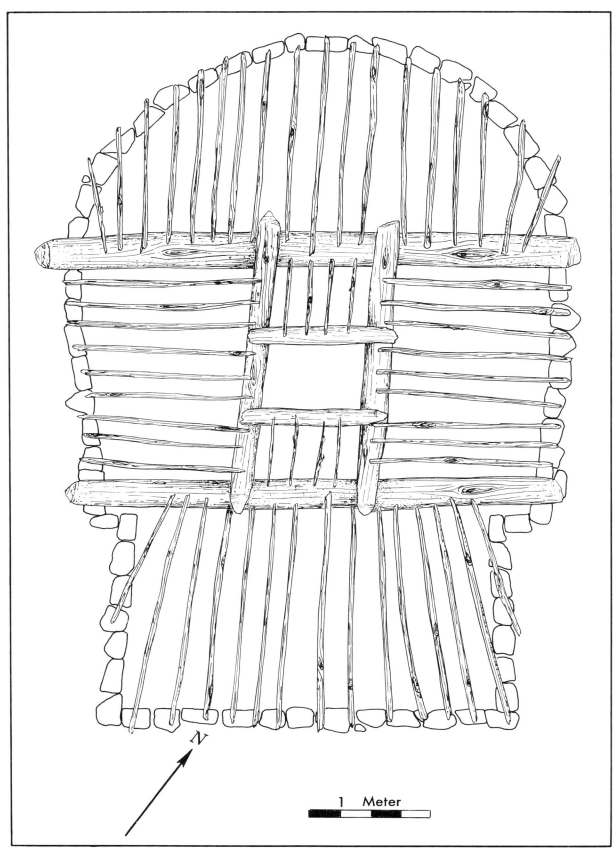

Fig. 77. Hypothetical reconstruction of the roof framework on the kiva at Site 4. This pattern was inferred by Charles A. Amsden from charred remains found upon the floor, where they lay in essentially their original relationships.

into a passageway that extended northwesterly to a point beneath one of the row of surface rooms that formed the pueblo, where a pit through the floor provided access to it. The bottom of this passageway was about 1.00 m. above the floor of the kiva and it was about 60 cm. wide, supported by parallel masonry walls, which had partly collapsed, however. Its height was indeterminate, and there remained no trace of a roof or lintel. This tunnel must have been a communicating link with the domestic rooms of the pueblo.

Several artifacts were found on the floor of the kiva, including a slab of sandstone with abraded channels, as if used for sharpening bone awls, a fragment of an ovoid mano, a roughly rounded hammerstone, and two squared stones suggesting floor smoothers. Beside these nondescript items were four badly charred wooden objects that somewhat resembled weaving battens. They were all elongated, flattened, and rounded along their edges and at their ends. Two were almost 50 cm. long and two considerably shorter, although the

latter may have been fragmentary. All lay on the floor, very close to the curved front wall and parallel to it. They are shown *in situ* in figure 75.

Of the numerous charred remnants of the roof that lay upon the floor, Edward T. Hall dated 36 specimens (some of which may have come originally from the same log) at dates between 1253±3 and 1257±2. He noted that outside rings were well preserved and that the logs had perhaps been cut and stock-piled over a short period of years before being incorporated into the structure, a custom that prevails among the Hopis and other Indians in the Southwest today.

Five of the same specimens were dated by the Laboratory of Tree-Ring Research of the University of Arizona at 1235, 1253, 1255, and 1275, respectively (Bannister, Robinson, and Warren 1967, p. 31). The authors of that report express the opinion that construction probably occurred just after 1255, and that the date of 1275 may represent later repair. They are thus in almost exact agreement with Hall.

KIVA AT SITE 4, SHERD COUNT

	Fill in Kiva		Fill in Passageway	
	No.	%	No.	%
Tusayan Gray Ware	15	16.1	—	—
Tusayan Corrugated	3	3.3	—	—
Tusayan White Ware	50	53.7	8	66.6
Kana-a Black-on-white	1	1.1	—	—
Tusayan Black-on-white	21	22.5	2*	16.6
— — ? — Black-on-white	—	—	1 bowl	8.4
— — ? — Black-on-red	2	2.2	—	—
— — ? — Black-on-orange	1 cup	1.1	1 bowl	8.4
Totals	93	100.0	12	100.0

* One was from a seed jar of Tularosa affiliation.

Three small charred branches found in the firepit were dated by Hall at 1282–83. He remarked that in each case the outer rings were present and the surfaces showed no effects of prolonged weathering, suggesting that they had been used in the firepit very soon after having been cut. Thus it may be inferred that the kiva was in use for approximately 30 years.

Although some components of the site may have been built and occupied during Pueblo II, it seems clear that the D-shaped kiva was built and used during middle or late Pueblo III.

In one of the small rectangular rooms at Site 4 was an unusual firepit and deflector. The firepit was almost square, although its exact dimensions

were not recorded. It was lined with upright slabs and finished with an adobe coping that rose about 5 cm. above the level of the floor. Immediately behind the firepit was the deflector. It was made of small-stone masonry, carefully laid in mortar, and was capped by heavy stone slabs. In the face toward the firepit there was a small rectangular niche, about halfway from floor to top of the deflector. The niche penetrated about halfway through the deflector, and contained nothing when excavated. The room in which this feature occurred could hardly have been a kiva because it was much too small, though it did contain a ventilator tunnel behind the deflector. These features are shown in figure 78.

THE KIVA AT SITE 4A

Site 4A was situated near the southeasterly escarpment of Antelope Mesa, about 5 miles northeast

of Awatovi and about a mile southwesterly from Jeddito Trading Post. It was very close to Site 4,

Fig. 78. A unique deflector in Site 4, Room 7, constructed of masonry and having a square niche in its face. This feature occurred in a small room that could hardly have been a kiva, although it contained a ventilator, deflector, and square firepit, as shown.

with which it was at first combined in the field notes, before excavation showed that they were quite distinct from each other.

Site 4A was mostly a complex of Basket Maker III or Pueblo I pithouses with associated structures, but several later rooms of masonry construction lay above or within some of the earlier rooms. Among this later group was a small D-shaped structure that was probably a kiva, and the discussion here will be limited to it. It was designated Room 22 and is illustrated in figures 79 and 80, which show it in relation to Room 17, one of the earlier pithouses.

The floor of this kiva was about 1.30 m. below the present ground surface, and had been excavated to a depth of about 30 cm. into bedrock. Well-made masonry walls stood about 1.00 m. above that level, but must originally have extended

at least 1.00 m. farther above the surface, so that the kiva was only semisubterranean, unless heavy erosion of the surface had occurred after its abandonment.

The kiva was D-shaped, its straight (rear) wall extending in a generally northeast–southwest orientation. It had been constructed above and partly within two earlier pithouses, Rooms 10 and 17, and its floor was about 30 cm. below the levels of those of the pithouses. The straight (rear) wall of the kiva cut through a segment of the northwest part of Room 10, and its curved (front) wall as well as its side walls encroached almost to the center of Room 17.

The walls of this kiva were well laid in even courses of carefully selected and perhaps deliberately shaped sandstone blocks, each of which measured from 30 to 50 cm. in length by 20 to 40 cm. in height. The wall was single-faced and about 25 cm. thick, the individual blocks smooth and even on their interior surfaces but irregular on the exterior. Vertical joints in successive courses were frequently but not always staggered. Mortar between the blocks was minimal and no spalls had been used. Remnants of gray mud plaster survived in a few areas on the wall surfaces.

The masonry was continuous around the entire periphery of the kiva, without angular junctions. The rear (southeast) wall was straight, about 1.75 m. long, blending at each end into the side walls along a curve of about 25 cm. radius. The side walls were at right angles to the rear wall and were straight for about 50 cm. before converging along a continuous curve whose radius increased from about 60 cm. at each end almost to infinity at the center, so that this part of the front wall was only slightly concave.

The room was very small for a kiva and was unusual in proportions, its width of about 2.60 m. being greater than its length of about 2.25 m. Orientation was approximately N. 20° W.

There were no benches, but at the center of the rear wall was the rectangular opening of a ventilator tunnel, 22 cm. wide and 19 cm. high, its sill 8 cm. above the floor of the kiva. The sill was a thin stone slab and the lintel was a heavier slab somewhat longer and thinner than the blocks used in the kiva walls. The lintel was supported at each end upon the bedrock surface. The tunnel penetrated the rear wall and extended about 30 cm. beyond its exterior, where it intersected a vertical masonry-lined shaft extending to the surface.

The floor of the kiva was of hard-packed earth, 3 to 5 cm. thick and laid directly on bedrock. About 1.00 m. in front of the rear wall and exactly

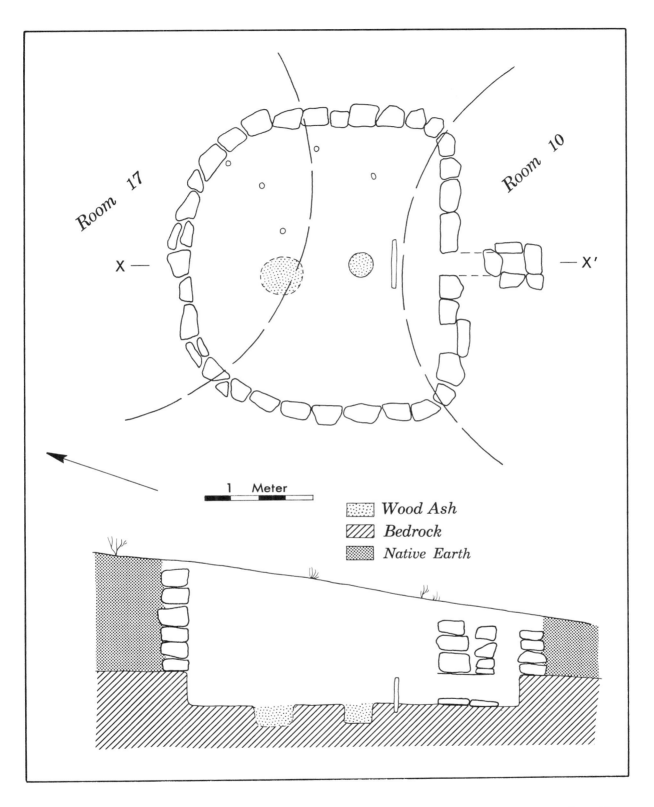

Room 17

Room 10

X —

— X'

1 Meter

Wood Ash
Bedrock
Native Earth

Fig. 79. Plan and profile of Site 4A, Room 22, showing its location relative to the earlier Rooms 10 and 17. Note that the lower part of Room 22 had been cut into bedrock.

a

Fig. 80. *a.* The D-shaped kiva, Room 22, in Site 4A, showing ventilator, deflector, basin-shaped firepit, and possible sipapu in the hard clay floor. Note characteristic Pueblo II masonry of the walls and large niche in rear wall toward the right.

b. Room 22, the D-shaped kiva at Site 4A, superimposed on an earlier pithouse, Room 17.

b

in the midline of the kiva was a roughly circular firepit 22 cm. deep and about 20 cm. in diameter. It was unlined, without a rim or coping, and contained wood ash. Between the firepit and the ventilator mouth, and slightly closer to the former, stood a thin deflector slab, 28 cm. high, 35 cm. wide, and only 3 cm. thick.

An irregular pit, perhaps functioning as a sipapu, lay halfway between the firepit and the front wall. Its dimensions and shape were uncertain because it had been damaged by tree roots.

Five circular holes, 5 to 8 cm. in diameter, occurred irregularly in the right half of the floor, and may have been used for loom anchors.

An almost square niche was let into the front wall at its midpoint, 77 cm. above the floor, 23 cm. wide, 19 cm. high, and 20 cm. deep. A second

niche existed in the rear wall, 57 cm. to the left of the ventilator, 9 cm. above the floor, 28 cm. wide, 28 cm. high, and 18 cm. deep. Its interior was plastered with the same gray mud that had been used on the surface of the walls.

The fill of Room 22 was well-consolidated sand, apparently water-laid, and almost perfectly clean in its lower strata, which did, however, contain fragments of two jars, one of gray corrugated ware, the other of an undetermined black-on-white type of Pueblo II character. In the higher strata there were a few sherds of Tusayan Polychrome, some undetermined black-on-white, and a considerable quantity of gray and corrugated sherds.

This pottery complex is extremely heterogeneous and represents a wide span of time, from Basket Maker III to Pueblo II. It may be a fair

KIVA AT SITE 4A, SHERD COUNT

Depth	0–110 cm.		110–130 cm.	
	No.	%	No.	%
Tusayan Gray Ware	150	71.7	75	70.7
Tusayan White Ware	20	9.5	12	11.3
Tusayan Black-on-white	2	1.0	15	14.1
Kana-a Black-on-white	4	2.0	1	1.0
— ? — Black-on-white	3	1.3	—	—
Tusayan Black-on-red	1	0.5	2	1.9
Tsegi Orange Ware	4	2.0	1	1.0
Lino Fugitive Red	25	12.0	—	—
Totals	209	100.0	106	100.0

guess that the kiva was built and occupied during Pueblo I or early Pueblo II, and that the large component of earlier sherds, represented by Lino Fugitive Red, came from the earlier pithouse.

No datable wood or charcoal was recovered

from the kiva, but 20 specimens from the fill of Room 10, beneath the kiva, were dated by Hall from 711 to 814, and by the Laboratory of Tree-Ring Research from 707 to 800 (Bannister, Robinson, and Warren 1967, p. 32).

THE KIVA (ROOM 24) AT PINK ARROW (SITE 7)

Close to the southeasterly escarpment of Antelope Mesa, about one-quarter mile northwest of Sites 4 and 4A, and about 1.25 miles southwesterly from the Jeddito Trading Post, was a moderately large masonry pueblo of late Pueblo III to Pueblo IV date.

This pueblo was called Site 7 or Pink Arrow because of the finding there of a small pink projectile point. The size of the village was not precisely determined but it may have contained more than a hundred rooms. In the summer of 1939, 32 rooms and one kiva were excavated, but we shall here consider only the kiva, which was designated Room 24 (fig. 81).

Room 24 was near the easterly edge of the village, about 9 m. back from the escarpment of the mesa. Whether it stood in isolation or was integrated into a complex of domiciliary rooms was not determined, since the immediately surrounding areas were not excavated.

Room 24 was very roughly rectangular, although its sides were irregular and slightly curved outward. The shape of the kiva had also been modified by the existence of a large boulder which encroached upon the right-rear (southwest) corner and made necessary the constriction of that region. It appeared that the boulder had fallen from an elevation just above and behind the kiva, but

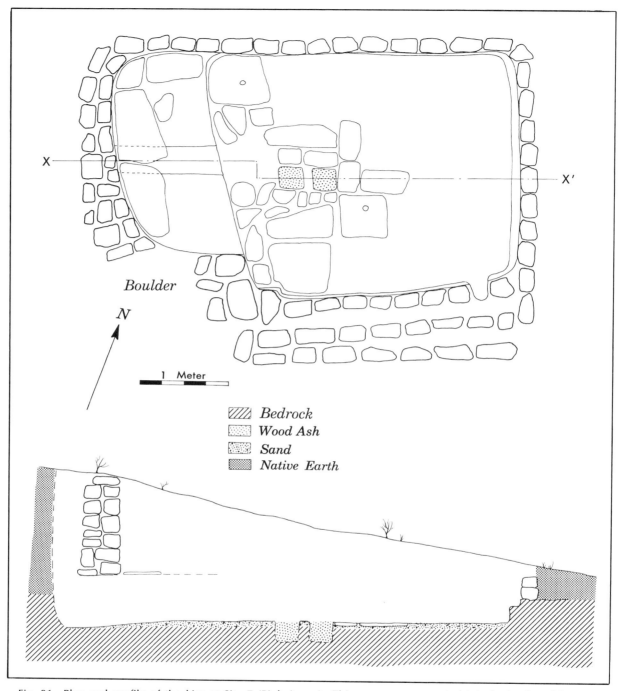

Fig. 81. Plan and profile of the kiva at Site 7 (Pink Arrow). This room was excavated into bedrock and its asymmetrical shape was due to the presence of a large boulder that had fallen from the slope above the kiva, necessitating the constriction of the right end of the rear bench.

whether during the period of construction or prior thereto was not certain. The walls seemed to have been adjusted to the position of the boulder, but it is strange that the kiva should have been placed in this position unless the boulder fell after construction had begun.

As said above, the outline of the kiva was that of a very irregular rectangle with rounded corners and slightly convex sides. Its maximum length along the midline was about 4.30 m. and the width varied from about 2.50 to 2.80 m. Orientation was about N. 60° E.

Across the rear extended a bench varying from about 90 cm. to 1.10 m. in breadth, although exact dimensions were difficult to make because both the face of the bench and the rear wall of the kiva were irregularly curved outward. The bench was about 2.40 m. long at its face, but slightly less at the rear, where the side walls of the kiva were rounded into the rear wall on arcs of about 55 cm. radius. The left end of the bench coincided with the left wall of the kiva, but its right end was 40 or 50 cm. inside the line of the right wall because of the intrusion of the boulder at that point. A part of the boulder had been chipped away to create a seat for the superimposed masonry of the kiva wall.

The lowest portions of the kiva had been excavated into bedrock, the original surface of which was uneven, to depths varying from 25 to 60 cm. or more. The top of the bench was indicated by a few irregular slabs, suggesting that it had once been completely paved. These slabs lay about 60 cm. above the floor, some of them directly on the higher area of bedrock, which here had been pecked to a relatively even surface.

A rectangular ventilator tunnel had been excavated through the ledge below the top of the bench, its floor level with that of the kiva. This tunnel extended through the rear wall of the room and varied in width from about 36 to 40 cm.

There may once have been a narrow bench along the right side of the kiva, but the irregularity of the masonry there made its existence uncertain. This right wall was unusually thick, up to about 80 cm., and the inner part of it may have been built later than the first construction as a repair or in order to make the kiva somewhat narrower.

The floor of the kiva was partly slab-covered, the slabs of irregular shapes and sizes and laid on a thin bed of sand upon native rock, into which the entire kiva had been sunk. Probably the floor had originally been completely paved.

About 1.00 m. in front of the mouth of the ventilator tunnel and slightly to the right of the midline of the kiva was a firepit about 30 cm. square, filled with wood ash, and showing evidence of heavy burning. Its depth was not determined, but it had been excavated into bedrock. About 15 cm. from the firepit toward the ventilator tunnel was another square pit of almost the same dimensions. It was also filled with wood ash, but showed no evidence of fire. The two pits had apparently been dug as a unit and subsequently separated by an inserted masonry wall.

In the surviving floor slabs were three small circular holes, one near each of the rear corners, the third about 30 cm. from the firepit and diagonally toward the right. No deflector was found.

The lower parts of the walls were formed by the bedrock into which the kiva had been dug, but above that and set slightly back so as to form a narrow ledge, rose very crudely built masonry walls, much of which along the rear and right sides had collapsed. The other walls still stood to a height of about 1.00 m. above the floor, but their upper limits were about 70 cm. below the modern ground surface. Thus the kiva was probably entirely subterranean.

A rounded niche occurred in the right wall about 25 cm. from the front corner. Its height above the floor was not recorded, but it was about 20 cm. in diameter and about 25 cm. deep.

The walls had once been plastered and at least partly painted, as evidenced by many fragments of plaster in the fill, one of which was coated with yellow paint.

The kiva had probably burned at some time after abandonment, because about 20 cm. of occupational debris lay on the floor beneath a layer

SITE 7, ROOM 24, SHERD COUNT

Depth	0–100 cm.		100 cm. to Charcoal Layer		Charcoal Layer to Floor	
	No.	%	No.	%	No.	%
Tusayan Gray Ware	18	7.5	43	10.1	87	14.3
Gray Corrugated	15	6.3	39	8.7	36	6.0
Jeddito Corrugated	27	11.4	46	10.2	92	15.2
Tusayan White Ware	3	1.4	27	6.0	20	3.4
Jeddito Black-on-orange	1	0.5	1	0.2	1	0.1
Awatovi Black-on-yellow	51	21.6	74	16.5	156	25.7
Jeddito and Equivocal Black-on-yellow	120	51.8	207	46.2	209	34.5
— ? — Black-on-red	1	0.5	5	1.0	3	0.5
Bidahochi Polychrome	—	—	6	1.1	2	0.3
Totals	236	100.0	448	100.0	606	100.0

of charred wood, apparently remnants of the burned and fallen roof. Above this layer the fill contained mostly building stones and adobe.

The pottery complex coincides generally with Ceramic Group A-3, except that the component of Sikyatki Polychrome is completely lacking. Room 24 would thus appear to have been approximately contemporaneous with the earlier kivas in the Western Mound at Awatovi, Rooms 218 and 229, and to have been constructed in early Pueblo IV, an estimate that is consistent with the tree-ring dates discussed below.

Among the supposed roof members were found numerous datable wood fragments, but none with the bark ring preserved. Dr. Hall dated 8 specimens at 1384±6, 3 specimens at 1387±4, and 14 specimens variously between 1256 and 1384. At the Laboratory of Tree-Ring Research 9 specimens were dated between 1376 and 1399, but with an uncertain number of lost rings. Their report (Bannister, Robinson, and Warren 1967, p. 26) states:

The 1378–82 cutting dates suggest construction of the room at that time with the later dates being reconstruction beams; however, it is possible that the room was constructed soon after 1399 and that the earlier beams are reused timbers. The dates thus confirm construction in the second half of the 14th century.

KIVAS AT SITE 107

Site 107 was situated on the northern rim of Tallahogan Canyon, nearly at its head, which placed it about 2 miles northeast from Awatovi. The site consisted of a collection of at least 14 rooms, representative of Pueblo I, II, and III. Most of the rooms appeared to have been built and occupied individually and were often unrelated to one another. In several instances one room overlay one or even two earlier rooms, and while the area of the site as a whole may have experienced almost continuous occupancy over several hundred years, only a few of the rooms were ever in use simultaneously. Since it is not the purpose here to analyze the entire complex, however, we shall discuss only certain rooms that may have served as kivas (fig. 82).

In the northeastern part of the area was a complex of three rooms, each apparently unrelated to

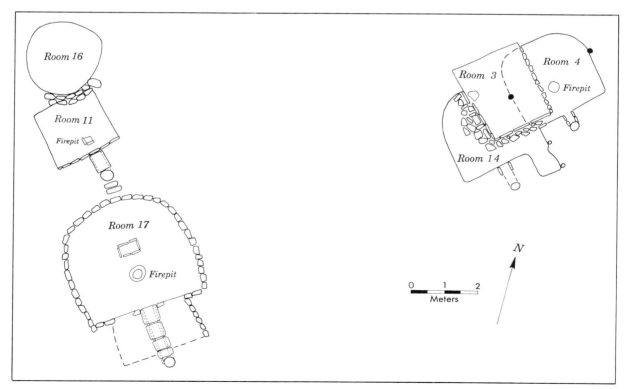

Fig. 82. General plan of Site 107.

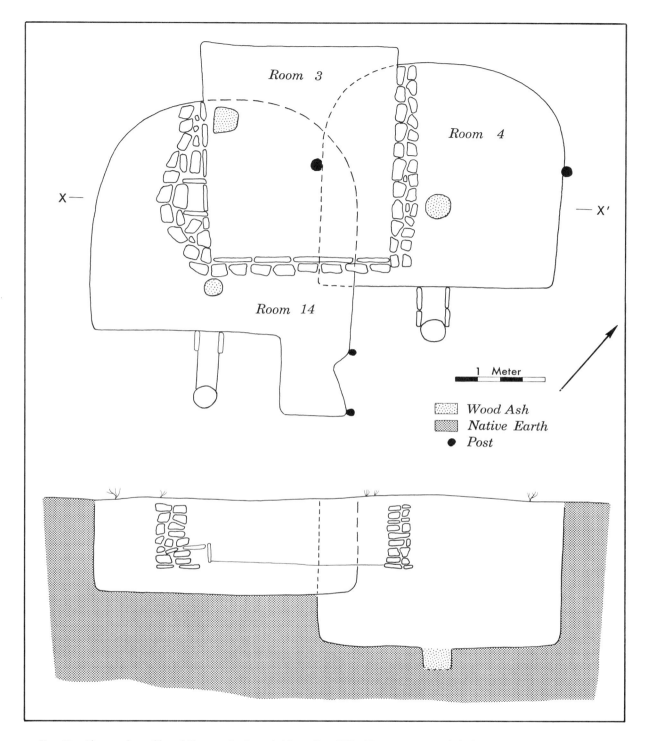

Fig. 83. Plan and profile of Rooms 3, 4, and 14 at Site 107. The sequence of their construction was: Room 4, Room 14, Room 3. Their relation to other rooms in Site 107 is indicated in figure 82.

the other two, and probably constructed and used independently. On the plan in figure 83 these rooms are designated Rooms 4, 14, and 3, and were probably built in that chronological order.

Each of the earlier two was partly destroyed by the construction of the subsequent one, so that only the latest, Room 3, remained essentially intact. It was roughly rectangular with walls partly of coursed masonry and partly of vertical slabs and earth, and was not a kiva. No precise date was ascertainable but it must have been built during middle or late Pueblo III times, and the sherds in the fill were entirely characteristic of that period. No datable wood specimens were recovered from Room 3.

ROOM 14

Room 14, which may or may not have been a kiva, was beneath Room 3 and had been partly destroyed by the construction of the latter. Its floor was of earth and lay from 30 to 60 cm. below that of Room 3. It appeared to have been D-shaped, with a horizontal ventilator tunnel that extended outward from the center of the straight (southeast) wall about 65 cm. where it intersected a vertical shaft. The floor and walls of the room were of earth and no benches had existed. It measured 2.65 m. across the straight (rear) side and 2.50 m. from that side to the center of the curved (front) side. Orientation was about N. 38° W.

Directly in front of the tunnel's mouth and 40 cm. from it was a circular, basin-shaped firepit 35 cm. deep and about 25 cm. in diameter.

An irregularly shaped alcove about 70 cm. wide extended 90 cm. backward and outward from the right end of the rear portion of the room, its right wall being a prolongation of the right wall of the room itself. The remains of two posts were found embedded in the right wall of this alcove, the purpose of which was not clear. It did not appear to have served as an entryway, since its floor did not slope upward to provide a ramp, nor was there evidence of steps. Perhaps a ladder had once been placed there? Although we have tentatively considered Room 14 a kiva, it might have served a domiciliary function (Smith 1952b, pp. 154–165).

No datable charcoal or wood specimens were recovered from Room 14, but the ceramics suggested a date around the beginning of the 12th century, which would correspond to late Pueblo II or early Pueblo III.

SITE 107, ROOM 14, SHERD COUNT

Depth	0–Floor	
	No.	%
Tusayan Gray Ware	7	13
Tusayan Corrugated	20	37
Moenkopi Corrugated	8	15
Tusayan White Ware	5	9
Flagstaff Black-on-white	9	17
Walnut Black-on-white	4	7
Tusayan Polychrome	1	2
Totals	54	100

ROOM 4

Room 4 was earlier than either Room 3 or Room 14. Its earthen floor lay about 75 to 85 cm. below that of Room 3 and about 50 to 60 cm. below that of Room 14. It, too, was D-shaped like Room 14 and was oriented in almost the same direction, with its straight (or rear) wall toward the southeast and its curved wall toward the northwest. All walls were of earth. A ventilator tunnel 30 cm. wide by 24 cm. high, lined with stone slabs, extended backward and outward from the center of the straight side a distance of about 40 cm. where it intersected a vertical shaft, the dimensions of which were not recorded. Orientation was N. 36° W.

Directly in front of the mouth of the tunnel and 75 cm. from it was a circular, basin-shaped firepit 25 cm. deep with a raised adobe coping. It contained wood ash.

Two posts had been emplaced in the side walls of the room, one on each side, about halfway between the straight (rear) wall and the foremost point of the curved (front) wall. Their outer edges were tangent with the faces of the walls, and they may once have been plastered over. Probably they had supported a single transverse roof beam.

No other features characterized Room 4 and it may or may not have been a kiva. Like Room 14 it could have served a domiciliary function (see Smith 1952b, pp. 154–165).

No datable wood specimens were recovered.

SITE 107, ROOM 4, SHERD COUNT*

Depth	0–100 cm.		100–168 cm.	
	No.	%	No.	%
Tusayan Gray Ware	15	38.5	—	—
Tusayan Corrugated	14	35.5	22	71.0
Tusayan White Ware	7	18.5	—	—
Black Mesa Black-on-white	1	2.5	—	—
Dogoszhi Black-on-white	1	2.5	—	—
Flagstaff Black-on-white	—	—	8	26.0
Tsegi Orange Ware	—	—	1	3.0
Tusayan Polychrome	1	2.5	—	—
Totals	39	100.0	31	100.0

* This ceramic complex suggests a date in late Pueblo II.

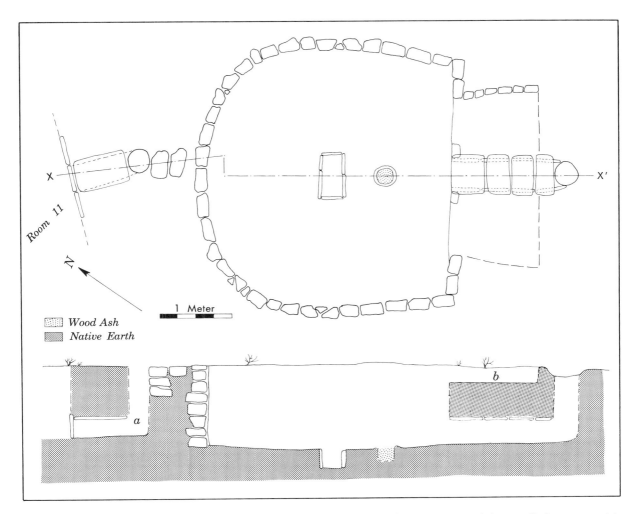

Fig. 84. Plan and profile of Room 17 at Site 107, showing also the relative position of the ventilating system (a) appurtenant to Room 11. A prepared earthen surface at b may have been the floor of an alcove or a bench.

ROOM 17

About 8 m. southwesterly from Room 14 lay a large D-shaped subterranean structure, numbered Room 17 on the field plan, that was certainly a kiva (fig. 84). The straight (rear) side was toward the southeast and the curved (front) side toward the northwest, in almost exactly the same orientation as Rooms 4 and 14. The hard earthen floor was about 1.15 m. below the surface.

The straight side was 3.30 m. long and the center point of the front curved wall was 3.40 m. from the straight side. The right and left sides formed a continuous curve with the front portion, although their radius of curvature was much greater than that of the latter. At both rear corners the side walls were directed slightly outward so that their interior angles with the rear wall were somewhat greater than right angles, and the maximum

width of the room was about 3.60 m. at a point about 1.29 m. forward of the rear wall. From that point forward the curved side walls converged until they coalesced at the front. Orientation was about N. 34° W.

The side and front walls were of well-laid masonry blocks in fairly even courses, the individual blocks mostly varying in length from 20 to 50 cm. and in thickness from 10 to 20 cm., although there were some thin slabs not more than 6 cm. thick. Mortar was just sufficient to form adequate bedding for the blocks and there were few spalls. The inner exposed faces of the walls were fairly even, and most of the blocks appeared to have been shaped on their exposed faces. The outer faces were, however, quite irregular (fig. 85).

The rear wall consisted only partially of masonry. At each end rose a single column of large, neatly dressed blocks contiguous to the side walls but not bonded into them. At floor level and almost exactly in the center of the rear wall a rectangular ventilator tunnel extended outward 1.60 m. where it intersected a roughly circular shaft. The tunnel was about 30 cm. wide by 42 cm. high. It was both lined and roofed with stone slabs, but its floor was of earth. Above the mouth of the tunnel the rear wall was composed of masonry similar to that elsewhere in the kiva, but the areas of the wall between this part and the masonry columns at the ends were of earth.

About 1.00 m. above the floor of the kiva and about 55 cm. above the ventilator roof was evidence of what may originally have been a recess or alcove extending outward behind the rear wall. There appeared to have been a prepared surface at that level, where also the three sections of masonry of the rear wall all terminated. At the same level and about 50 cm. inward from the right end of the rear wall, a single course of masonry extended backward and outward about 1.25 m. at an interior angle of about 100° with the line of the rear wall. Assuming the former existence of a corresponding boundary at the left side, there would have been an alcove about 2.20 m. wide at the front and perhaps 2.60 m. wide at the back. Its breadth was problematical but could not have exceeded 1.40 m. because the vertical ventilator shaft rose about 20 cm. beyond that point. This shaft was roughly circular and opened at the top into a small, irregularly shaped pit that was largely filled with coal ash. No obvious relation existed

between this pit and the shaft, and it was probably of a later date than that of the shaft.

The floor of the kiva sloped markedly downward toward the center, which was perhaps 50 cm. lower than the level along the edges.

Directly in front of the mouth of the tunnel and 80 cm. from it was a roughly circular, basin-shaped firepit about 36 cm. in diameter and about 16 cm. deep. Its sides and hearth were of heavily burned earth and it was surrounded at floor level by a raised earthen coping. It was filled with wood ash.

In the midline of the kiva and 45 cm. in front of the firepit was a rectangular subfloor pit, 30 cm. deep and 65 cm. transversely by 35 cm. fore-and-aft. All four sides were lined with vertical stone slabs, their upper edges flush with the floor. The bottom was of earth, and the fill was of sand and wood ash, over which the hard plastered floor had been extended, indicating that the pit had been in use during an earlier period but had later been abandoned and sealed.

Each side wall contained a single rectangular niche at about the point of greatest width of the kiva. That in the right wall was 12 cm. high, its sill 84 cm. above the floor. That in the left wall was only 8 cm. high, its sill 1.04 m. above the floor. No objects were found in either niche.

That Room 17 was a kiva was indicated by its size, which greatly exceeded that of any other room in the site, its shape, its floor features, and the probable southeasterly alcove. It closely resembled the kiva at Site 4 (fig. 75).

SITE 107, ROOM 17, SHERD COUNT

Depth	0–50 cm.		50–115 cm.	
	No.	%	No.	%
Tusayan Gray Ware	24	6.6	28	10.5
Tusayan Corrugated	254*	70.0	172	64.5
Moenkopi Corrugated	9	2.4	—	—
Tusayan White Ware	13	3.6	28	10.5
Flagstaff Black-on-white	25	6.9	—	—
Kiet Siel Polychrome	—	—	1	0.4
Little Colorado White Ware	2	0.6	7	2.7
Walnut Black-on-white	35*	9.6	20	7.2
Jeddito Yellow Ware	1	0.3	4	1.5
Jeddito Black-on-yellow	—	—	4	1.5
Sikyatki Polychrome	—	—	2	0.8
Wingate Black-on-red	—	—	1	0.4
Totals	363	100.0	267	100.0

* Includes one complete jar.

Specimens of charcoal from the lower fill of Room 17 were dated by Hall at 1180+x and 1190+x, and by the Laboratory of Tree-Ring Research at 1179vv, 1190vv, and 1202vv (Bannister, Robinson, and Warren, 1967, p. 36).

In general, both the tree-ring and the ceramic evidence fairly well corroborate an inferred date of early or middle 13th century, or late Pueblo III. The presence of a small component of yellow types suggests a considerably later date, but the

a

b

Fig. 85. *a.* Room 17 at Site 107, showing the partial masonry of the rear bench, with ventilator tunnel and basin-shaped firepit. Raised alcove appears in upper background.

b. Room 17 at Site 107, showing front and side walls.

sherds are so few as to be almost insignificant and may have drifted into the fill fortuitously.

ROOM 11

One other room at site 107 had some features of a kiva but may have been a domiciliary room. This was Room 11, situated about 1.50 m. northwesterly from Room 17. It was oriented N. 55° W. and was roughly rectangular, measuring 1.80 m. along its right and left sides, 1.90 m. across its front and 2.10 m. across its rear. The walls were of earth but a row of vertical slabs extended along the base of the rear wall. The floor was of hard earth 1.42 m. below the surface.

At a point 1.00 m. from the left wall, 65 cm. from the right wall and exactly at floor level, a rectangular ventilator tunnel 45 cm. wide and 24 cm. high, penetrated the rear wall, its mouth blocked by one of the vertical slabs of that wall. This slab appeared to be movable and probably served when needed as a deflector. The floor and sides of the tunnel were of earth, but it was roofed by a single large slab that extended rearward a distance of 60 cm. where the tunnel intersected a circular vertical shaft, the sides of which were of earth except for a column of stones at its rear. This stone column on its outer face abutted the front wall of Room 17.

Directly in front of the mouth of the tunnel and only about 25 cm. from it was a rectangular firepit, about 25 by 20 cm. and of unrecorded depth, filled with wood ash. Vertical slabs stood at two sides flush with the floor and others may once have existed at the other sides as well.

A fragment of charcoal with preserved bark from the lower fill was dated 1216 by both Hall and the Laboratory of Tree-Ring Research (Bannister, Robinson, and Warren 1967, p. 36), but whether it had been a part of the original roof structure could not be determined. No sherds were saved from the fill.

Collectively the dates from Site 107 were not very conclusive, but they are consistent with an inferred occupation of the site from the early 12th to the middle 13th century.

THE KIVA (ROOM 2) AT SITE 108

Site 108 was located on a bench below the southeastern escarpment of Antelope Mesa about halfway between Awatovi and Kawaika-a. It comprised a small masonry surface pueblo of eight or nine approximately rectangular rooms with a partly subterranean D-shaped kiva, designated as Room 2, situated about 5.25 m. southeasterly from the surface structure, its curved (front) wall toward the latter (figs. 86, 87).

The floor of the kiva lay almost 2.00 m. below the surface, so that the walls must originally have extended somewhat above the surface to provide sufficient headroom. This extrusion need not have been more than 50 cm., however.

Like all D-shaped kivas the rear end of the main area, which was also the face of a broad bench, was straight and 3.20 m. long. The side walls diverged slightly from this bench face, forming interior angles of about 96° with it. They reached maximum divergence at a point about 1.50 m. forward of the bench face, where they were about 3.40 m. apart, and then converged in a continuous curve until they blended into the curved front wall, which was built on a circular curve of about 1.70 m. radius, its midpoint 3.50 m. from the bench face. The rear wall had disappeared, but must have been about 1.60 m. behind the face of the bench, thus making the kiva about 5.10 m. long. Orientation was about N. 36° W.

The lower portion of this kiva had been dug through soft native sandstone, and the walls up to about 75 cm. above the floor were formed by the sides of the pit unfinished with masonry, although they may once have been plastered. Above that level the side and front walls were built of good, evenly coursed masonry, with dressed rectangular blocks of sandstone from 20 to 50 cm. long by 10 to 30 cm. thick. Their exposed inner faces formed an even, perpendicular surface, but their exterior faces were irregular. Mortar was sufficient for adequate bearing, and there were no spalls. A small rectangular niche occurred in the right wall, but its dimensions and exact position were not recorded.

The face of the bench was of native sandstone, to which some plaster still adhered, and it extended back into an alcove across the full width of the room, its ends at right angles to its face but its breadth indeterminate because of the complete erosion of the rear wall.

Beneath the bench a rectangular ventilator tunnel, 30 cm. wide by 45 cm. high, had been excavated into the native sandstone. Its mouth was al-

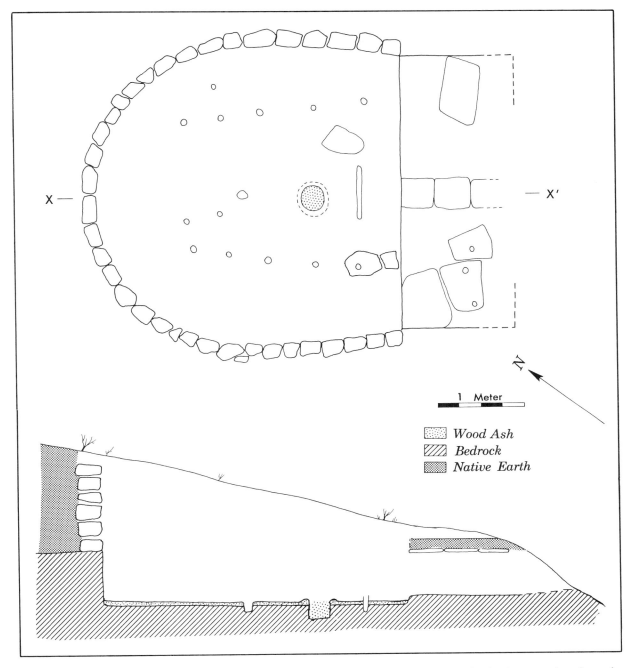

Fig. 86. Plan and profile of the kiva at Site 108, which had been dug partly into bedrock, the natural surface of which formed the surface of the rear bench. The depressed area above the cover slabs of the ventilator tunnel, however, had been filled with earth.

most exactly in the midline of the kiva, its floor at the mouth about 10 cm. above the floor of the kiva and sloping upwards toward the rear. This

tunnel had originally been excavated into the sandstone from above, in the form of a trench. Later, horizontal slabs had been inserted at a

Fig. 87. Room 2 at Site 108, a D-shaped kiva, showing rear bench, with ventilator tunnel, deflector, circular firepit, and loom-anchor holes in hard clay floor. Note characteristic Pueblo II masonry.

level about 30 cm. lower than the top of the bench to form a cover, and earth was then placed above them up to the surface of the bench. A few irregular paving slabs lay upon the bench, the entire surface of which may once have been paved. The character and position of the vertical ventilator shaft were not determined.

The floor of the kiva was made of a layer of sand and adobe laid directly on the native sandstone surface. This floor had been repaired at various times, the adobe patches being of various colors, some overlapping others, and many displaying the fingerprints of the workmen. A few flat stone slabs had also been inserted into the floor here and there.

A vertical stone slab serving as a deflector stood directly in front of the mouth of the ventilator and 45 cm. from it. It was about 65 cm. long

at the base and about 80 cm. at the top, and stood about 70 cm. above the floor.

In front of the deflector and 35 cm. from it was a basin-shaped circular firepit about 30 cm. in diameter, surrounded by a very low adobe coping and filled with wood ash. Its depth was not recorded.

Fifteen small circular holes penetrated the adobe floor. Two rows of five each extended longitudinally, each row about 1.80 m. long with the holes at nearly equal intervals of about 42 cm. One row was almost parallel to the left wall and from 65 to 75 cm. from it, the other almost parallel to the right wall and from 55 to 70 cm. from it. These had doubtless served as holes for loom anchors. The five other similar holes in the floor as well as three in the slabs of the bench appeared to be haphazardly placed. One in the middle of the kiva and 50 cm. in front of the firepit may have been a sipapu.

One human burial had been inserted into the fill subsequent to abandonment of the kiva, and other human bones were scattered throughout the debris. No datable specimens of wood or charcoal were recovered.

The relatively small change in the ceramic con-

SITE 108, ROOM 2, SHERD COUNT

Depth	0–75 cm.		75–100 cm.		100–150 cm.		150–200 cm.	
	No.	%	No.	%	No.	%	No.	%
Tusayan Gray Ware	81	25.8	79	33.9	124	28.0	13	31.0
Tusayan Corrugated	137	43.7	93*	40.1	187*	42.5	13	31.0
Tusayan White Ware	41	13.1	—	—	42	9.5	6	14.3
Black Mesa B/W	3	0.9	—	—	—	—	—	—
Flagstaff B/W	28	8.9	36	15.5	42	9.5	6	14.2
Tusayan B/W (incl. Kayenta Variety)	12	3.9	16	6.9	34	7.8	2	4.7
Little Colorado White Ware	1	0.3	—	—	—	—	—	—
Tsegi Orange Ware	—	—	3	1.2	3	0.7	—	—
Tusayan Polychrome	7	2.2	1	0.4	1	0.2	1	2.4
Kayenta Polychrome	1	0.3	3	1.2	2	0.5	—	—
Sikyatki Polychrome	1	0.3	—	—	—	—	—	—
St. Johns Polychrome **	2	0.6	2	0.8	6	1.3	1	2.4
Totals	314	100.0	233	100.0	441	100.0	42	100.0

* Includes one restorable jar.
** Some of these may have been Jeddito Polychrome.

tents of the several strata suggests a fairly rapid filling of the kiva after abandonment. And while no very precise dates can be inferred, the ceramic evidence is consistent with a hypothetical date for the filling between late Pueblo II and early Pueblo III, which in turn suggests that the kiva may have been constructed, occupied, and abandoned during the period from about 1050 to 1125.

KIVAS AT SITE 111

Site 111 was situated about one-half mile north of the head of Tallahogan Canyon, and about 2.5 miles northeast of Awatovi. It was a scatteration of at least six rooms with three or four isolated pits or outdoor fireplaces. Each of the structures was physically unconnected with any of the others, and there seemed no logical arrangement among them. All were at least partially subterranean, two rectangular in plan, one roughly circular, and three more complex in shape, possibly having served as kivas (fig. 88).

Except in one corner of one of the rectangular rooms no masonry walls were found. Whether such walls had originally existed could not be determined, but if they had not, there must once have been jacal or similar walls above ground, since no part of the floor was deep enough to have provided adequate headroom without some sort of superstructure. This architectural character was especially notable inasmuch as the ceramic de-bris and the available tree-ring dates suggested occupation during the 11th century, a time in late Pueblo II when most sites in the region contained clusters of small masonry surface rooms.

Moreover, it is hardly credible that so small a village, apparently occupied for a fairly short period, could have contained more than a single kiva. It seems likely, therefore, that not more than one room had served as such; but we shall consider the three rooms that exhibited at least some kiva characteristics (see Smith 1952b, pp. 154–165).

ROOM 8

The structure most closely resembling a kiva was Room 8 in the extreme westerly part of the village (fig. 89). Its floor was D-shaped, with diameters between 3.10 and 3.30 m., the straight side forming the face of a raised rectangular alcove that extended outward from the southeasterly

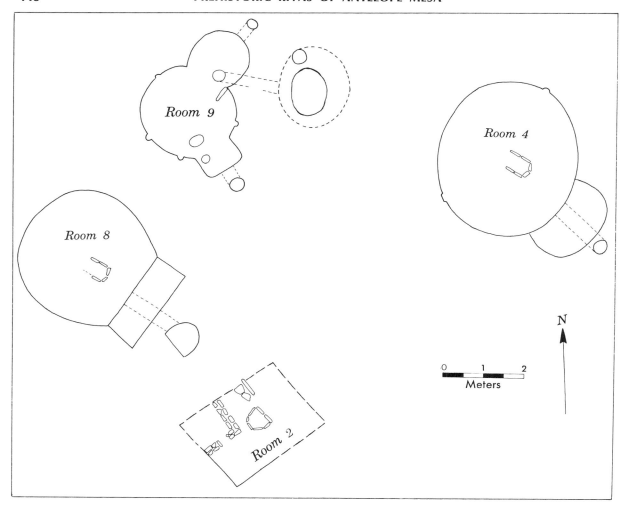

Fig. 88. General plan of a part of Site 111.

side. This main floor was 1.75 m. below the surface and had been excavated a few centimeters
into bedrock. The walls above bedrock were of
earth and the floor was of roughly surfaced native
rock. Orientation was about N. 65° W.

The alcove was 2.10 m. wide, 80 cm. broad at
its midline, and about 60 cm. above the main
floor. Its end and rear walls were straight and bat-
tered outward very slightly, and were formed of
native earth (fig. 90, a). The plan of the main floor
and alcove together was in the form of a keyhole.

Beneath the alcove was a horizontal ventilator
tunnel 35 cm. wide by 45 cm. high, 75 cm. from
the left wall of the alcove, and 1.00 m. from its
right wall. The tunnel was at floor level where it

entered the kiva, but rose gradually as it extended
backward. Its sides and roof, which arched upward in a barrel vault, were plastered with gray
adobe. The tunnel extended a distance of 1.10
m. to an intersection with a large D-shaped vertical
shaft. The latter measured 75 cm. along its
straight side, which was about parallel to the direction of the ventilator tunnel and to the left
of it; the curved side extended toward the right,
its apex being 70 cm. from the straight side.

A slab-lined firepit lay along the midline of the
kiva, 1.00 m. in front of the face of the bench or
raised alcove. It was U-shaped and about 50 by
30 cm. in plan, the longer, straight sides extending fore-and-aft, the curved side across the rear.

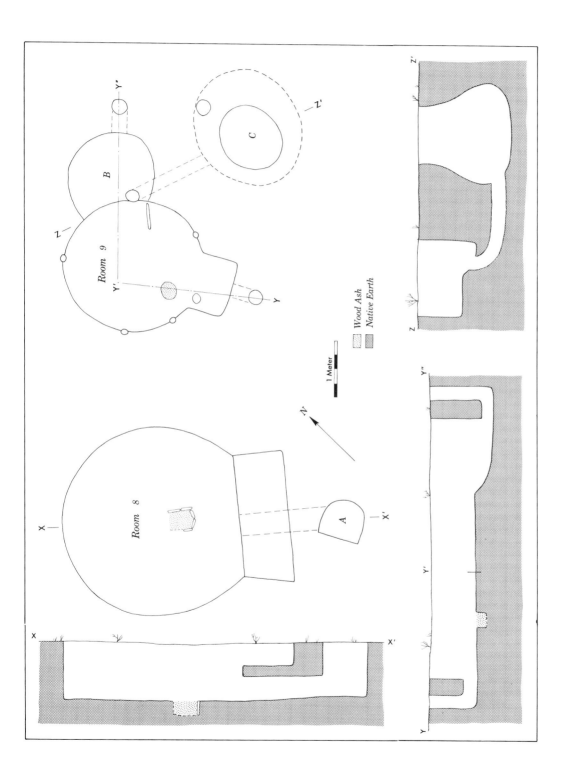

Fig. 89. Plans and profiles of Rooms 8 and 9 at Site 111. Room 8 was a D-shaped kiva, with an unusual D-shaped ventilator shaft (A), as discussed on page 148. Room 9 may not have been a kiva at all, but it was part of an unusual complex that included a roughly circular alcove (B) and a large bell-shaped pit (C) connected to the main room by a subterranean tunnel.

It closely resembled the firepit in Room 4 and contained wood ash. If the open end had once had a straight side, the entire firepit would have been D-shaped like that in Room 2, described below. No other floor features were discovered in Room 8 of Site 111.

SITE 111, ROOM 8, SHERD COUNT

Depth	0–50 cm.		50–125 cm.		125–175 cm.	
	No.	%	No.	%	No.	%
Tusayan Gray Ware	10	5.5	22	21.5	—	—
Tusayan Corrugated	100	55.0	51	50.0	32	58.2
Tusayan White Ware	52	28.6	19	18.6	16	29.0
Black Mesa Black-on-white	5	2.8	—	—	1	1.9
Dogoszhi Black-on-white	4	2.1	—	—	6	10.9
Flagstaff Black-on-white	10	5.5	10	9.9	—	—
Kiet Siel Polychrome	1	0.5	—	—	—	—
Totals	182	100.0	102	100.0	55	100.0

One charcoal specimen from the fill in the ventilator shaft, the outer ring an undetermined distance from the bark, was dated by Hall at 1069+x and by the Laboratory of Tree-Ring Research at 1074vv (Bannister, Robinson, and Warren, 1967, p. 37). Six other charcoal specimens found just above the floor were dated by Hall at 1006+x, 1014+x, 1064+x, and 1084+10 (3 specimens), respectively.

Room 8 could thus have been occupied during late Pueblo II or even early Pueblo III, in the late 11th or early 12th centuries.

ROOM 4

Another structure with considerable resemblance to Room 8 was Room 4 (fig. 91). It was at the eastern edge of the village about 7.00 m. northeasterly from Room 8, and was elliptical in plan, with a north–south diameter of 3.85 m. and an east–west diameter of 3.35 m. Orientation was N. 45° W.

Floor was on bedrock, 1.50 m. below the surface, and walls were of native earth. Two posts had been recessed into the walls almost opposite each other on the right and left sides, and had evidently supported a single main roof beam.

From the southeast (rear?) side of the kiva there extended outward a raised alcove, its floor 95 cm. above that of the main room. The walls of this alcove were also of native earth, and formed a continuous curve approximately circular along both sides, but somewhat flattened at the rear. Extreme width of the alcove was 1.95 m. and its breadth 1.05 m. (fig. 90, b).

A ventilator tunnel 40 cm. wide and of undetermined height passed under the alcove along its midline. It intersected a vertical circular shaft immediately outside the rear wall of the alcove. The method of roofing the tunnel was not determined.

In the main floor of the kiva, in front of the mouth of the tunnel and 1.10 m. from it, was a firepit in the shape of a U, its two straight and one curved sides lined with slabs. The front end was not slabbed. If this end had originally had a straight side supported by slabs, the entire firepit would have been D-shaped, like that in Room 2,

SITE 111, ROOM 4, SHERD COUNT

Depth	0–50 cm.		50–100 cm.		100–150 cm.	
	No.	%	No.	%	No.	%
Tusayan Gray Ware	58	19.3	7	20.7	19	23.4
Tusayan Corrugated	190	63.3	22	64.5	41	50.7
Tusayan White Ware	35	11.7	4	11.8	10	12.4
Black Mesa Black-on-white	6	2.0	—	—	4	4.9
Dogoszhi Black-on-white	8	2.7	—	—	—	—
Flagstaff Black-on-white	—	—	—	—	7	8.6
Tsegi Orange Ware	3	1.0	—	—	—	—
Awatovi Black-on-yellow	—	—	1	3.0	—	—
Totals	300	100.0	34	100.0	81	100.0

a

b

c

Fig. 90. *a.* Room 8 at Site 111, from the front, showing the rear alcove with ventilator tunnel and D-shaped vertical shaft. The walls were of native earth and the floor of bedrock. Room 9 appears at the upper left.

b. Room 4 at Site 111, from the front, showing its elliptical outline, rear alcove, and ventilator tunnel. The walls were of native earth and the floor of bedrock.

c. The peculiarly shaped Room 9 at Site 111. A rectangular alcove, extending outward, appears at the upper left, and a horseshoe-shaped alcove at the lower left. In the floor of the main area was a clay-lined firepit, and recesses for four roof-support posts were set into the earthen walls.

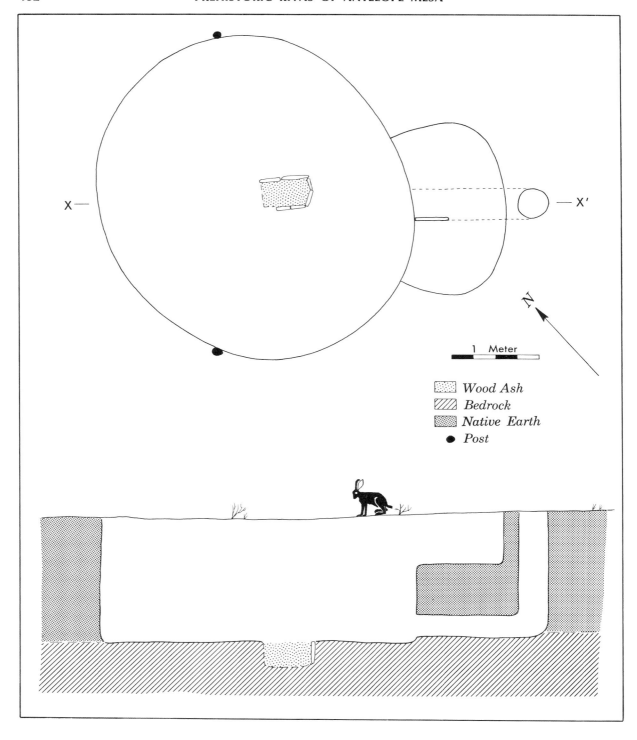

X —

— X'

1   Meter

Wood Ash
Bedrock
Native Earth
● Post

Fig. 91. Plan and profile of Room 4 at Site 111. The room was excavated very slightly into bedrock. The manner in which the ventilator tunnel was lined and roofed was not ascertained.

described below, and perhaps like that in Room 8. It contained wood ash. There was no deflector.

One tree-ring specimen from the fill, its outer ring an indeterminate distance from the bark, was dated by Hall at 1040+x and by the Laboratory of Tree-Ring Research at 1033vv (Bannister, Robinson, and Warren 1967, p. 37).

Room 4, thus, could have been occupied during late Pueblo II or even early Pueblo III, at the end of the 11th century or beginning of the 12th.

ROOM 2

Room 2 was not a kiva, but a small, isolated, rectangular, domiciliary room, located about 5.75 m. southwest of Room 4 and about 2.50 m. southeast of Room 8. It is mentioned here only because its earth floor contained near its center a slab-lined, D-shaped firepit, about 50 by 55 cm. in dimensions, the straight side of the D being across the northeast end. The firepits in Rooms 4 and 8, discussed above, may originally have resembled this one.

The floor of Room 2 was 65 cm. below the surface, its walls of native earth without masonry reinforcement. In the western corner was an almost square "closet" set off by masonry partitions nearly parallel to the walls of the main room. A narrow doorway penetrated the southeast partition, its sill 20 cm. above the floor. Against the northwest wall of the room was a stone box formed by two upright slabs perpendicular to the wall and supporting a horizontal slab cover.

ROOM 9

Room 9 at this site was a very peculiar structure, unlike any other known in the area (figs. 89, 90). It was in the northwesterly part of the village about 1.60 m. northerly from Room 8. It consisted essentially of a nearly circular pit with a small horseshoe-shaped alcove extending from its northerly arc, a roughly rectangular alcove extending outward from its southwesterly arc, and no less than three ventilatorlike tunnels.

The main structure was almost perfectly circular, 2.25 to 2.40 m. in diameter, its floor 80 cm. below the surface. Walls and floor were of native earth. Irregularly spaced along the periphery and recessed into the walls had been four posts which could have supported a frame for a rectangularly cribbed roof.

In the floor of the main area, about 60 cm. south of the center and close to the south wall, was a roughly circular firepit about 35 cm. in diameter, its vertical sides lined with fired clay.

A rectangular alcove extended outward toward the southeast, 90 cm. wide at its opening into the main area and expanding slightly to a width of 1.00 m. at the rear. Its floor was continuous with that of the main area. At the rear a short ventilator tunnel penetrated the outer wall for a distance of 40 cm. where it intersected a circular ventilator shaft.

Near the left-front corner of this alcove was a small bell-shaped pit in the floor, 20 to 25 cm. in diameter, containing sand and wood ash. It showed no evidence of fire. About 30 cm. from the pit but within the periphery of the main area and to the left of the alcove was a basin-shaped elliptical firepit, 30 by 40 cm. in diameter, lined with adobe and heavily burned, but containing no ash. It was without a raised coping. There were no other floor features in the main room.

Another alcove extended beyond the periphery of the main area from its northerly arc. This feature was horseshoe-shaped with the open end on the arc of the main area and 1.10 m. wide. From there the arc of the shoe extended outward 1.25 m. and reached a maximum width of 1.25 m. about halfway from base to apex. The floor of this alcove sloped downward unevenly to a depth at its apex of about 40 cm. below that of the floor of the main area. Both floor and walls of the alcove were of native earth.

A ventilator tunnel extended outward from the apex of the alcove a distance of 35 cm. where it intersected a circular vertical shaft. Exact details of this feature were not recorded.

At a point in the floor just to the left of the midline of the alcove and just within the arc of contact with the main floor was a circular pit about 25 cm. in diameter. This led downward into a tunnel which in turn extended eastwardly beyond the limits of the alcove about 1.50 m., where it entered a large, isolated, bell-shaped pit that had been excavated to bedrock 1.55 m. below the surface, or about 35 cm. below the floor level of the horseshoe-shaped alcove. This large pit was 2.00 m. in diameter just above the bottom and 1.16 m. at the surface. It contained nothing beyond undifferentiated debris and showed no evidence of fire. The tunnel was not carefully examined but the field notes indicate some doubt whether it was man-made or the result of an animal burrowing.

A statement of orientation for Room 9 is difficult because of its complex form, but if we consider

Fig. 92. In August, 1939, Dr. A. V. Kidder visited the Jeddito excavations. At Room 8 of Site 111, accompanied by the Field Director, Dr. J. O. Brew, his keen archaeological eye noted certain remarkable morphological coincidences, which he recorded in the field drawing reproduced herewith.

the rectangular alcove as indicative of the rear of the structure it was oriented N. 34° W.

The date of the construction and occupation of Room 9 cannot be determined very precisely, but it may be inferred as having been during the lat-ter part of Pueblo II and the early part of Pueblo III, and thus approximately contemporaneous with Rooms 4 and 8.

No datable wood or charcoal specimens were recovered.

SITE 111, ROOM 9, SHERD COUNT

Depth	0–50 cm.		50–80 cm.	
	No.	%	No.	%
Tusayan Gray Ware	49	22.5	7	11.1
Tusayan Corrugated	105	48.0	35	55.5
Tusayan White Ware	43	19.9	14	22.2
Black Mesa B/W	5	2.3	4	6.3
Dogoszhi B/W	5	2.3	—	—
Flagstaff B/W	11	5.0	2	3.2
Tsegi Orange Ware	—	—	1	1.7
Totals	218	100.0	63	100.0

VII

Hopi-like Kivas in Adjacent Areas

Our earth is degenerate in these latter days. Bribery and corruption are common. Children no longer obey their parents. Every man wants to write a book. The end of the world is evidently approaching.

Incised on a stone slab in Assyria, c. 2800 B.C.

HOMOLOVI

Several large villages of Pueblo IV date were located along the right bank of the Little Colorado River from three to six miles below (north of) the city of Winslow, Arizona. They are thus approximately 60 miles southwest of Awatovi. Dr. Fewkes excavated there on several occasions in the late 1890s (Anonymous 1896, p. 253; 1898a, pp. 517–539; 1904, pp. 23–32) and although his work was not centered on kivas as such, he noted that the pottery was "distinctly Hopi in character."

In 1962, however, Mr. Gordon Pond excavated one kiva at Homolovi Ruin No. 2, which he has described carefully (Pond 1966). Although only 11 feet, 5 in. long by 7 ft. wide, this kiva resembled those in the Jeddito villages, except that its rear bench was only 15 in. broad, and it lacked a sunken firepit. Instead two stone slabs, laid directly on the flagged floor, had served as hearths

on which small fires of brushwood had been kindled.

Numerous layers of plaster, to a thickness of one inch, covered the walls, and at least one of them was painted with a design of anthropomorphic figures. The kilts and bare feet with toes of two such figures survived.

The Homolovi villages must have been closely affiliated with those of the Hopi and Jeddito areas, and Fewkes recorded Hopi legends that some Hopi clans had lived there at one time (Fewkes 1904, p. 24; Anonymous 1896).

Twenty-four whole vessels of what appeared to be Awatovi Black-on-yellow pottery were recovered by Mr. Pond from the fill and on the floor of the kiva (Pond 1966, figs. 3–7), a fact indicative of a date of occupancy generally during middle Pueblo IV.

KOKOPNYAMA

Although the Peabody Museum Awatovi Expedition did not excavate any kivas in the several other large Pueblo IV ruins that are located along the southerly escarpment of Antelope Mesa, some excavations have been made there by earlier investigators. The most definitive work was done in 1929 by Lyndon L. Hargrave in the village of Kokopnyama, which lies about a mile east of the Jeddito trading post. The major purpose of that work was the recovery of datable beams for Dr. A. E. Douglass, who was at that time developing his method of dendrochronology, but there were

incidental dividends in the information gained of architectural and ceramic features.

Three rectangular kivas were excavated at Kokopnyama, and are fully described in the report (Hargrave 1931, pp. 103–115, figs. 33–35, pls. 23–26). It is not necessary here to repeat these descriptions in detail, but we can usefully summarize the general character of the kivas in relation to those of Awatovi and Kawaika-a.

Two of them (Rooms 4 and 24) were essentially indistinguishable in nearly every feature from those already discussed. Both were rectangular, approximately 15 by 10 ft. in size, with broad, rear, masonry-faced benches, rectangular ventilator tunnels, slab paving on the floors as well as on bench surfaces, no side or front benches, rectangular slab-lined firepits filled with wood ash, upright slab deflectors between firepit and ventilator mouth, multi-layered plaster on interior walls (at least one layer painted), niches and pegs in walls, rows of four loom-anchor holes in floors parallel to side walls, and orientation respectively N. 45° W. and N. 60° W.

In only two features did these kivas differ notably from the "standard." Neither contained a sipapu or footdrum, and one (Room 4) possessed a unique fireplace in addition to its square sub-floor pit. This feature was so unusual as to warrant particular description. It was integral with the deflector, which constituted its back wall. At each edge of the deflector was built an arm of sandstone and adobe extending forward at right angles, 1 ft. long, 5 in. thick, and 7 in. high, the entire construction resembling an armchair without legs (Hargrave 1931, pls. 23(2), 24). Between the arms was a fireplace of two levels, the rear portion against the deflector being at floor level, the front portion in a pit 10 in. deep. There was no enclosing wall or slab between the forward ends of the side arms, but a cover slab had been laid horizontally over them.

The third kiva (Room 23) at Kokopnyama was unusual in being almost square, and without a rear bench. Its ventilator entered the rear wall at floor level and intersected a circular shaft within the core of the wall itself. Otherwise this kiva was fairly "standard," with flagged floor, rectangular firepit, slab deflector, and a row of loom-anchor holes. A second pit or ash receptacle was situated, however, in the abnormal area between the deflector and the mouth of the ventilator. It may have served as the base for a ladder to an overhead hatchway. The orientation of this kiva was also unusual, being about S. 30° W.

Several datable remnants of roof members were recovered from Rooms 23 and 24. Those from the former indicated a building date of about 1400, and from the latter, exactly 1380 (Hargrave 1931, pp. 116–117; Bannister, Robinson, and Warren 1967, pp. 18–19). Room 4 was not dated.

KIN TIEL

At the Pueblo IV village of Kin Tiel, or Wide Ruin, about 45 miles southeast of Awatovi in an upper tributary of Leroux Wash, Hargrave in 1929 excavated two kivas, which have been fully described and illustrated in his report (Hargrave 1931, pp. 80–95, figs. 24, 25, pls. 21, 22). They were closely similar to those at the Jeddito ruins and need not be further discussed here in detail. It is appropriate to remark, however, that they represent the earliest and most easterly examples of kivas of Hopi character that have been reported up to this time.

Very large numbers of wood and charcoal specimens were recovered from these two kivas, of which no less than 174 showed cutting dates, based on the survival of the outside ring, which sustained the conclusion that both kivas had been built in 1275 or 1276 (Hargrave 1931, pp. 94–95; Bannister, Hannah, and Robinson 1966, pp. 25–29).

This date is somewhat surprising, inasmuch as it places the Kin Tiel kivas in a period prior to the supposed time of construction of the earliest excavated kivas at Awatovi, namely Rooms 218, 229, and Test 14, Room 10, all of which were hypothetically dated on the basis of ceramic evidence at early Pueblo IV, which is to say not before about 1300. There may well be earlier kivas, as yet unexcavated, in the lower levels of the Western Mound at Awatovi, which would show contemporaneity with those at Kin Tiel, but it is remarkable that Hopi-style kivas should occur at so considerable a geographical remove from what has been considered their homeland.

One of the Kin Tiel kivas was peculiar in that the walls of its main portion (excluding the area of the rear bench) were simply the plastered sides of the original excavation, unsupported by masonry. Whether this feature can be interpreted as suggesting an earlier evolutionary stage, however, seems dubious.

Pottery recovered from the fill in both kivas is not adequately described in the published report but is referred to therein as black-on-white, black-on-orange, and corrugated, without further specification. On the basis of this meagre characterization, however, this ceramic complex can be accepted as indicative of the period of transition from Pueblo III to Pueblo IV, consistent with the dendrochronological data referred to above.

Questions of possible routes of migration or diffusion arise to plague the observer. Did this type of rectangular kiva originate at, say, places like Betatakin in the Tsegi area, and was it then carried simultaneously southward and southeastward to the Hopi country, Homolovi, the Jeddito area, and the vicinity of Kin Tiel and Klagetoh? Or did it reach these several places progressively,

and was its ultimate form influenced by factors coming up from the south? Dr. Fewkes (1904, pp. 124–125) suggested the possibility that certain Hopi clans had previously lived at both Homolovi and Kin Tiel, perhaps with Zuni affiliations. And there are kivas with generally similar features at Four Mile and other sites in the Upper Little Colorado area.

At this point we cannot know the answers, but the speculation points provocatively toward directions for further investigation.

REFERENCES CITED

References Cited

Anonymous
 1896. "Southern Extension of Prehistoric Tusayan,"
  American Anthropologist, vol. 9, no. 7, p. 253.
Bandelier, Adolph F. A.
 1890– *Final Report of Investigations among the In-*
 1892. *dians of the Southwestern United States.*
  Archaeological Institute of America, American
  Series, Papers, vols. 3, 4.
Bannister, Bryant, John W. Hannah, and
 William J. Robinson
 1966. *Tree-Ring Dates from Arizona K: Puerco–Wide*
  Ruin–Ganado Area. Laboratory of Tree-Ring
  Research, University of Arizona. Tucson.
Bannister, Bryant, William J. Robinson, and
 Richard L. Warren
 1967. *Tree-Ring Dates from Arizona J: Hopi Mesas*
  Area. Laboratory of Tree-Ring Research, Uni-
  versity of Arizona. Tucson.
Bourke, John G.
 1884. *The Moquis of Arizona.* Charles Scribner's
  Sons, New York.
Brew, John Otis
 1937. "The First Two Seasons at Awatovi," *Ameri-*
  can Antiquity, vol. 3, no. 2, pp. 122–137.
 1939a. "Preliminary Report of the Peabody Museum
  Awatovi Expedition of 1937," *American An-*
  tiquity, vol. 5, no. 2, pp. 103–114.
 1939b. "Peabody Museum Excavations in Arizona,"
  Harvard Alumni Bulletin, vol. 41, no. 27, pp.
  870–875. Cambridge, Mass.
 1941. "Preliminary Report of the Peabody Museum
  Awatovi Expedition of 1939," *Museum of*
  Northern Arizona, Plateau, vol. 13, no. 3, pp.
  37–48. Flagstaff.
 1946. *Archaeology of Alkali Ridge, Southeastern*
  Utah. Papers of the Peabody Museum, Harvard University, vol. 21. Cambridge, Mass.
Colton, Harold S.
 1953. *Potsherds: An Introduction to the Study of*
  Prehistoric Southwestern Ceramics and Their
  Use in Historic Reconstruction. Museum of
  Northern Arizona, Bulletin no. 25. Flagstaff.
Daifuku, Hiroshi
 1961. *Jeddito 264: A Report on the Excavation of*
  a Basket Maker III–Pueblo I Site in Northeast-
  ern Arizona with a Review of Some Current
  Theories in Southwestern Archaeology. Pa-
  pers of the Peabody Museum, Harvard Uni-
  versity, vol. 33, no. 1. Reports of the Awatovi
  Expedition, no. 7. Cambridge, Mass.
Dorsey, George A., and H. R. Voth
 1902. *The Mishongnovi Ceremonies of the Snake*
  and Antelope Fraternities. Field Columbian
  Museum, Publication no. 66, Anthropological
  Series, vol. 3, no. 3. Chicago.

Fewkes, J. Walter
 1893. "A-wá-to-bi: An Archaeological Verification
  of a Tusayan Legend," *American Anthropolo-*
  gist, vol. 6, no. 4, pp. 363–375.
 1898a. "Preliminary Account of an Expedition to the
  Pueblo Ruins near Winslow, Arizona, in 1896,"
  Annual Report for 1896, pp. 517–539, Smithsonian Institution. Washington, D.C.
 1898b. "Archeological Expedition to Arizona in
  1895," *Seventeenth Annual Report*, pt. 2, pp.
  519–744, Bureau of American Ethnology,
  Smithsonian Institution. Washington, D.C.
 1904. "Two Summers' Work in Pueblo Ruins," *Twen-*
  ty-second Annual Report, pp. 1–195, Bureau
  of American Ethnology, Smithsonian Institution. Washington, D.C.
Hack, John T.
 1942a. *The Changing Physical Environment of the*
  Hopi Indians of Arizona. Papers of the Peabody Museum, Harvard University, vol. 35,
  no. 1, Reports of the Awatovi Expedition, no.
  1. Cambridge, Mass.
 1942b. *Prehistoric Coal Mining in the Jeddito Val-*
  ley, Arizona. Papers of the Peabody Museum,
  Harvard University, vol. 35, no. 2, Reports of
  the Awatovi Expedition, no. 2. Cambridge,
  Mass.
Hackett, Charles Wilson, editor
 1937. *Historical Documents Relating to New Mexi-*
  co, Nueva Vizcaya, and Approaches Thereto,
  to 1773. Collected by Adolph F. A. and Fan-
  ny R. Bandelier. English translation, edited
  with an introduction and annotations by
  Charles Wilson Hackett. Carnegie Institution
  of Washington, Publications, no. 330, 3 vols.
  Washington, D.C.
Hall, Edward T., Jr.
 1951. "Southwestern Dated Ruins: VI," *Tree-Ring*
  Bulletin, vol. 17, no. 4, pp. 26–28. Tucson.
Hargrave, Lyndon L.
 1931. "Excavations at Kin Tiel and Kokopnyama,"
  in Haury and Hargrave, 1931, pp. 80–120.
Haury, Emil W., and Lyndon L. Hargrave
 1931. *Recently Dated Pueblo Ruins in Arizona.*
  Smithsonian Institution, Miscellaneous Collec-
  tions, vol. 82, no. 11. Washington, D.C.
Hodge, Frederick Webb
 1939. "A Square Kiva at Hawikuh," in: *So Live the*
  Works of Men. Seventeenth anniversary vol-
  ume honoring Edgar Lee Hewett, edited by
  Donald D. Brand and Fred E. Harvey, pp. 195–
  214. University of New Mexico and School of
  American Research. Albuquerque.

Hough, Walter
  1903. "Archeologic... Arizona: Th... 1901," Annu... United States... D.C. ...

Judd, Neil M.
  1930. *The Excavat...* United State... vol. 77, art. ... D.C.

Kidder, Alfred V.
  1958. *Pecos, New...* Phillips Acad... tion, Papers,...

Kidder, Alfred V., and...
  1919. *Archeologica...* *Arizona.* Bu... letin no. 65... ington, D.C...

Lawrence, Barbara
  1951. *Part I: Mam...* *Part II: Po...* *Deer, Prong...* *on Bos anc...* Museum, H... Reports of... Cambridge,...

Mindeleff, Victor
  1891. "A Study o... and Cibola,"... Bureau of E... Washington,...

Montgomery, Ross G., Watson Smith, and
  John Otis Brew
  1949. *Franciscan Awatovi: The Excavation and Conjectural Reconstruction of a 17th-Century Spanish Mission Establishment at a Hopi Indian Town in Northeastern Arizona.* Papers of the Peabody Museum, Harvard University, vol. 36. Reports of the Awatovi Expedition, no. 3. Cambridge, Mass.

Olson, Alan P.
  1966. "A Mass Secondary Burial from Northern Arizona," *American Antiquity,* vol. 31, no. 6, pp. 822–826.

Parsons, Elsie Clews
  1939. *Pueblo Indian Religion,* 2 vols. University of Chicago Press, Chicago.

Pond, Gordon G.
  1966. "A Painted Kiva near Winslow, Arizona," *American Antiquity,* vol. 31, no. 4, pp. 555–558.

Smiley, Terah L.
  1951. *A Summary of Tree-Ring Dates from Some Southwestern Archaeological Sites.* Laboratory

... of Tree-Ring Research, no. 5, Univer-...rizona, Bulletin, vol. 22, no. 4. Tucson.

...ural Decorations at Awatovi and Ka-... With a Survey of Other Wall Paint-...the Pueblo Southwest. Papers of the ... Museum, Harvard University, vol. 37. ... of the Awatovi Expedition, no. 5. ...ge, Mass.

...ions in Big Hawk Valley, Wupatki ... Monument, Arizona. Museum of ...n Arizona, Bulletin, no. 24. Flagstaff.

...enth-Century Spanish Missions of the ... Pueblo Area. The Smoke Signal, no. ...son, Arizona.

... Ceramics of the Western Mound at ... Papers of the Peabody Museum, ... University, vol. 38. Reports of the ... Expedition, no. 8. Cambridge, Mass.

...ichard B. Woodbury, and ... Woodbury

...avation of Hawikuh by Frederick Webb ... Report of the Hendricks-Hodge Ex-..., 1917–1923. Museum of the Ameri-...lian, Heye Foundation, Contributions, ... New York.

...ler M.

...urnal. Edited by Elsie Clews Parsons. ...ia University, Contributions to Anthro-... vol. 23, 2 vols. Columbia University ...New York.

...G., and Nancy Tucker

...ssacre at Hopi," *Abstracts of Papers,* ...wenty-third Annual Meeting, Society for American Archaeology, pp. 41–42. Sante Fe.

Turner, Christy G., and Nancy T. Morris
  1970. "A Massacre at Hopi," *American Antiquity,* vol. 35, no. 3, pp. 320–331.

Valverde, Fray José Narváez
  1732. "Notes upon Moqui and Other Recent Ones
  (1937) upon New Mexico [written at Senecú, October 7, 1732]," in Charles Wilson Hackett, editor, 1937, vol. 3, pp. 385–387.

Vivian, Gordon, and Paul Reiter
  1965. *The Great Kivas of Chaco Canyon and Their Relationships.* The School of American Research, Monograph no. 22. Santa Fe.

Wilson, John P.
  1972. "Awatovi — More Light on a Legend," *Museum of Northern Arizona, Plateau,* vol. 44, no. 3, pp. 125–130. Flagstaff.

Woodbury, Richard B.
  1954. *Prehistoric Stone Implements of Northeastern Arizona.* Papers of the Peabody Museum, Harvard University, vol. 34. Reports of the Awatovi Expedition, no. 6. Cambridge, Mass.